DEFINING MOMENTS
PLESSY v. FERGUSON

DEFINING MOMENTS
PLESSY v. FERGUSON

Laurie Collier Hillstrom

155 W. Congress, Suite 200
Detroit, MI 48226

Omnigraphics, Inc.

Kevin Hillstrom, *Series Editor*
Cherie D. Abbey, *Managing Editor*

Peter E. Ruffner, *Publisher*
Matthew P. Barbour, *Senior Vice President*

Elizabeth Collins, *Research and Permissions Coordinator*
Kevin M. Hayes, *Operations Manager*

Mary Butler, *Researcher*
Shirley Amore, Joseph Harris, Martha Johns, and Kirk Kauffmann, *Administrative Staff*

Library of Congress Cataloging-in-Publication Data

Hillstrom, Laurie Collier, 1965-
  Plessy v. Ferguson / By Laurie Collier Hillstrom.
    pages cm.
  Includes bibliographical references and index.
  Summary: "Provides a comprehensive account of the legal drama that established the 'separate but equal' doctrine. Details the postwar Reconstruction era; the legal issues involved in Plessy v. Ferguson; the spread of discriminatory Jim Crow laws; the effects of segregation on African Americans; and the efforts to overturn Plessy. Includes biographies, primary sources, and more"-- Provided by publisher.
  ISBN 978-0-7808-1329-8 (hardcover : alk. paper) 1. Plessy, Homer Adolph--Trials, litigation, etc. 2. Segregation--Law and legislation--United States 3. Segregation in transportation--Law and legislation--Louisiana--History 4. United States--Race relations--History. I. Title.
    KF223.P56H55 2013
    342.7308'73--dc21

2013019044

The information in this publication was compiled from sources cited and from sources considered reliable. While every possible effort has been made to ensure reliability, the publisher will not assume liability for damages caused by inaccuracies in the data, and makes no warranty, express or implied, on the accuracy of the information contained herein.

This book is printed on acid-free paper meeting the ANSI Z39.48 Standard. The infinity symbol that appears above indicates that the paper in this book meets that standard.

Printed in the United States of America

TABLE OF CONTENTS

NARRATIVE OVERVIEW

BIOGRAPHIES

PRIMARY SOURCES

PREFACE

Throughout the course of America's existence, its people, culture, and institutions have been periodically challenged—and in many cases transformed—by profound historical events. Some of these momentous events, such as women's suffrage, the civil rights movement, and U.S. involvement in World War II, invigorated the nation and strengthened American confidence and capabilities. Others, such as the McCarthy era, the Vietnam War, and Watergate, have prompted troubled assessments and heated debates about the country's core beliefs and character.

Some of these defining moments in American history were years or even decades in the making. The Harlem Renaissance and the New Deal, for example, unfurled over the span of several years, while the American labor movement and the Cold War evolved over the course of decades. Other defining moments, such as the Cuban missile crisis and the terrorist attacks of September 11, 2001, transpired over a matter of days or weeks.

But although significant differences exist among these events in terms of their duration and their place in the timeline of American history, all share the same basic characteristic: they transformed the United States' political, cultural, and social landscape for future generations of Americans.

Taking heed of this fundamental reality, American citizens, schools, and other institutions are increasingly emphasizing the importance of understanding our nation's history. Omnigraphics' *Defining Moments* series was created for the express purpose of meeting this growing appetite for authoritative, useful historical resources. This series will be of enduring value to anyone interested in learning more about America's past—and in understanding how those historical events continue to reverberate in the twenty-first century.

Each individual volume of *Defining Moments* provides a valuable resource for readers interested in learning about the most profound events in our nation's history. Each volume is organized into three distinct sections—Narrative Overview, Biographies, and Primary Sources.

- The **Narrative Overview** provides readers with a detailed, factual account of the origins and progression of the "defining moment" being examined. It also explores the event's lasting impact on America's political and cultural landscape.

- The **Biographies** section provides valuable biographical background on leading figures associated with the event in question. Each biography concludes with a list of sources for further information on the profiled individual.

- The **Primary Sources** section collects a wide variety of pertinent primary source materials from the era under discussion, including official documents, papers and resolutions, letters, oral histories, memoirs, editorials, and other important works.

Individually, each of these sections is a rich resource for users. Together, they comprise an authoritative, balanced, and absorbing examination of some of the most significant events in U.S. history.

Other notable features contained within each volume in the series include a glossary of important individuals, places, and terms; a detailed chronology featuring page references to relevant sections of the narrative; an annotated bibliography of sources for further study; an extensive general bibliography that reflects the wide range of historical sources consulted by the author; and a subject index.

New Feature—Research Topics for Student Reports

Each volume in the *Defining Moments* series now includes a list of potential research topics for students. Students working on historical research and writing assignments will find this feature especially useful in assessing their options.

Information on the highlighted research topics can be found throughout the different sections of the book—and especially in the narrative overview, biography, and primary source sections. This wide coverage gives readers the flexibility to study the topic through multiple entry points.

Special Note about *Defining Moments: Plessy v. Ferguson*

Some of the quoted material in this volume contains offensive terminology in reference to African Americans. We chose to retain such terminology when it appeared in the original source material in order to provide readers with an accurate picture of the racial atmosphere during the Jim Crow era in U.S. history.

Acknowledgements

This series was developed in consultation with a distinguished Advisory Board comprised of public librarians, school librarians, and educators. They evaluated the series as it developed, and their comments and suggestions were invaluable throughout the production process. Any errors in this and other volumes in the series are ours alone. Following is a list of board members who contributed to the *Defining Moments* series:

Gail Beaver, M.A., M.A.L.S.
Adjunct Lecturer, University of Michigan
Ann Arbor, MI

Melissa C. Bergin, L.M.S., NBCT
Library Media Specialist
Niskayuna High School
Niskayuna, NY

Rose Davenport, M.S.L.S., Ed.Specialist
Library Media Specialist
Pershing High School Library
Detroit, MI

Karen Imarisio, A.M.L.S.
Assistant Head of Adult Services
Bloomfield Twp. Public Library
Bloomfield Hills, MI

Nancy Larsen, M.L.S., M.S. Ed.
Library Media Specialist
Clarkston High School
Clarkston, MI

Marilyn Mast, M.I.L.S.
Kingswood Campus Librarian
Cranbrook Kingswood Upper School
Bloomfield Hills, MI

Rosemary Orlando, M.L.I.S.
Library Director

St. Clair Shores Public Library
St. Clair Shores, MI

Comments and Suggestions

We welcome your comments on *Defining Moments: Plessy v. Ferguson* and suggestions for other events in U.S. history that warrant treatment in the *Defining Moments* series. Correspondence should be addressed to:

Editor, *Defining Moments*
Omnigraphics, Inc.
155 West Congress, Suite 200
Detroit, MI 48231

HOW TO USE THIS BOOK

*D*efining Moments: Plessy v. Ferguson provides users with a detailed and authoritative overview of events surrounding the infamous 1896 Supreme Court decision that legalized racial segregation, as well as background on the principal figures involved in this pivotal episode in U.S. history. The preparation and arrangement of this volume—and all other books in the *Defining Moments* series—reflect an emphasis on providing a thorough and objective account of events that shaped our nation, presented in an easy-to-use reference work.

Defining Moments: Plessy v. Ferguson is divided into three main sections. The first of these sections, the **Narrative Overview**, provides a comprehensive account of the legal drama that established "separate but equal" as the law of the land. It chronicles the postwar Reconstruction era, which gave rise to hopes of equality among freed slaves but also engendered fierce resistance among white Southerners. It describes the political battle over passage of the Separate Car Law in Louisiana and the formation of the Citizens' Committee to challenge it in court. The overview then details the legal arguments on both sides of the *Plessy v. Ferguson* case and the reasoning behind the Supreme Court's controversial ruling. It also follows the spread of discriminatory Jim Crow laws throughout the South in the aftermath of the decision and shows how segregation affected the lives of African Americans. Finally, this section covers the courageous efforts by civil rights activists to overturn *Plessy v. Ferguson* and gain legal and social equality for black citizens.

The second section, **Biographies**, provides valuable biographical background on key figures involved in the *Plessy v. Ferguson* case. Among the individuals profiled are Homer Plessy, the mixed-race New Orleans shoemaker who volunteered to challenge the Separate Car Law; John Howard Ferguson, the New Orleans judge who first ruled against Plessy; Albion Tourgée, the Republican activist and attorney who argued Plessy's case before the Supreme Court;

Supreme Court justice John Marshall Harlan, who delivered a scathing dissent in *Plessy v. Ferguson;* and Thurgood Marshall, the civil rights lawyer who helped overturn the notorious decision nearly six decades later. Each biography concludes with a list of sources for further information on the profiled individual.

The third section, **Primary Sources**, collects essential and illuminating documents related to *Plessy v. Ferguson* and its importance in American history. This diverse collection includes the full text of Louisiana's Separate Car Law; period newspaper articles discussing the pros and cons of racial segregation in public transportation; excerpts from the Supreme Court's majority opinion in *Plessy v. Ferguson,* as well as Harlan's famous dissenting opinion; first-hand accounts of the daily humiliation, constant wariness, and horrific violence that characterized African-American life in the Jim Crow South; and assessments of the state of race relations in the United States since the election of Barack Obama as the nation's first black president.

Other valuable features in *Defining Moments: Plessy v. Ferguson* include the following:

- A list of Research Topics that provides students with starting points for reports.
- Attribution and referencing of primary sources and other quoted material to help guide users to other valuable historical research resources.
- Glossary of Important People, Places, and Terms.
- Detailed Chronology of events with a *see reference* feature. Under this arrangement, events listed in the chronology include a reference to page numbers within the Narrative Overview wherein users can find additional information on the event in question.
- Photographs of the leading figures and major events associated with the *Plessy v. Ferguson* ruling, the Jim Crow era, and the civil rights movement.
- Sources for Further Study, an annotated list of noteworthy works about *Plessy v. Ferguson* and its impact.
- Extensive bibliography of works consulted in the creation of this book, including books, periodicals, and Internet sites.
- A Subject Index.

RESEARCH TOPICS FOR
DEFINING MOMENTS:
PLESSY V. FERGUSON

W hen students receive an assignment to produce a research paper on a historical event or topic, the first step in that process—settling on a subject for the paper—can be one of the most vexing. In recognition of this reality, each book in the *Defining Moments* series now highlights research areas/topics that receive extensive coverage within that particular volume.

Potential research topics for students using *Defining Moments: Plessy v. Ferguson* include the following:

- Although the South lost the Civil War, it ultimately "won the peace" by dismantling most of the social and political changes that the North had imposed during Reconstruction. Examine the various factors that encouraged "Redeemers" in the South to resist the North's Reconstruction efforts. What, if anything, could the federal government have done differently to make lasting change possible?

- Discuss some of the political, social, and economic factors that led to the segregation of people by race in the United States.

- Homer Plessy was arrested for refusing to comply with a segregated seating policy in 1892, and Rosa Parks was arrested for the same crime in 1955. Compare and contrast these two individuals' personal backgrounds, as well as the circumstances and results of their protest actions.

- List the main reasons Justice Henry Billings Brown provides for upholding the lower court's ruling in *Plessy v. Ferguson* and finding "separate but equal" accommodations constitutional. How does Justice John Marshall Harlan respond to each of Brown's justifications in his dissent? Which man's legal arguments are most convincing? Which seem most consistent with the U.S. Constitution?

- To what extent did the *Plessy v. Ferguson* decision merely reflect public opinion of the time? To what extent did it inflame race hate and promote the spread of segregation?

- The Supreme Court overturned *Plessy v. Ferguson*'s "separate but equal" doctrine with its *Brown v. Board of Education* decision. Explain the main legal arguments behind the unanimous 1954 decision.

- From Homer Plessy to the Montgomery Bus Boycott to the Freedom Rides, public transportation has been a flashpoint in the battle against segregation. Discuss reasons why this might be the case.

- Many Americans believe that political, economic, and cultural gains by blacks and other minorities—most notably the election of the nation's first black president in 2008—show that racism in the United States is mostly a thing of the past. Many others, however, contend that the deck is still stacked against black Americans in numerous respects. Present facts to support both sides of this argument.

- Discuss the legacy of *Plessy v. Ferguson* and explore the relevance this episode in U.S. history holds for Americans today.

NARRATIVE OVERVIEW

PROLOGUE

On the hot and muggy afternoon of June 7, 1892, a thirty-year-old man named Homer Plessy walked into the Press Street Depot in New Orleans, Louisiana. Making his way through the crowded, bustling train station, Plessy approached the ticket window and purchased a first-class ticket on the East Louisiana Railroad. His train was scheduled to depart at 4:15 P.M. for a two-hour trip to Covington, Louisiana—a tourist town with popular beaches that was advertised as "the healthiest spot in America." When the train began its journey northward, it would pass through woodlands and swamps, cross a seven-mile-long bridge over Lake Pontchartrain, and stop at several small towns before reaching the end of the line at Covington, near the Mississippi border.

As Plessy made his way to the boarding platform, he noticed signs posted in prominent locations informing travelers about a law that had recently been passed by the Louisiana state legislature. Known as the Separate Car Law, this controversial measure required railroad passengers traveling within Louisiana to be segregated into separate cars by race. The statute was described as:

> An Act to promote the comfort of passengers on railway trains; requiring all railway companies carrying passengers on their trains, in this State, to provide equal but separate accommodations for the white and colored races, by providing separate coaches or compartments so as to secure separate accommodations; defining the duties of the officers of such railways; directing them to assign passengers to the coaches or compartment set aside for the use of the race to which such passengers belong; authorizing them to refuse to carry on their train such passengers as may refuse to occupy the coaches or compartments to which he or she is assigned; to exonerate such railway companies from any and all blame or damages that might proceed or result from such a refusal; to prescribe penalties for all violations

3

of this act; to put this act into effect ninety days after its pro-mulgation, and to repeal all laws or parts of laws contrary to or inconsistent with the provisions of this act.[1]

Plessy belonged to a group of prominent black and mixed-race New Orleans residents who believed that racial segregation violated the U.S. Constitution. They called themselves the Citizens' Committee to Test the Constitutionality of the Separate Car Law. Plessy's train journey that day was part of a carefully arranged plan to challenge the law—and the entire discriminatory "Jim Crow" system that relegated blacks to a position of second-class citizenship—in court. The committee selected Plessy because he had light skin and could easily pass for white, yet he was still considered "colored" under Louisiana law since one of his great-grandparents was African American.

As a colored person, Plessy was required to sit in the railroad car that was designated for black passengers. Instead, he intentionally boarded the first-class car that was only open to white passengers. Plessy sat down on a plush, cushioned seat and looked around at the elegant mahogany paneling and shiny brass light fixtures. None of the white passengers noticed anything out of the ordinary about the quiet, well-dressed man in their midst until East Louisiana Railroad conductor J. J. Dowling stopped by to collect Plessy's ticket.

Proceeding according to plan, Plessy informed the railroad employee that he was a colored man according to state law. When Dowling told him that he was required to move to the car reserved for blacks, Plessy refused to comply. He was then removed from the train and placed under arrest for violating the Separate Car Law. Plessy's arrest set in motion a series of legal events that eventually brought the issue of racial segregation before the U.S. Supreme Court. According to historian Keith Weldon Medley, "The future of constitutional rights for blacks in America would ride on his day in court."[2]

Notes

[1] Louisiana Railway Accommodations Act of 1890. Louisiana Laws, No. 111, pp. 153-54. Retrieved from http://railroads.unl.edu/documents/view_document.php?id=rail.gen.0060.

[2] Medley, Keith Weldon. "The Sad Story of How 'Separate but Equal' Was Born." *Smithsonian*, February 1994, p. 104.

Chapter One

RECONSTRUCTION IN THE SOUTH

⟨⟨⟨⟨∩∩⟩⟩⟩⟩

In the case of civil war, where the contending parties must rest face to face after peace, there can be no quick and perfect peace. When to all this you add a servile and disadvantaged race, who represent the cause of war and who afterwards are left near naked to their enemies, war may go on more secretly, more spasmodically, and yet as truly as before the peace. This was the case in the South after Lee's surrender.

—W. E. B. Du Bois

The first African-American people to arrive in the land that eventually became the United States were brought by force in the mid-1600s to serve as slaves for white colonists of European ancestry. Slavery—and efforts to abolish the practice and overcome its insidious effects—dominated the first two centuries of black-white relations in America. Although the North's victory in the Civil War ended the practice of slavery in the South in 1865, changing the law did not necessarily change people's long-held racial attitudes or patterns of behavior. "There was no easy way," historian Keith Weldon Medley wrote, "for four million ex-slaves, just freed and without education, to be integrated into a racist, bitterly defeated, and economically collapsing South."[1]

During the postwar Reconstruction era, the federal government passed a series of laws and amendments designed to eliminate racism and discrimination in American society. These measures, though, encountered fierce opposition from white Southerners, who resorted to intimidation and violence in an attempt to reclaim their dominant position in the social order.

Slavery and the Abolitionist Movement

Slavery existed in North America almost from the time that the first Europeans set foot on the continent. As newly arriving colonists worked to carve a new life out of the wilderness, they needed a cheap source of labor to help them clear land, build homes, and plant and harvest crops. Some filled this need by forcing fellow human beings into slavery. Although some colonists enslaved local Native Americans, most slaves were Africans who were kidnapped by slave traders, transported across the ocean on ships, and sold to white masters in the New World.

Since these transplanted Africans had dark skin and spoke unfamiliar languages, it was easy for slave owners to view them as different and somehow less human than white people of European origin. They justified the practice of slavery by claiming that the African race was inferior, incapable of advanced learning or independent living, and thus destined for servitude. Slaves were considered the property of their owners, along the same lines as livestock or farming equipment. They could be bought and sold at will, forced to work without pay, and punished for disobedience or disrespectful behavior.

Some masters treated their slaves well, out of either basic human decency or a desire to preserve the value and working condition of their property. Most masters at least provided their slaves with the simple necessities of life, such as food, clothing, and shelter. But some owners treated their slaves like animals and beat them severely for the slightest misstep. Escaped slave Harriet Tubman claimed that children in slave-owning families learned from an early age to treat their slaves with indifference or cruelty. "Make the little slaves mind you, or flog them, was what they said to their children, and they were brought up with the whip in their hand," she stated. "Now, that wasn't the way on all plantations. There were good masters and mistresses, as I've heard tell. But I didn't happen to come across any of them."[2]

Slavery was controversial from the beginning. Religious groups like the Quakers argued that owning fellow human beings was immoral and fought to abolish the practice. Critics of slavery supported their stand by reminding Americans of their country's origins. When the thirteen American colonies gained their independence from England in 1783, they combined to form a new nation based on the principles of freedom, equality, and democracy. Abolitionists pointed out that slavery violated these founding principles and demanded that it be outlawed.

This drawing by editorial cartoonist Thomas Nast contrasts scenes of African-American life in the South under slavery (left) with visions of the future of free blacks in the United States (right).

Crusaders against slavery, though, could not cite explicit condemnations of the practice in America's founding documents. The framers of the U.S. Constitution worried that banning slavery would weaken support for the newly created federal government, so they avoided dealing with the contentious issue. They included an article in the Constitution that postponed government regulation of the slave trade for twenty years. Their hope was that the practice would die out on its own during this time.

Slavery did fade in popularity in the North, which developed an industrial economy. Most Northern states passed laws abolishing slavery by the early 1800s. But the practice became even more deeply ingrained in the South, which maintained an agricultural economy based on labor-intensive crops like cotton and tobacco. The 1793 invention of the cotton gin, a machine that separated seeds from cotton fibers, led to a massive increase in cotton production in the South—and an accompanying increase in demand for slave labor on

7

large cotton-growing plantations. As a result, the number of African-American slaves in the United States grew from 700,000 in 1790 to around 4 million by 1860. The "peculiar institution" of slavery became a generally accepted part of the region's society and culture.

As slavery grew in the South, abolitionists in the North became better organized and more vocal in their opposition to it. They gave speeches and published articles and books about the inhumanity of slavery, and they pressured both state and federal governments to take a firm stand against it. In 1808 they succeeded in convincing the U.S. Congress to outlaw the transatlantic slave trade, making it illegal to import slaves from Africa to the United States. The slave population in the South continued to grow, though, as new generations of blacks were born into bondage. Abolitionists also helped slaves escape to freedom on the Underground Railroad, a secret network of homes and businesses that offered food, shelter, and guidance on the journey northward.

Some of the most heated arguments over slavery concerned its spread into new states and territories as the United States expanded westward (see "The Supreme Court Protects Slavery," p. 9). Even if they were unable to uproot slavery in the South, abolitionists were determined to prevent it from taking hold in new areas. At the same time, pro-slavery forces recognized that preserving the institution depended upon maintaining a balance of political power between Northern free states and Southern slave states. Congress adopted a series of compromise measures during the 1850s that were designed to ease the escalating tension between the two regions. Ultimately, though, it took a war to settle the arguments over slavery.

The Civil War

Slavery and states' rights were the most pressing issues in the 1860 presidential election. Republican candidate Abraham Lincoln won the presidency on the basis of his promise to halt the spread of slavery. Southern slave owners believed that Lincoln's victory posed a serious threat to their way of life. Within a short time, eleven Southern states announced their decision to withdraw or secede from the United States and form a new country called the Confederate States of America. Lincoln argued that secession was unlawful and proclaimed his determination to preserve the Union.

The armed conflict known as the Civil War began on April 12, 1861, when Confederate troops attacked a U.S. Army garrison at Fort Sumter in Charleston,

The Supreme Court Protects Slavery

In 1857 the U.S. Supreme Court gave legal protection to the institution of slavery in its highly controversial *Dred Scott v. Sandford* decision. The case concerned a slave named Dred Scott who sued to obtain freedom for himself and his family. His argument centered around the fact that he and his owners had lived for ten years in states and territories where slavery was not allowed.

The Supreme Court rejected Scott's petition in a 7-2 decision. Writing for the majority, Chief Justice Roger B. Taney declared that African Americans were not citizens of the United States, and therefore Scott had no standing to bring a lawsuit or exercise any other constitutional rights. In fact, Taney claimed that blacks were "so far inferior that they had no rights which the white man was bound to respect."

The infamous *Dred Scott* decision invalidated the Missouri Compromise, which Congress had passed to regulate the spread of slavery to new states and territories. In effect, it legalized the practice of slavery throughout the United States by allowing slave owners to take their slaves anywhere and still maintain their property rights. The ruling fanned the flames of controversy over slavery and helped bring about the Civil War. After the war ended in victory for the Union, the Thirteenth and Fourteenth Amendments to the Constitution outlawed slavery and granted the rights of citizenship to African Americans.

Source

"The Dred Scott Case: The Supreme Court Decision." PBS, n.d. Retrieved from http://www.pbs.org/wgbh/aia/part4/4h2933t.html.

South Carolina. The Confederates quickly overcame the federal defenders and took control of the fort. As news of the attack spread, thousands of African Americans expressed a desire to join the Union Army and help put an end to slavery. Lincoln initially resisted the idea. He knew that Confederate leaders would find the presence of black soldiers offensive, and he still held out hope of bringing the Southern states back into the Union peacefully.

Lincoln's attitude changed after the Confederates won a string of battles in the first year of the war. On July 17, 1862, Congress passed a law allowing

After President Abraham Lincoln issued the Emancipation Proclamation in 1863, thousands of freed slaves joined the Union Army as it marched across the South.

black men who were free before the war to enlist in the Union Army. African-American soldiers and sailors did not serve alongside whites, though. Instead, they were placed in all-black, segregated units under the command of white officers. In many cases these units, known as the U.S. Colored Troops, received the least desirable duty assignments, which included digging graves, handling sanitation, and building forts, barracks, and bridges. The Colored Troops also received less pay than their white counterparts. They put up with such unfairness, however, to prove their loyalty to the Union and help end slavery.

As the Confederates continued to pile up victories on the battlefield in 1862, Northern morale declined. Hoping to restore support for the Union cause, Lincoln decided to forge a direct link between the war's outcome and the goal of abolishing slavery. On January 1, 1863, he issued the Emancipation Proclamation, which declared that "all the slaves of persons who shall hereafter be engaged in rebellion against the Government of the United States … shall be forever free of their servitude, and not again held as slaves."

This historic document did not have much immediate impact on the lives of African Americans in the South. It did not apply to slaves held in border states that remained part of the Union, and it would not take effect in Confederate states until the North won the war. Still, it played an important role in revitalizing the North's enthusiasm for the war. Abolitionists rejoiced upon hearing the news. "We shout for joy that we live to record this righteous moment," said former slave and abolitionist leader Frederick Douglass. "'Free forever.' Oh! long enslaved millions... Suffer on a few days in sorrow, the hour of your deliverance draws nigh!"[3]

Six months later, the tide finally began to turn when Union forces repelled a Confederate invasion of the North in the three-day Battle of Gettysburg in Pennsylvania. From that time forward, Union leaders effectively used their advantages in manpower, industrial capacity, and transportation to wear down the enemy. As Union troops slowly but steadily advanced across the South and captured Confederate territory, they were often greeted joyously by former slaves who were now free. Thousands of freed slaves joined the Union Army, while thousands of others simply followed along with the troops for protection and rations. These followers became known as "contrabands," since they were technically considered property confiscated from the enemy.

"There was no easy way," historian Keith Weldon Medley wrote, "for four million ex-slaves, just freed and without education, to be integrated into a racist, bitterly defeated, and economically collapsing South."

The surrender of Confederate general Robert E. Lee on April 9, 1865, marked the end of the Civil War. Only five days later, on April 14, Lincoln was shot and killed by a Confederate sympathizer, and Vice President Andrew Johnson assumed the presidency. The conflict had lasted four long years and taken the lives of 620,000 soldiers on both sides, as well as countless civilians. An estimated 190,000 black men enlisted in the Union Army before the end of the war, nearly half of whom were former slaves from Confederate states. African Americans served bravely in 449 battles, and twenty-one black soldiers and sailors received the Congressional Medal of Honor for their wartime service.

Reconstruction

At the conclusion of the Civil War, homes, farms, schools, churches, factories, roads, and railroad lines lay in ruins across the defeated South. During the postwar period known as Reconstruction, the federal government helped to rebuild the South's shattered infrastructure. It also established conditions for

President Andrew Johnson, who took office following the assassination of President Lincoln, clashed with Congress during the postwar Reconstruction era.

the Confederate states to be readmitted to the Union. Opponents of slavery in the victorious North also viewed the Reconstruction era as an opportunity to overthrow the old social order in the South and create a new system based on racial equality. They wanted the federal government to pass laws granting civil rights to freed slaves and protecting them from discrimination.

Lincoln's original plan for Reconstruction had involved distributing 850,000 acres of land in the South to freed slaves. Black families would receive "forty acres and a mule" to help them start a new life. Since this land had been confiscated from Confederate plantation owners, the plan also provided a means of punishing leaders of the rebellion. But President Johnson, a Democrat who hailed from the South, did not follow his predecessor's plan. On May 29, 1865, while Congress was not in session, Johnson signed a Proclamation of Amnesty that pardoned Confederate soldiers who took an oath of allegiance to the United States. The proclamation also returned most Southern farmland to white ownership.

Still, the end of the war brought a number of beneficial changes to the lives of African Americans in the South. Many former slaves, known as freedmen, felt jubilation upon gaining their freedom. They immediately set about locating and reuniting with lost family members, building their own churches and businesses, and becoming active participants in their communities and government. Thousands of other freedmen migrated north in search of better living conditions and job opportunities. Many settled in Canada, which had outlawed slavery decades earlier, while others moved to cities in the North or to western U.S. states like Kansas.

Some former slaves, however, felt bewildered or frightened by their sudden transition to freedom. After all, generations of blacks in the South had been trained to be subservient to whites. They depended on their masters for food, shelter, and work assignments, and they had little knowledge of the world beyond the plantations where they lived. Since teaching slaves to read and write had been illegal in the pre-war South, only 10 to 15 percent of African Americans were literate. Lacking education, property, and marketable skills, they worried about whether they would be able to support their families. As a result, many former slaves—particularly elderly people and families with children—chose to accept low-paying jobs on the plantations owned by their former masters.

Southern Resistance and the Black Codes

Many white Southerners found the changes of the postwar Reconstruction era disconcerting as well. The abolition of slavery meant that they had to establish a new kind of relationship with African Americans, who made up nearly 40 percent of the population of the South. Many people considered blacks inferior and found it very difficult to overcome their old racial attitudes and prejudices. In addition, many white Southerners were determined to maintain the position of power and privilege they had long enjoyed. Finally, many whites worried that if blacks gained too many rights, freedmen would rise up and take violent revenge against their former masters.

The combination of these factors led to a great deal of resistance to Reconstruction among white Southerners, and Johnson's lenient policies allowed these resentments to flourish. Southern Democrats elected a postwar delegation to Congress that included many former Confederate military and political leaders—including the man who had served as vice president of the Confederacy, Alexander H. Stephens of Georgia. They also introduced a series of repressive laws, known as Black Codes, that were designed to restrict the rights and freedoms of former slaves and prevent them from gaining any political or economic power.

Federal officials were unprepared for this combative stance. "There was no strategy for cleansing the South of the economic and intellectual addiction to slavery," wrote historian Douglas A. Blackmon.

> The resistance to what should have been the obvious consequences of losing the Civil War—full emancipation of the slaves and shared political control between blacks and whites—was so virulent and effective that the tangible outcome of the military struggle between the North and the South remained uncertain even twenty-five years after the issuance of President Abraham

This 1874 political cartoon depicts white Southern Democrats using various means to restrict the voting rights of newly freed slaves during Reconstruction.

Lincoln's Emancipation Proclamation.... In the first decades of that span, the intensity of southern whites' need to reestablish hegemony over blacks rivaled the most visceral patriotism of the wartime Confederacy.[4]

The Black Codes dictated nearly every aspect of existence for African Americans in the South. In many states, these rules prohibited freedmen from living in certain cities and towns, entering certain stores and hotels, using public transportation, or owning weapons. They also restricted blacks from meeting in groups, purchasing property, entering legal contracts, or testifying in court. African Americans were only allowed to hold certain jobs, such as farmer or house servant. To obtain an exception to this rule, a black worker had to apply for permission from the local justice of the peace. Black workers were expected to behave in a servile manner toward their white employers and obey all orders without question. If they quit a job or got fired, they risked being arrested for "vagrancy" and sentenced to work without pay.

The penalties for disobeying the elaborate and confusing Black Codes included beating, whipping, and hanging (see "Albion Tourgée Describes Reconstruction-Era Violence in the South," p. 143). These rules effectively restored the relationship between blacks and whites in the South to something very similar to slavery. "Some white plantation owners attempted to coerce their former slaves into signing 'lifetime contracts' to work on the farms," Blackmon explained. "More common were year-to-year contracts that obligated black workers to remain throughout a planting and harvest season to receive their full pay, and under which they agreed to extraordinarily onerous limitations on personal freedom that echoed slave laws in effect before emancipation."[5]

Radical Republicans Step In

The Black Codes and other examples of white Southern resistance to Reconstruction infuriated people in the North. They concluded that the former Confederates had not learned any lessons from their defeat, since conditions in the South appeared to be reverting back to the way they had been before the war. Many outraged Northerners wanted to punish white Southerners for their arrogance and establish much harsher terms for Reconstruction. Abolitionists and so-called Radical Republicans in Congress expressed renewed determination to destroy the old social order in the South and create a new system based on racial equality.

When Congress met again in December 1865, the Radical Republicans immediately took a number of steps to reverse Johnson's lenient Reconstruction policies and dismantle the white-dominated Southern state governments. They refused to seat incoming representatives who had supported the Confederacy, for instance, and they established strict new rules for the Southern states to rejoin the Union. They also passed a series of laws designed to protect the rights of freed slaves, and they sent federal military troops into the South to enforce them.

The Thirteenth Amendment to the Constitution, passed in 1865, abolished slavery in the United States and freed all slaves in border states who were not covered under the Emancipation Proclamation. The Fourteenth Amendment extended the rights of U.S. citizenship to all persons "born or naturalized in the United States," including freed slaves. It also guaranteed all citizens equal protection under the law and forbade states from denying citizens their rights without due process of law. The Fifteenth Amendment extended voting rights to black men. It forbade states from denying or abridging a citizen's right to vote "on account of race, color, or previous condition of servitude." Radical Republicans in Congress also passed the Civil Rights Act of 1866 over Johnson's veto. This law eliminated the Black Codes that restricted the activities of African Americans in the South.

"We are part and parcel of this nation, which has done more than any other on earth to illustrate the great idea that all races of men may dwell together in harmony," declared Richard Cain, a black minister who was elected to the U.S. House of Representatives from South Carolina during Reconstruction.

Perhaps the most sweeping law passed during this period was the Reconstruction Act of 1867. This legislation divided the former Confederate states into five military districts, each of which was overseen by a Union general who had the power to enforce laws and punish crimes. It also established the Freedmen's Bureau to help former slaves make a successful transition to new lives. With the help of various religious and charitable organizations, the Freedmen's Bureau provided food, clothing, medical care, farmland, and assistance with resettlement to former slaves—as well as to poverty-stricken whites—across the postwar South. Before it was disbanded in 1872, the bureau also established 4,000 schools, including several colleges, to improve the educational opportunities for African Americans.

In an effort to ensure that blacks in the South gained political power, Congress required each former Confederate state to draft a new state constitution and ratify the Fourteenth and Fifteenth Amendments. Voters across the South

Once the federal government sent military troops to the South to enforce Reconstruction laws, African Americans were elected to political office for the first time across the South.

elected delegates to their states' constitutional conventions. With federal troops in place to protect black voting rights, every former Confederate state elected at least some black delegates, and most states elected African Americans in about the same proportion as their population. A few states, including South Carolina, elected a majority of black delegates.

Most of the state conventions developed progressive constitutions that eliminated the discriminatory Black Codes and established protections for civil rights and voting rights that applied to black and white citizens alike. Although some white Southerners expressed reservations about including African Americans in the conventions, many black delegates earned the respect of their white counterparts. "Beyond all question, the best men in the convention are the colored members," wrote the *Daily News* of Charleston, South Carolina. "They have assembled neither to pull wires like some, nor to make money like others; but to legislate for the welfare of the race to which they belong."[6]

As the reconstructed Southern states were readmitted to the Union, they held free elections that resulted in African Americans serving in local, state, and national government positions for the first time. Hiram Revels, a Republican from Mississippi, became the first black member of the U.S. Senate in 1870. Twenty more black candidates won election to the U.S. House of Representatives. "We are part and parcel of this nation, which has done more than any other on earth to illustrate the great idea that all races of men may dwell together in harmony," declared Richard Cain, who was elected as a representative from South Carolina in 1873. "Anglo-Saxon and Afro-American can together work out a common destiny, until universal liberty, as announced by this nation, shall be known throughout the world."[7]

Notes

[1] Medley, Keith Weldon. "The Sad Story of How 'Separate but Equal' Was Born in 1896." *Smithsonian,* February 1994, p. 104.

[2] Quoted in Conrad, Earl. *Harriet Tubman.* Washington, DC: Associated Publishers, 1943, p. 10.

[3] Douglass, Frederick. "Emancipation Proclaimed." *Douglass' Monthly,* October 1862. Retrieved from http://www.lib.rochester.edu/index.cfm?PAGE=4406.

[4] Blackmon, Douglas A. *Slavery by Another Name: The Re-Enslavement of Black Americans from the Civil War to World War II.* New York: Doubleday, 2008, p. 41.

[5] Blackmon, p. 27.

[6] Quoted in Du Bois, W. E. B. *Black Reconstruction in America, 1860-1880.* 1935. Reprint. New York: Free Press, 1998, p. 390.

[7] Quoted in Middleton, Stephen. *Black Congressmen during Reconstruction: A Documentary Sourcebook.* Westport, CT: Greenwood Press, 2002, p. 57.

Chapter Two

THE RISE OF JIM CROW

The Reconstruction era ended in 1877 with the withdrawal of federal troops from the former Confederate states. African Americans quickly lost most of the civil rights they had won during the postwar period. As white Democrats regained political control across the South, many city and state governments passed strict new laws that segregated people by race and returned blacks to a position of second-class citizenship. These so-called "Jim Crow" laws, which restricted African Americans' use of public facilities like schools, parks, and transportation, amounted to a form of legalized discrimination. "Blacks watched with despair while the foundations for the Jim Crow system were laid and the walls of segregation mounted around them," wrote historian C. Vann Woodward. "The American commitment to equality, solemnly attested by three amendments to the Constitution and elaborate civil rights acts, was virtually repudiated. What had started as a retreat in 1877, when the last federal troops were pulled out of the South, had turned into a rout.... A tide of racism was mounting in the country unopposed."[1]

The Ku Klux Klan Launches a Campaign of Terror

The political, economic, and educational gains of the Radical Reconstruction era led many blacks in the South to hope that they were on the road

Toward the end of Reconstruction, federal troops were the only thing standing between freedmen and angry white Southerners determined to regain a dominant position in society.

to true equality. But racist attitudes continued to simmer among white Southerners, many of whom deeply resented the changes imposed by the federal government. Such feelings led to the formation of the Ku Klux Klan (KKK), a shadowy terrorist group made up of white supremacists who were determined to regain their dominant position in Southern society. The KKK waged a relentless campaign of intimidation and violence aimed at reversing the changes of the Reconstruction era and putting blacks back "in their place." Thomas Dixon's 1905 novel *The Clansman: An Historical Romance of the Ku Klux Klan* described Reconstruction as "the darkest hour of the life of the South, when her wounded people lay helpless amid rags and ashes under the beak and talon of the Vulture." It proclaimed that the KKK "enacted a drama of fierce revenge"[2] against blacks who dared to try to improve their lives.

Some of the tactics employed by the KKK included beatings, whippings, lynchings, rapes, and wholesale destruction of black property. Dressed in white robes and hoods, these self-appointed vigilantes rode on horseback through the night and burned down black schools and churches. Former slave Andrew Flowers received a severe whipping from KKK members in 1870 after he defeated a white candidate in an election. "They said they had nothing particular against me, that they didn't dispute I was a very good fellow," he recalled, "but they did not intend any nigger to hold office in the United States."[3] Although Congress passed a law in 1871 that made racial hate crimes a federal offense, it had only a limited impact on the KKK's campaign of terror.

As white Southern resistance to Reconstruction continued into the mid-1870s, support for federal intervention slowly drained away in the North. Many people simply grew tired of the seemingly endless fight to secure black civil rights. "The Negro is now a voter and a citizen," declared an Illinois newspaper editorial. "Let him hereafter take his chances in the battle of life."[4] Others felt that Reconstruction was an expensive failure and argued that the government needed to direct its attention and resources toward a looming economic downturn.

> *"The Negro is now a voter and a citizen," declared an Illinois newspaper editorial. "Let him hereafter take his chances in the battle of life."*

A controversy surrounding the 1876 presidential election led to the end of Reconstruction. Democratic candidate Samuel J. Tilden received 250,000 more popular votes than Republican candidate Rutherford B. Hayes, but neither man received enough Electoral College votes to win the election. Most of Tilden's support came from the South, while Hayes was favored in the North. Congress came up with a compromise to resolve the dispute. It declared Hayes the winner, but it also placated Tilden supporters by promising to withdraw federal troops from the South and provide the former Confederate states with additional funds for public works projects.

Redeemers Take Control of Southern Politics

After Republican president Rutherford B. Hayes ordered federal troops to leave the South in 1877, white Democrats known as Redeemers gradually reclaimed control over politics across the region. Their primary goal was to reverse the postwar changes that had granted equal rights to African Americans. They described their mission as "redeeming" the South from the influence of freed slaves and their Northern supporters. As a result, most of the social, political, and economic gains African Americans had made during the Reconstruction era quickly eroded.

The Redeemers understood that black voting rights presented a key obstacle to their quest for political power. During Reconstruction, black men voted in large numbers and influenced elections in many states. They also gained representation in government on the local, state, and national levels. As long as black voter turnout remained high, white Democrats knew that it would be difficult to regain political control. Suppressing the black vote thus became a priority for the Redeemers. Among the means they used to achieve this goal were intimidation and violence. African Americans who tried to register or vote ran the risk of being fired from their jobs, evicted from their homes, or targeted for violent crimes.

The Redeemers also used legal tools to prevent blacks from voting. Although the Fifteenth Amendment to the U.S. Constitution prohibited states from denying citizens the right to vote "on account of race, color, or previous condition of servitude," states across the South found countless ways to circumvent it. They passed laws that restricted voting rights on the basis of something other than race—but they always chose restrictions that applied mainly to blacks. For example, some Southern states required prospective voters to pass a literacy test, knowing that many former slaves did not know how to read and write. Others charged prospective voters a fee known as a poll tax or required voters to own property. These restrictions eliminated many African Americans who lived in poverty.

Mississippi enacted a whole series of restrictions designed to prevent blacks from voting. In order to register to vote, men had to prove that they were residents of the state, provide documentation that all of their property taxes had been paid, pay a poll tax, and pass a literacy test. Of course, these restrictions also had the potential to disqualify many white voters, especially men who came from poor families. Some Southern states avoided this complication by enacting a "grandfather clause." This type of law offered an exemption from voter-registration requirements to anyone who had been eligible to vote prior to 1867 or whose ancestors had voted before that time. Since African Americans did not gain the right to vote until 1867, the exemptions only applied to white men. Grandfather clauses passed in every Southern state but Kentucky and West Virginia during the 1890s.

Literacy tests, poll taxes, and other state-imposed restrictions had a dramatic impact on the number of black registered voters in the South. In South Carolina, where 100,000 black men had voted in the 1876 presidential election, the number dropped to 14,000 by 1888. Advocates of black voting rights challenged the legality of such restrictions before the U.S. Supreme Court in 1898.

This 1883 political cartoon depicts Justice as an elderly woman who sleeps through riots and lynching as Redeemers use violence to retake control of the South.

In the case of *Williams v. Mississippi*, however, the Court ruled that the restrictions did not violate the Fifteenth Amendment because they did not target voters specifically on the basis of race. This decision gave legal cover to the discriminatory voter-registration laws that effectively denied black voting rights in the South for the next sixty years.

Without the right to vote, African Americans quickly lost their opportunities to participate in government. Robert Brown Elliott, who was forced to resign from his position as attorney general of South Carolina when white

Democrats took over the state government in 1877, expressed his anger and frustration at the unfairness of the situation: "I desire to place on the record, in the most public and unqualified manner, my sense of the great wrong which thus forces me practically to abandon rights conferred on me, as I fully believe, by a majority of my fellow citizens of the State."[5]

As their political influence waned, blacks throughout the South once again found themselves at the mercy of white lawmakers. George Henry White, a Republican from North Carolina, was the last black man to serve in the U.S. House of Representatives from the South until 1972. "This is perhaps the Negroes' temporary farewell to the American Congress, but let me say, Phoenix-like he will rise up some day and come again," White declared in his farewell speech, delivered on January 29, 1901. "These parting words are in behalf of an outraged, heart-broken, bruised and bleeding, but God-fearing people; faithful, industrious, loyal, rising people—full of potential force"[6] (see "George H. White Makes His 'Defense of the Negro Race' Speech," p. 173).

Jim Crow Laws

Prior to the Civil War, the institution of slavery had defined the boundaries of social interaction between blacks and whites. Because most African Americans in the South were legally considered the property of white people, it was simply understood that they would behave in a subservient manner and defer to white authority. The end of slavery and the passage of civil rights laws and amendments during Reconstruction knocked down these long-established boundaries, but they did not change white Southerners' attitudes about the inferiority and lower social standing of blacks. After Reconstruction ended, many cities and states took steps to reestablish strict boundaries between the races.

"Violence was instrumental for Jim Crow," noted one historian. "It was a method of social control."

Once white Democrats gained control of city councils and state legislatures across the South, they enacted a wide variety of laws aimed at dismantling the civil rights gains that African Americans had made during Reconstruction and returning blacks to the status of second-class citizens. These discriminatory regulations became known as "Jim Crow" laws, after a negative caricature of black people that was popularized by white performers in minstrel shows in the mid-1800s. Such laws legitimized racism and created a racial caste system throughout the South.

Jim Crow laws served as a constant reminder that blacks were considered inferior to whites and that black-white social interactions should be strictly limited. A Mississippi law made it illegal for anyone even to suggest that blacks and whites might be equal: "Any person … who shall be guilty of printing, publishing or circulating printed, typewritten or written matter urging or presenting for public acceptance or general information, arguments or suggestions in favor of social equality or of intermarriage between whites and negroes, shall be guilty of a misdemeanor and subject to fines not exceeding five hundred (500.00) dollars or imprisonment not exceeding six (6) months or both."[7]

Preventing interracial relationships was a major focus of Jim Crow laws. Nearly every Southern state passed laws prohibiting blacks and whites from living together, getting married, and having or adopting children. "Under Jim Crow any and all sexual interaction between black men and white women

Discriminatory anti-black laws became known as "Jim Crow" after a negative caricature of African Americans that was popularized in minstrel shows.

was illegal, illicit, socially repugnant, and within the Jim Crow definition of rape," explained historian David Pilgrim. "[Racist whites believed that] sexual relations between blacks and whites would produce a mongrel race which would destroy America."[8]

In addition to explicit anti-black laws, the Jim Crow system included a maze of unwritten rules to guide social interaction between blacks and whites. All of these social rules reinforced the idea that blacks occupied a lower place in Southern communities. Black men could not offer to shake hands with white men, for instance, because that might imply social equality. Black men were also strictly forbidden from looking at, speaking to, or touching white women. Black people were required to address white people using formal titles, such as Mr., Mrs.,

Sir, or Ma'am. White people, on the other hand, never addressed black people using formal titles. Instead, they addressed blacks using their first names or common nicknames like "boy" or "Auntie." Finally, a black person could never laugh at a white person or imply that a white person might be wrong.

Segregation Policies

In addition to the etiquette rules of the Jim Crow system, Southern Democrats passed laws that formally separated people by race in order to limit social contact between blacks and whites. Segregation laws restricted the use of public facilities—such as schools, hospitals, orphanages, court houses, parks, restrooms, and drinking fountains—to either white or "colored" people. Most white-owned private businesses in the South, including hotels, restaurants, theaters, and stores, only catered to white customers and refused service to blacks.

The Civil Rights Act of 1875, which had been passed shortly before the end of Reconstruction, had prohibited discrimination in businesses that served the public, like restaurants and hotels. On October 15, 1883, however, the U.S.

Bishop Henry McNeal Turner was an outspoken opponent of racial segregation.

Supreme Court overturned the law. The majority ruled that Congress did not have the authority to regulate the practices of private businesses. They also said that the protections of the Fourteenth Amendment only applied to discrimination by state governments, rather than by individual citizens. The lone dissenter, Justice John Marshall Harlan, argued that the Court's decision reduced the Fourteenth Amendment to "splendid baubles, thrown out to delude those who deserved fair and generous treatment at the hands of the nation."[9]

The Supreme Court's ruling essentially legalized racial segregation. It freed cities and states across the South to force black citizens to build separate lives outside of white society. Southern legislatures subsequently passed numerous laws that went to great lengths to prevent any interracial social contact. The city code of Durham, North Carolina, for instance, made it illegal to serve both black and white customers in a restaurant unless they ate in separate rooms or on either side of a solid partition made of wood, plaster, or brick that extended from floor to ceiling. The city of Birmingham, Alabama, passed a law making it illegal for blacks and whites to play cards, dice, checkers, baseball, football, basketball, or any similar games together. The state of Georgia prohibited all-black and all-white baseball teams from playing within two blocks of each other. The state of Louisiana required circus operators to provide separate ticket booths, entrances, and seating areas for white and colored spectators, while the state of Oklahoma required blacks and whites to use separate boat launches, fishing piers, and swimming areas.

On the surface, segregation laws did not necessarily appear discriminatory. They merely required the facilities provided to blacks and whites to be separate. In practice, though, the public facilities available to African Americans were far inferior to those offered to whites. "The world has never witnessed such barbarous laws entailed upon a free people as have grown out of the decision of the United States Supreme Court, issued October 15, 1883," declared abolitionist Henry McNeal Turner.

> For that decision alone authorized and now sustains all the unjust discriminations, proscriptions and robberies perpetrated by public [institutions] upon millions of the nation's most loyal defenders. It fathers all the 'Jim-Crow cars' into which colored people are huddled and compelled to pay as much as the whites, who are given the finest accommodations. It has made the ballot of the black man a parody, his citizenship a nullity and his freedom a burlesque. It has engendered the bitterest feeling between the whites and blacks, and resulted in the deaths of thousands, who would have been living and enjoying life today.[10]

Enforcement of the Jim Crow laws and segregation policies often involved violence. "Violence was instrumental for Jim Crow. It was a method of social control," Pilgrim wrote. "The most extreme forms of Jim Crow violence were lynchings. Lynchings were public, often sadistic, murders carried out by mobs.... Lynching served many purposes: it was cheap entertainment; it served as a rallying, uniting point for whites; it functioned as an ego-massage for low-income, low-status whites; it was a method of defending white domination and helped stop or retard the fledgling social equality movement."[11] Lynching victims could be beaten, hanged, shot, burned at the stake, castrated, or dismembered by angry mobs. In 1892 a record 230 lynchings of African Americans took place in the United States. More than 95 percent of these incidents occurred in former Confederate states or border states.

The Question of Public Transportation

Many segregation laws and policies focused on the issue of public transportation. The late 1800s and early 1900s saw the development and expansion of public transportation networks throughout the United States. Streetcars and subways carried passengers around the nation's rapidly growing urban centers, while steamboats and railroads took travelers on longer journeys.

Segregationists seeking to minimize social contact between blacks and whites were determined to segregate these forms of transportation as well. They faced a difficulty, however, in that public transportation systems had been designed for the use of all citizens. "Railroads were subject to common-law requirements that public carriers accept all customers, subject only to reasonable regulations imposed for public convenience,"[12] wrote legal scholar Michael J. Klarman. Segregationists could not simply exclude black passengers from certain means of travel, because alternative means often were not available. In addition, many transportation systems operated across state lines, so they came under the regulatory authority of the federal government rather than the individual states.

Segregationists were encouraged, however, by the knowledge that some forms of public transportation already divided people by social class. After the war concluded, many wealthy white passengers felt more comfortable sharing a first-class railroad car with refined, neatly dressed black passengers than with dirty, uncivilized, lower-class whites. Many railroad lines thus provided well-appointed luxury accommodations for those who could afford them, and bare-bones "smoking cars" for the masses. Some postwar Black Codes forbade black passengers from riding in first-class cars, but such laws generally disappeared during Reconstruction.

Once Reconstruction ended, though, cities and states across the South revisited the question of segregating their public transportation systems by race. As was the case with other segregation laws, some of the laws concerning transportation were crafted so as to hide their racist intentions. For example, they guaranteed equal access to public transportation for black and white citizens

Booker T. Washington Suggests a Compromise

During the 1890s, African Americans in the South watched the political and economic gains of the Reconstruction era disappear in an atmosphere of Jim Crow laws and racial violence. Black leaders throughout the United States debated about the best way to counteract these changes and secure civil rights for African Americans. On September 15, 1895, the respected black educator Booker T. Washington addressed this question in a speech before a mostly white audience at the Cotton States and International Exposition in Atlanta, Georgia.

In his Atlanta Exposition address, Washington urged African Americans to proceed slowly in their quest for full equality. He suggested that they should accept segregation, social inequality, and the concentration of political power in the hands of whites in exchange for basic education, increased job opportunities, and equality under the law. He believed that African Americans would eventually earn the respect of whites and gain the rights of citizenship through hard work and accommodation. "In all things that are purely social, we can be as separate as the fingers, yet one as the hand in all things essential to mutual progress," he declared. "The wisest among my race understand that the agitation of questions of social equality is the extremest folly, and that progress in the enjoyment of all the privileges that will come to us must be the result of severe and constant struggle rather than of artificial forcing."

Although Washington's prescription for improving race relations made him popular among white segregationists, it drew criticism from African-American activists like W. E. B. Du Bois, who argued that blacks should continue fighting for full political and social equality.

Source

Washington, Booker T. "Atlanta Exposition Speech," September 15, 1895. Retrieved from http://myloc.gov/Exhibitions/naacp/prelude/ExhibitObjects/BookerTWashington Speech.aspx.

Some of the biggest battles over segregation took place in the area of public transportation, as shown in this cartoon depicting an airship with a Jim Crow trailer.

even as they required them to ride in separate cars. Supporters of segregation claimed that these laws would minimize the potential for conflict between the races. A Florida statute, for instance, specified that "no white person shall be permitted to ride in a Negro car or to insult or annoy Negroes in such car."[13] Some African Americans initially welcomed the passage of such laws. They hoped that separate accommodations might be of a higher quality than the ones they usually used, and they believed riding separately might reduce their mistreatment at the hands of white passengers or employees (see "Booker T. Washington Suggests a Compromise," p. 29).

Over time, however, it became apparent that the true intent of segregated public transportation was to increase the comfort of white passengers by eliminating the need for them to come into contact with African Americans. A New Orleans newspaper editorial argued that segregation of railroad cars was necessary because "one is thrown in much closer communication in the car with one's traveling companions than in the theatre or restaurant," and train passengers were "crowded together, squeezed close to each other in the same seats, using the same conveniences, and to all intents and purposes in social intercourse."[14] According to this perspective, white passengers should not be forced to share accommodations with black passengers who were inherently inferior.

Once the real motive for segregating public transportation became clear, most African Americans opposed such measures. They were often joined by railroad companies, which resisted the regulations for a number of reasons. Some railroad companies were based in the North and did not feel segregation was necessary. Others argued that providing separate cars for black and white passengers increased their operating costs. It meant that every train running in the South had to include at least four passenger cars—first-class and smoking cars for both white passengers and black passengers. Many lines did not have enough passengers to fill that many cars, so trains ended up pulling empty cars. Finally, the railroad companies felt uncomfortable about requiring their conductors and other employees to enforce segregation laws. Like the passengers, however, the railroad companies had little choice but to follow the regulations once the segregation laws passed.

Notes

[1] Woodward, C. Vann. "The Case of the Louisiana Traveler." In *American Counterpoint*. Boston: Little, Brown, 1971, p. 163. Retrieved from http://www.soc.umn.edu/~samaha/cases/van%20woodward,%20plessy.htm.

[2] Dixon, Thomas, Jr. *The Clansman: An Historical Romance of the Ku Klux Klan*. New York: Grosset & Dunlap, 1905. Retrieved from http://www.pbs.org/wgbh/amex/reconstruction/plantation/ps_dixon.html.

[3] Quoted in Foner, Eric. *Reconstruction: America's Unfinished Revolution*. New York: Harper and Row, 1988, p. 427.

[4] Quoted in Medley, Keith Weldon. *We as Freemen:* Plessy v. Ferguson. Gretna, LA: Pelican, 2003, p. 104.

[5] Quoted in Hine, Darlene Clark. *The African-American Odyssey*. Upper Saddle River, NJ: Prentice Hall, 2005, p. 310.

[6] White, George H. "Defense of the Negro Race—Charges Answered." Speech before the U.S. House of Representatives, January 29, 1901. Washington, DC: Government Printing Office, 1901.

[7] "Examples of Jim Crow Laws." Jim Crow Museum of Racist Memorabilia, Ferris State University, 2012. Retrieved from http://www.ferris.edu/htmls/news/jimcrow/links/misclink/examples/homepage.htm.

[8] Pilgrim, David. "What Was Jim Crow?" Jim Crow Museum of Racist Memorabilia, Ferris State University, 2012. Retrieved from http://www.ferris.edu/jimcrow/what.htm.

[9] Quoted in Schwartz, Bernard. *A History of the Supreme Court*. New York: Oxford, 1993, p. 167.

[10] Quoted in Wormser, Richard. "Civil Rights Act of 1875 Declared Unconstitutional." *The Rise and Fall of Jim Crow*, PBS. Retrieved from http://www.pbs.org/wnet/jimcrow/stories_events_uncivil.html.

[11] Pilgrim, "What Was Jim Crow?"

[12] Klarman, Michael J. *From Jim Crow to Civil Rights: The Supreme Court and the Struggle for Racial Equality.* New York: Oxford University Press, 2004, p. 17.

[13] Quoted in Chafe, William H., ed. *Remembering Jim Crow: African-Americans Tell about Life in the Segregated South.* New York: New Press, 2001, p. 72.

[14] Quoted in Ayers, Edward L. *Promise of the New South: Life after Reconstruction.* New York: Oxford University Press, 1992, p. 139.

Chapter Three

HOMER PLESSY TAKES A STAND

~✦~

It is the imperative duty of oppressed citizens to seek redress
before the judicial tribunals of the country. In our case, we find
it is the only means left us. We must have recourse to it, or sink
into a state of hopeless inferiority.

—Appeal by the Citizens' Committee, September 5, 1891

One of the most celebrated battles against racial segregation in public transportation took place in New Orleans, Louisiana, in the 1890s. When the
state legislature passed a controversial measure known as the Separate Car
Law, which divided railroad passengers into different cars by race, a group of black
and mixed-race activists based in New Orleans organized a campaign to challenge
the law in court. The test case involved a thirty-year-old shoemaker named
Homer Plessy, who received the assignment because he was "white enough to gain
access to the train and black enough to be arrested for doing so,"[1] according to
historian Keith Weldon Medley. The ultimate goal was to convince the U.S.
Supreme Court to declare the Separate Car Law unconstitutional, which would
nullify similar segregation laws all across the Jim Crow South.

Race Relations in Louisiana

As the civil rights and social standing of African Americans deteriorated
across the South following the end of Reconstruction, the situation changed
more slowly in the state of Louisiana. Louisiana—and especially the city of New
Orleans—had always been different from most of the surrounding region in
terms of race relations. Louisiana had been founded by French traders in the
1700s and still showed a strong French influence in the late 1800s. New

This photograph of Canal Street in New Orleans from the late 1800s shows a mule-drawn streetcar and a statue of Henry Clay, a politician known for promoting compromises over the issue of slavery.

Orleans, located at the mouth of the Mississippi River on the Gulf of Mexico, was a major international port that had long served as a hub for the African slave trade. However, it also attracted many free black settlers from nearby Caribbean island nations such as Haiti and Cuba.

Louisiana became part of the United States in 1803 through the Louisiana Purchase, a territorial expansion that doubled the size of the nation. It became a state nine years later. In the early 1800s the population of New Orleans included 25,000 slaves as well as 20,000 free people of color. The city also had a large population of Creoles, or descendants of French colonists, including mixed-race people of black and French ancestry. Most Creoles of color had never been slaves, and many had light enough skin that they could easily blend in with the city's white population. As a group, Creoles tended to be relatively wealthy and well-educated, and they made many important contributions to the city's economy and culture. Thanks to its melting pot of racial, ethnic, and language groups, New Orleans was a unique and vibrant city that had a history of harmonious interaction between races.

34

Union forces captured New Orleans in April 1862 and occupied it for the remaining three years of the Civil War. The federal troops initiated many progressive political and social changes during the occupation—long before Reconstruction brought such changes to the rest of the South. They ended slavery, for instance, and granted increased civil rights and voting rights to African Americans. As a result, New Orleans served as "somewhat of a laboratory for one of the great democratic experiments in history," according to Medley. "Ex-slaves now relished their newfound freedoms of speech, religion, association, and mobility. They heartily pursued their right to increased citizenship, access to education, and reconstruction of family"[2] (see "The New Orleans Streetcar Boycott," p. 37).

Since it contained a large free black population ready to take full advantage of equal rights, Louisiana emerged as a major focus of federal Reconstruction efforts. The state went further than many others in the South by integrating its public schools and legalizing interracial marriage. In 1872 it became the first state in U.S. history with an African-American governor. Lieutenant Governor Pinckney Benton Stewart (P. B. S.) Pinchback took office in December of that year when his predecessor stepped down during impeachment proceedings. Pinchback's term only lasted thirty-five days, though, until the next election.

In 1873 a group of prominent African-American, Creole, and white businessmen, military leaders, and politicians formed the Louisiana Unification Movement. Its membership included P. G. T. Beauregard, a Creole and former Confederate general; C. C. Antoine, an African-American politician and former Union Army captain; and Jewish businessman Isaac Marks, who served as chairman. The main goal of the Unification Movement was interracial cooperation. On June 16 it issued a manifesto proclaiming its intention to "advocate by speech, and pen, and deed, the equal and impartial exercise by every citizen of

Louisiana became the first state in U.S. history with an African-American governor when P. B. S. Pinchback took office in 1872.

35

Louisiana of every civil and political right guaranteed by the Constitution and the laws of the United States."[3] The Unification Movement encountered resistance from white Democrats, however, and failed to take root. The group's goals of equal rights and cooperative race relations turned out to be ahead of their time. "Their pronouncements were perhaps the most advanced thinking on race to appear anywhere during Reconstruction," one historian noted, "and resembled closely what Congress would enact almost a century later in the Civil Rights Act of 1964."[4]

Even after Reconstruction ended and white Democrats regained control in Louisiana, the state government did not immediately act to reverse the gains that had been made by black citizens. Democrat Francis Tillou Nicholls (see biography, p. 130), a Confederate war hero, became governor in the disputed election of 1876 as part of the political compromise that gave Republican Rutherford B. Hayes the presidency in exchange for his promise to withdraw federal troops from the South. Nicholls pledged to "obliterate the color line in politics and consolidate the people on the basis of equal rights and common interests."[5] Although white supremacists slowly gained power in the state, black and mixed-race Louisianans fought bravely to maintain their rights. As a result, black men still accounted for half of all registered voters by 1888, while the state legislature included eighteen black members.

The Separate Car Act

In the end, though, Louisiana could not resist the flood of Jim Crow laws that washed over the South after the end of Reconstruction. In May 1890 the state legislature debated House Bill 42, commonly known as the Separate Car Act, which would require racial segregation in railroad transportation. Specifically, the bill proposed to "promote the comfort of passengers in railway trains" by requiring railroad companies to provide separate cars for black and white passengers. According to the bill's provisions, any passenger who boarded a car that was designated for people of a different race faced a $25 fine or twenty days in jail. Any railroad employee who failed or refused to enforce segregation—by physically preventing passengers from entering the wrong cars, if necessary—faced a $50 fine or a jail term. Railroad companies that did not provide separate cars incurred a fine of $500. The bill did not make an exception to allow interracial couples to ride together, although it did allow colored nurses to ride in cars designated for white passengers in order to assist their patients.

The New Orleans Streetcar Boycott

Shortly after the Civil War ended, New Orleans' black and Creole communities won an early battle over segregation of public transportation. In 1867 they successfully challenged a law that reserved two-thirds of the city's mule-drawn streetcars for the exclusive use of white passengers and relegated African Americans to cars marked with a black star.

If a person of color boarded an unmarked car, the streetcar company instructed its drivers to refuse to move the vehicle. Those who were seeking to end segregation decided to use this policy to their advantage. A loosely organized protest erupted in which African Americans boarded whites-only streetcars all over the city, bringing traffic to a standstill. As more and more people joined the sit-in, the New Orleans public transportation system was forced to shut down.

Police Chief Thomas Adams responded to the civil disobedience by issuing an order that integrated the city's streetcars. "Have no interference with negroes riding in cars of any kind," he warned in the *New Orleans Crescent*. "No passenger has a right to reject any other passenger, no matter what his color. If he does so, he is liable to arrest for assault, or breech of the peace." The successful streetcar boycott of 1867 demonstrated the power of New Orleans' black community and led to an era of increased equality.

Source

Medley, Keith Weldon. *We as Freemen:* Plessy v. Ferguson. Gretna, LA: Pelican, 2003, p. 80.

The Separate Car Act generated spirited public debate, with passionate voices on both sides of the issue. An editorial in the *New Orleans Times Democrat* argued that it was logical and proper to segregate public transportation, since many other public facilities already divided people by race: "A man that would be horrified at the idea of his wife or daughter seated by the side of a burly negro in the parlor of a hotel or at a restaurant cannot see her occupying a crowded seat in a car next to a negro without the same feeling of disgust."[6]

A weekly African-American newspaper called the *Crusader* led the opposition to the Separate Car Act. Founded in 1889 by Creole attorney Louis A. Mar-

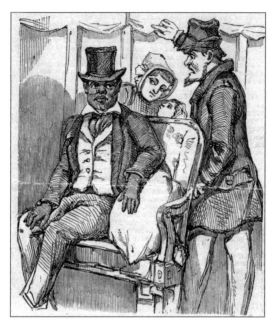

As state after state passed laws segregating railroad travel, African-American passengers ran the risk of being evicted from whites-only cars.

tinet (see biography, p. 127), the *Crusader* described itself as "newsy, spicy, progressive, liberal, stalwart, and fearless"[7] in its support for black rights. *Crusader* contributor Rodolphe Lucien Desdunes (see biography, p. 114) condemned House Bill 42 with particular passion. "Among the many schemes devised by the Southern statesmen to divide the races, none is so insulting as the one which provides separate cars for black and white people on railroads running through the state," he wrote. "It is like a slap in the face of every member of the black race, whether he has the full measure or only one-eighth of that blood."[8]

Opponents of the Separate Car Act formed an interracial organization called the American Citizens' Equal Rights Association (ACERA), which included many former members of the Unification Movement. They held a rally in the state capital, published newspaper editorials and pamphlets, and sent telegrams to legislators in an effort to derail the legislation. "We do not think that citizens of a darker hue should be treated by law on different lines than those of a lighter complexion," an ACERA spokesman declared. "Citizenship is national and has no color. We hold that any attempt to abridge it on account of color is simply a surrender of wisdom to the appeals of passion."[9]

At first it appeared that the state legislature, which included sixteen black members in 1890, might reject the Separate Car Act. But then the bill became caught up in a political controversy surrounding the reauthorization of the Louisiana lottery. The lottery had been created in 1868 by the state legislature, and it was run by the Louisiana Lottery Company under a twenty-five-year lease arrangement. During its existence, the lottery had grown into a multimillion dollar business. In the city of New Orleans alone, there were more than one hundred lottery shops that sold tickets for the monthly drawings. Opponents of gambling, however, criticized the lottery for contributing to what they viewed as moral decay in the city. They pointed out that New Orleans contained some 650 saloons, dance parlors, gambling dens, and related businesses of questionable repute.

The lottery lease came up for review before the state legislature in 1890, around the same time as the Separate Car Act. The controversial measure split both the Democratic and Republican parties into pro- and anti-lottery factions and created unusual alliances between members from different parties. With several black legislators voting in favor of reauthorizing the lottery, the bill passed. Governor Nicholls vetoed it, but the Senate judiciary committee ruled that he did not have the authority to do so because the lottery lease was part of the state constitution. The proposed lottery renewal amendment appeared on the ballot during the next election, and it was approved by popular vote.

In the meantime, a group of anti-lottery state legislators, led by Senator Murphy J. Foster, threw their support behind the Separate Car Act. Martinet, Desdunes, and other opponents of racial segregation claimed that Foster resurrected the bill as a form of revenge against the black legislators who had voted for the lottery. When the Separate Car Act came up for a vote, eight white senators switched sides and voted in favor of it. Although opponents begged Governor Nicholls to veto the legislation, he ignored their pleas and signed it into law on July 10, 1890 (see "Louisiana Passes the Separate Car Law," p. 148).

"Among the many schemes devised by the Southern statesmen to divide the races, none is so insulting as the one which provides separate cars for black and white people on railroads running through the state," wrote Rodolphe Desdunes. *"It is like a slap in the face of every member of the black race."*

Opponents Challenge the Law

As soon as the Separate Car Law took effect, the *Crusader* began encouraging the black citizens of Louisiana to support efforts to challenge it in court. "We are American citizens and it is our duty to defend our constitutional rights against the encroachments and attacks of prejudice," Desdunes wrote. "The courts are open for that purpose, and it is our fault if we do not seek the redress they alone can afford in cases of injustice done or of wrongs endured."[10] Although passions ran high, it took opponents of the law over a year to raise funds for a legal challenge, get advice from attorneys, and devise a strategy for overturning the measure.

The challenge began to take shape on September 1, 1891, when the respected Republican activist Aristide Mary gathered a group of eighteen prominent black

Haitian-born Arthur Esteves, who founded a successful sailmaking business in New Orleans, served as president of the Citizens' Committee to Test the Constitutionality of the Separate Car Law.

and Creole community leaders to form the Comité des Citoyens, or Citizens' Committee to Test the Constitutionality of the Separate Car Law. The members of the Citizens' Committee were an elite group of well-educated, bilingual, politically active businessmen, educators, lawyers, journalists, artisans, and government workers. The group included Martinet, Desdunes, and former Unification Movement member Antoine. Arthur Esteves, owner of a successful sailmaking business in New Orleans, was elected president of the committee.

To help develop its legal strategy, the Citizens' Committee consulted with Albion W. Tourgée (see biography, p. 136), a well-known white attorney from New York. Tourgée had been a leader in the fight to abolish slavery before the Civil War, and he remained a vocal advocate of African-American rights during Reconstruction and the early Jim Crow era. He had published several articles about the Separate Car Act and the battle to prevent its passage in the Louisiana state legislature. Tourgée offered to waive his usual attorney's fees and provide his legal expertise for free. Given his busy schedule and the time and expense involved in traveling to New Orleans, however, he recommended that the Citizens' Committee find a local lawyer to take the case through the Louisiana court system. The organization subsequently hired Louisiana attorney James C. Walker for this purpose, but Tourgée promised to take over if the legal challenge went all the way to the U.S. Supreme Court.

The Citizens' Committee believed that the best way to test the constitutionality of the Separate Car Law was to break it. They decided to find a "colored" volunteer who was willing to intentionally disobey the law by boarding a railroad car that was designated for white passengers only. If all went according to plan, the person would be arrested and charged with a crime for failing to comply with the Separate Car Law. Then the courts would be forced to confront the issue of whether racial segregation of public transportation violated the U.S. Constitution. If the U.S. Supreme Court ultimately ruled in the group's favor, it would not only overturn Louisiana's Separate Car Law, but it would also nullify similar segregation laws all across the South.

In order to demonstrate the absurdity of the law, the Citizens' Committee wanted a volunteer with certain characteristics. It sought a person who would be defined as colored under the law, but who had such light skin that they ordinarily would not be questioned for sitting in a whites-only car. It also wanted a well-mannered, respectable, law-abiding citizen whose civil disobedience would be taken seriously. The Citizens' Committee also decided to seek the cooperation of railroad officials in its test case. Members knew that the railroad companies generally disliked the Separate Car Law and were reluctant to enforce it. After the committee presented its plan to several different railroads, representatives of the Louisville and Nashville line agreed to participate.

The initial test of the Separate Car Law took place on February 24, 1892. Musician Daniel Desdunes, the son of journalist and Citizens' Committee member Rodolphe Desdunes, attempted to board a first-class, whites-only railroad car on Canal Street in New Orleans. Before the train embarked on its journey to Mobile, Alabama, Desdunes informed the conductor that he was not allowed to ride in a car designated for white passengers because he was one-eighth black. In other words, one of his eight great-grand-parents had been African American. Desdunes was then arrested and charged with violating the Separate Car Law.

Before Desdunes's case went to trial, however, the state dismissed the charges against him. The Louisiana Supreme Court—now led by Chief Justice Francis T. Nicholls, the former governor who had signed the Separate Car Act into law—ruled in the unrelated case *Abbott v. Hicks* that the state's segregation laws did not apply to interstate travel. The court noted that the Commerce Clause of the U.S. Constitution gave the federal government, rather than the individual states, authority to regulate transportation that crossed state borders. The trial judge appointed to hear the Desdunes case, John Howard Ferguson, cited

> *"It is hoped that what [Judge Ferguson] says will have some effect on the silly negroes who are trying to fight this law,"* declared an editorial in the New Orleans Times-Picayune. *"The sooner they drop their so-called crusade against 'the Jim Crow car,' … the better for them."*

the higher court's ruling in dismissing the charges against Desdunes. Martinet viewed the ruling as a major victory for the Citizens' Committee. "The Jim Crow car is ditched and will remain in the ditch,"[11] he declared.

Homer Plessy Rides into History

Although the outcome of the Desdunes case was encouraging, members of the Citizens' Committee knew that the Separate Car Law still applied to railroad lines that operated wholly within the state of Louisiana. They decided to arrange another test in hopes of gaining a favorable court ruling that would decisively end racial segregation in public transportation. They also recognized that a highly publicized legal drama could draw national attention to the erosion of black civil rights in the Jim Crow South. "The people of the North must be educated to conditions in the South, & this can only be done through the press," Martinet wrote in the *Crusader*. "We must expose continually to the people of the North the hideous sores of the South & the ever-recurring outrages to which we are subjected & the lurking therein to the Nation."[12]

For its second test case, the Citizens' Committee turned to a quiet, unassuming, thirty-year-old shoemaker named Homer Adolph Plessy (see biography, p. 133). Plessy's parents had been free people of color in New Orleans before the Civil War, and his stepfather had been a member of the Unification Movement during Reconstruction. Having grown up during the federal occupation of New Orleans, Plessy was determined to do his part to preserve the civil rights that the city's black community had worked so hard to achieve. On June 7, 1892, he purchased a first-class ticket on an East Louisiana Railroad train that was scheduled to travel from New Orleans to Covington, Louisiana, around fifty miles away. When the train arrived, Plessy boarded a car designated for white passengers only. Since he had light skin, none of the other passengers questioned his right to sit in the car.

East Louisiana Railroad conductor J. J. Dowling had been notified in advance of Plessy's intention to violate the Separate Car Act. When Dowling approached Plessy and inquired about his race, Plessy acknowledged that he was considered "colored" under Louisiana law. When Dowling asked Plessy to move to the car designated for black passengers, Plessy refused. He was then placed under arrest and taken to jail, although he was released a short time later when six members of the Citizens' Committee arrived to post his bail. Plessy appeared in court the following morning. At that time, Dowling and another

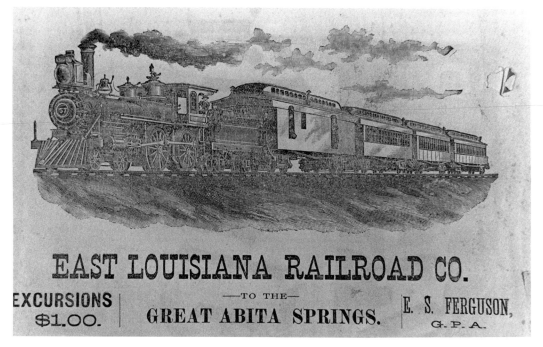

EAST LOUISIANA RAILROAD CO.

EXCURSIONS $1.00.

—TO THE—
GREAT ABITA SPRINGS.

E. S. FERGUSON, G. P. A.

On June 7, 1892, Homer Plessy intentionally boarded an East Louisiana Railroad car designated for white passengers only as a test of the Separate Car Law.
Photo Credit: The Historic New Orleans Collection, Acc. No. 1974.25.37.57.

witness swore affidavits that Plessy had boarded the wrong train car and refused orders to move. The case, then titled *Louisiana v. Plessy,* was scheduled for trial before Judge John H. Ferguson (see biography, p. 117) in the Criminal Court of the Parish of New Orleans on October 13, 1892.

When Plessy got his day in court, he was represented by James C. Walker, the New Orleans attorney retained by the Citizens' Committee. Walker immediately asked Ferguson to dismiss the charges against his client. He argued that the Separate Car Law was unconstitutional because it violated the Thirteenth and Fourteenth Amendments. The Thirteenth Amendment had outlawed slavery and involuntary servitude. Walker claimed that segregating African Americans in public spaces was one of the features of slavery and was therefore illegal. The Fourteenth Amendment had declared all U.S. citizens to be equal before the law. By creating artificial distinctions between citizens on the basis of race, Walker argued, the Separate Car Law discarded equal treatment in favor of white superiority. Walker also urged Ferguson to invalidate the

Separate Car Law because it was unclear about the status of mixed-race people and light-skinned blacks. Finally, he claimed that the law gave train conductors unwarranted authority to determine the race of passengers.

Lionel Adams was the prosecuting attorney who represented the State of Louisiana in Ferguson's court. He argued that the Separate Car Law served a legitimate state interest. He claimed that the intent of the law was to reduce racial tensions and promote the comfort and safety of passengers during railroad travel within the state. Adams also pointed out that the law required the cars provided to white and black passengers to provide equal accommodations. According to Adams, this meant that the act did not discriminate on the basis of race.

After considering the arguments for both sides, Judge Ferguson issued his decision on November 18. He ruled against Plessy, asserting that the Separate Car Law was, in fact, constitutional. White segregationists celebrated the ruling and tried to convince the Citizens' Committee to give up the fight. "It is hoped that what [Judge Ferguson] says will have some effect on the silly negroes who are trying to fight this law," declared an editorial in the *New Orleans Times-Picayune*. "The sooner they drop their so-called crusade against 'the Jim Crow car,' … the better for them."[13] But Plessy and the Citizens' Committee remained determined to pursue the matter all the way to the U.S. Supreme Court if necessary. As the next step in that process, they appealed Ferguson's ruling to the Louisiana Supreme Court. At this point the case became known as *Plessy v. Ferguson*.

Opponents of the Separate Car Law had little hope of success in the state Supreme Court. After all, the court was led by Chief Justice Francis Nicholls, who had signed the bill into law during his tenure as governor. The Louisiana Supreme Court heard the case on November 22 and, as expected, upheld the lower court's ruling a few weeks later. Justice Charles E. Fenner, who wrote the decision, claimed that the law was not discriminatory because it applied equally to blacks and whites. Whites were not allowed to ride in train cars designated for black passengers, just as blacks could not ride in those designated for white passengers. He also said that the state had acted within its authority to regulate railroad travel within its borders. Finally, he concluded that forcing black passengers and white passengers to ride together in the same car "would foster and intensify repulsion between them."[14] Although Plessy, his lawyers, and the members of the Citizens' Committee were disappointed with the decision, they looked forward to taking the battle against segregation in public transportation to the highest court in the land.

Notes

[1] Medley, Keith Weldon. *We as Freemen:* Plessy v. Ferguson. Gretna, LA: Pelican, 2003, p. 17.

[2] Medley, p. 74.

[3] Quoted in Williams, T. Henry. "The Louisiana Unification Movement of 1873." In *The Journal of Southern History,* Vol. IX, No. 1. Nashville, TN: Vanderbilt University Press, 1945, p. 359.

[4] Nystrom, Justin A. "Reconstruction." In *KnowLA Encyclopedia of Louisiana.* Louisiana Endowment for the Humanities, December 21, 2012. Retrieved from http://www.knowla.org/entry.php?rec=463.

[5] Quoted in Fischer, Roger A. *The Segregation Struggle in Louisiana, 1862-77.* Urbana: University of Illinois Press, 1974, p. 134.

[6] Quoted in Olsen, Otto H. *The Thin Disguise: Turning Point in Negro History*—Plessy v. Ferguson. New York: American Institute for Marxist Studies, 1967, p. 53.

[7] Quoted in Medley, p. 104.

[8] Quoted in Esty, Amos. *The Civil Rights Movement:* Plessy v. Ferguson. Greensboro, NC: Morgan Reynolds, 2012, p. 48.

[9] *Official Journal of the Proceedings of the House of Representatives.* Baton Rouge, LA: 1890, p. 62.

[10] Desdunes, Rodolphe. "To Be or Not to Be." *Crusader,* July 4, 1891.

[11] Martinet, Louis. "Jim Crow Is Dead." *Crusader,* July 1892.

[12] Quoted in Medley, p. 157.

[13] Quoted in Stevens, Leonard. *Equal! The Case of Integration vs. Jim Crow.* New York: Coward, McCann, and Geohagen, 1976, p. 48.

[14] Fenner, Charles E. *Ex parte Plessy.* In McKinney, William M., ed. *The American and English Railroad Cases.* Long Island, NY: Edward Thompson, 1894, p. 556.

Chapter Four
SEPARATE BUT EQUAL

The arbitrary separation of citizens, on the basis of race, while they are on a public highway, is a badge of servitude wholly inconsistent with the civil freedom and the equality before the law established by the constitution. It cannot be justified upon any legal grounds.

—U.S. Supreme Court justice John Marshall Harlan, dissenting opinion in *Plessy v. Ferguson*

The *Plessy v. Ferguson* case finally reached the U.S. Supreme Court in 1896. The prominent civil rights advocate Albion W. Tourgée, appearing on behalf of Homer Plessy, argued that Louisiana's Separate Car Law was unconstitutional. Attorney Alexander Porter Morse, representing Louisiana, argued that the state legislature had acted within its authority in segregating public transportation. The Supreme Court's landmark 7-1 decision upheld the lower court's ruling that racial segregation did not violate the U.S. Constitution, as long as the accommodations provided to black and white citizens were "separate but equal." This controversial ruling gave legal sanction to segregation, which soon encompassed virtually all aspects of life in the South. As Justice John Marshall Harlan predicted in his scathing dissent, however, the *Plessy v. Ferguson* decision also stained the Court's reputation for decades to come.

The *Plessy* Case Reaches the U.S. Supreme Court

It took longer than many people expected to bring Homer Plessy's challenge of Louisiana's Separate Car Law before the U.S. Supreme Court. After receiving the unfavorable ruling from the Louisiana Supreme Court in late 1892, the Citizens' Committee could have filed an immediate appeal and had the case heard in the spring of 1893. But the committee members and Tourgée decided to take some time to raise funds for the ongoing legal battle. In the meantime, they hoped that the makeup of the Supreme Court—as well as the political and social climate of the nation—might shift in their favor (see "The U.S. Supreme Court," p. 50).

Looking at the Supreme Court in early 1893, Tourgée determined that only one of the justices, John Marshall Harlan, was clearly supportive of protecting African-American civil rights. Five of the other justices had issued rulings that made it appear as if they were strongly opposed to the cause. Tourgée felt uncertain about the leanings of the three remaining justices. Since he needed a majority of the nine-member Court to decide in Plessy's favor in order to overturn the Separate Car Law, he did not feel optimistic about his chances before that particular Court. He felt that the situation might improve if new justices joined the Court.

As Tourgée had hoped, two new justices were confirmed in 1895 to replace justices who had died. Unfortunately, President Grover Cleveland appointed two men who did not seem likely to be sympathetic to Plessy's position. Justice Edward D. White was a former Confederate soldier from Louisiana. Justice Rufus Wheeler Peckham hailed from New York, but he was generally viewed as a pro-business conservative.

Unfavorable changes also took place in the nation's political and social climate in the intervening years. The equal rights laws that had been passed during Reconstruction continued to be replaced with discriminatory Jim Crow laws across the South. But Northerners and Republican lawmakers showed little interest in intervening to protect the rights of African Americans. Many people viewed Reconstruction as a failure, and they longed to reconcile the two halves of the country and move forward—even if that meant leaving blacks to fend for themselves. Meanwhile, the state of Louisiana fell in line with the rest of the South in terms of racial segregation. In 1894 the state legislature strengthened its railroad segregation law to require separate black and white waiting areas in train stations, and it also took steps to limit interracial marriage. In addition, white supremacists continued to consolidate power in the state through intimidation and violence. One-third of the lynchings that occurred in the United States in 1893 took place in Louisiana.

The U.S. Supreme Court reflected the souring national mood toward Reconstruction and African-American rights by issuing several decisions that

This composite photograph shows the eight U.S. Supreme Court justices who decided the *Plessy v. Ferguson* case in 1896 (Justice Brewer abstained).

The U.S. Supreme Court

The Supreme Court is the highest judicial body in the United States. Its role in the U.S. government is to ensure that all laws passed by Congress and actions taken by the president are legal under the Constitution. It is made up of eight associate justices and one chief justice who are nominated by the president and confirmed by Congress. Supreme Court justices have life tenure, meaning that they serve until they die or decide to retire.

Thousands of cases are submitted to the Court for review each year, but the justices only accept about 150 that represent important legal issues. The Supreme Court's annual term lasts from October to June. During this time, the justices alternate between two-week sessions of hearing oral arguments in court and two-week recesses in which they read legal briefs and write opinions. Most cases have a total of one hour allotted for oral arguments before the Court, half an hour of which is used by each side to present key legal issues and answer questions from the justices.

The Supreme Court underwent many changes during and after Reconstruction. In the decade leading up to the *Plessy v. Ferguson* ruling in 1896, seven justices left the Court. In general, they were replaced by new justices who did not believe that the federal government should intervene when state governments passed laws that limited the civil rights of African Americans. The following list provides basic information on the Supreme Court justices who heard *Plessy v. Ferguson,* in order of seniority:

Stephen J. Field: The oldest member of the Court at eighty, Field had been appointed by Abraham Lincoln in 1863. Although he was a Republican from Connecticut, he had dissented in previous Court decisions that upheld the right of black men to serve on juries.

narrowed the scope of the Thirteenth, Fourteenth, and Fifteenth Amendments to the Constitution. The Court refused to invalidate state laws that restricted black voting rights through literacy tests and poll taxes, for instance. The majority held that such laws were constitutional because they were race-neutral on their surface, even if they had discriminatory effects. The Court also found laws requiring segregation of public schools to be constitutional. The justices did

John Marshall Harlan: Appointed by Rutherford B. Hayes in 1877, the sixty-three-year-old former slave owner from Kentucky had often clashed with his colleagues over civil rights issues and was considered the most likely justice to vote in favor of Plessy.

Horace Gray: A sixty-eight-year-old Republican from Massachusetts, Gray had been appointed by Chester B. Arthur in 1882. He placed tremendous value on precedent and was considered unlikely to support Plessy.

Melville W. Fuller: The sixty-three-year-old chief justice, appointed by Grover Cleveland in 1888, hailed from Maine and was a Democrat and states' rights supporter.

David J. Brewer: A Republican appointed by Benjamin Harrison in 1890, the fifty-nine-year-old Brewer was considered a wild card because he had supported both states' rights and the abolition of slavery. He recused himself from hearing the *Plessy* case without offering an explanation.

Henry Billings Brown: Appointed by Harrison in 1891, the sixty-year-old Brown came from a wealthy Massachusetts family. He was considered a moderate Republican as well as a supporter of states' rights.

George Shiras Jr.: The sixty-four-year-old Republican from Pennsylvania, appointed by Harrison in 1892, tended to vote with the majority throughout his judicial career.

Edward D. White: Appointed by Grover Cleveland in 1894, the fifty-one-year-old Democrat from Louisiana had served as an officer in the Confederate Army.

Rufus W. Peckham: The fifty-eight-year-old Democrat from New York, appointed by Cleveland in 1896, had a reputation as a pro-business conservative.

decide that the Reconstruction amendments protected the rights of blacks to serve on juries, but they did not go so far as to overturn the convictions of black defendants by all-white juries.

After surveying the legal, political, and social situation in which the *Plessy* case would be heard, *Crusader* publisher Louis Martinet expressed deep reservations in a letter to Tourgée. "The question forces itself upon me, are we not fighting a hopeless battle—a battle made doubly hopeless by the tyranny and cruelty of the Southern white?" he asked. "If our fight is fruitless, or rather our own manner of fighting ... what is to be done?"[1]

Tourgée Argues on Behalf of Plessy

Despite such reservations, the Citizens' Committee submitted *Plessy v. Ferguson* to the U.S. Supreme Court for review in late 1895. The Court agreed to hear the case on April 13, 1896. Tourgée traveled to Washington, D.C., from New York to argue on behalf of Plessy. James Walker, who had presented the case to Judge Ferguson and to the Louisiana Supreme Court, was too ill to make the trip from New Orleans. In his place, Tourgée called upon Samuel F. Phillips, a former U.S. solicitor general who had unsuccessfully defended the Civil Rights Act of 1875 before the Court in 1883.

Tourgée, Walker, and Phillips all provided the justices with lengthy written arguments called briefs that outlined the main legal points supporting their position that the Separate Car Law was unconstitutional (see "Plessy's Lawyers Present Their Arguments in a Legal Brief," p. 155). Tourgée also made a thirty-minute oral argument before the Court, during which the justices had the opportunity to raise questions and ask for clarification. Although the oral arguments were not recorded or transcribed at that time, Tourgée kept a written copy of his remarks.

Tourgée and his colleagues asked the Court to adopt a broad interpretation of the three constitutional amendments that had grown out of the North's victory in the Civil War. They argued that the outcome of the war had fundamentally changed the nature of citizenship in the United States, redefining it without reference to race or color. "The old citizenship of the United States was determined by race or descent," Tourgée declared. "In the new citizenship color is expressly ignored and the sole condition of citizenship is birth in the United States."[2]

The Fourteenth Amendment, Plessy's defenders argued, made state citizenship subordinate to national citizenship and gave the federal government new powers to protect African Americans against discrimination by state governments. It prohibited states from abridging the "privileges or immunities" of citizens, depriving them of "life, liberty, or property, without due process of law," or denying them "the equal protection of the laws." Tourgée claimed that the Separate Car Law violated the Four-teenth Amendment by abridging Plessy's freedom to occupy his seat of choice. He also noted that enforcement of the Sep-arate Car Law deprived Plessy of prop-erty, including the first-class railroad ticket he had purchased, and cast a shadow over his public reputation. Tourgée described the law as a blatant "attempt to evade the constitutional requirements of equality of right and legal privilege to all citizens."[3]

Plessy's lawyers also said that the law ran afoul of the Fourteenth Amend-ment by denying Plessy and other black railway passengers equality under the law. Although proponents claimed that the Separate Car Law applied equally to black and white passengers, Tourgée argued that its true purpose was to pro-mote the comfort of white passengers at the expense of black passengers. "The claim that this act is for the common advantage of both races … is farcical," he

Abolitionist, author, and attorney Albion W. Tourgée led the U.S. Supreme Court challenge of the Separate Car Law.

asserted. "The question is not as to the equality of the privileges enjoyed, but the right of the State to label one citizen as white and another as colored in the common enjoyment of a public highway."[4]

Tourgée and his colleagues also claimed that the Separate Car Law violated the Thirteenth Amendment, which outlawed slavery and involuntary servitude. Court decisions from the Reconstruction era had expanded the interpretation of the amendment to include "conditions of subjection and inferiority" that resembled slavery, as well as "burdens and disabilities of a servile character" that created a legalized caste system. Tourgée argued that forcing Plessy to sit in a Jim Crow car had humiliated him, placed him in an inferior condition, and bur-dened him with a "badge of servitude." He claimed that the federal government had a responsibility to protect African Americans from state-imposed discrim-ination that subjected them to second-class citizenship.

> *"The old citizenship of the United States was determined by race or descent,"* attorney Albion W. Tourgée declared. *"In the new citizenship color is expressly ignored and the sole condition of citizenship is birth in the United States."*

Plessy's defenders also attacked the Separate Car Law on the grounds that it was vague and deceptive. The Due Process Clause of the Fourteenth Amendment requires laws to be clearly written and applied fairly to all citizens. Tourgée argued that the Louisiana statute violated the amendment because it contained inexact terms, such as "persons of colored race." Tourgée claimed that in the case of a light-skinned person like Plessy, it was impossible to determine his race or classify him by "color" in an objective manner.

Finally, Plessy's lawyers argued that the law violated the Due Process Clause by giving unwarranted legal powers to train conductors. The Separate Car Law made train conductors responsible for determining passengers' race in order to decide whether they should be allowed to sit in cars reserved for whites. The conductors' enforcement of the law carried legal consequences for passengers, including arrest and a fine. But the Separate Car Law made railroads and their employees exempt from civil liability, meaning that passengers could not sue for damages if they wrongfully applied the law. By leaving railroad passengers without legal recourse, Tourgée claimed that the Separate Car Law deprived them of their right to Due Process. He concluded by warning that the law served only to "perpetuate the stigma of color—to make the curse immortal, incurable, inevitable."[5]

The State of Louisiana Presents Its Case

On the other side of the *Plessy v. Ferguson* case was the legal team representing the state of Louisiana. Its job was to convince the justices of the U.S. Supreme Court to uphold Judge John H. Ferguson's 1892 ruling that the Separate Car Law was constitutional. State attorney general Milton Cunningham submitted a brief that summarized the findings of the Louisiana Supreme Court. But neither he nor Lionel Adams, who had argued the original case before Judge Ferguson, made the trip to Washington, D.C. Instead, the task of presenting oral arguments in favor of the Separate Car Law fell to Alexander Porter Morse, a Louisiana native who specialized in federal appeals cases.

Morse and his legal team argued that the Louisiana state legislature had acted within its constitutional authority when it required railroad cars to be segregated by race. Under the Tenth Amendment, any powers not reserved for the federal government fell under the domain of the states. These so-called "police powers" gave states the right to enact reasonable regulations of public accommodations in order to protect the health, safety, or morality of citizens. Morse claimed that the Separate Car Law was "designed to prevent problems that could prove harmful to society if such regulation were left entirely to the whims and passions of each passenger riding the train."[6] Rather than abridging the rights of African Americans, he claimed that the legislation promoted the common good by protecting black passengers from harassment and violence at the hands of whites.

Morse and his colleagues mentioned a number of precedents, or previous court decisions, that supported states' rights to pass segregation laws. They pointed out that such laws were commonplace across the South, and they noted that Washington, D.C., and many states in the North, Midwest, and West had passed laws segregating their public schools. In addition, the Union Army had maintained segregated units during the Civil War. The lawyers claimed that segregation laws were so common because they reflected public opinion. Most Americans believed that there were fundamental differences between blacks and whites, Morse argued, and that these differences precluded any close social interaction between the races.

Morse acknowledged that the Thirteenth, Fourteenth, and Fifteenth Amendments had granted citizenship and civil rights to African Americans. But he insisted that there was a distinction between civil rights, which were protected by federal law, and social rights, which were defined by the states to reflect the opinions and beliefs of their citizens. Morse argued that the Separate Car Law did not discriminate against blacks or deny their civil rights because it required railroads to provide equal accommodations to both races. He described the Louisiana statute as a legitimate use of state authority to define social rights in accordance with public opinion and thus promote the common good.

The Supreme Court Reaches a Verdict

On May 18, 1896—one month after hearing oral arguments—the U.S. Supreme Court announced its decision in the case of *Plessy v. Ferguson*. In a 7-1 ruling (Justice David J. Brewer excused himself from participating), the Court declared Louisiana's Separate Car Act constitutional and rejected Plessy's request to overturn Ferguson's original finding. Justice Henry Billings Brown (see biography, p. 111) wrote the majority opinion. The son of a wealthy Massachusetts

Justice Henry Billings Brown wrote the majority opinion in *Plessy v. Ferguson.*

businessman and a graduate of both Yale and Harvard, Brown had been appointed to the Court by President Benjamin Harrison in 1890. Chief Justice Melville Fuller generally turned to Brown to write opinions that favored business interests and private property rights, so Tourgée took it as a bad sign when he learned that Brown had prepared the Court's decision (see "Justice Brown Announces the Majority Opinion in *Plessy v. Ferguson,*" p. 158).

Brown started out by agreeing with Louisiana's position that a fundamental difference existed between blacks and whites. He said this difference was "founded in the color of the two races" and "must always exist so long as white men are distinguished from the other race by color."[7] Brown acknowledged Tourgée's point that the Fourteenth Amendment granted civil rights to African Americans and made the two races equal before the law. He claimed, however, that the law could not change people's attitudes about race, which created unavoidable social distinctions between blacks and whites. "If the civil and political rights of both races be equal, one cannot be inferior to the other civilly or politically," he declared. "If one race be inferior to the other socially, the Constitution of the United States cannot put them on the same plane."[8]

Brown also rejected the idea that the Separate Car Law violated the Thirteenth Amendment. He said that segregation could not be compared to slavery because it was not intended to "destroy the legal equality of the two races, or to reestablish a state of involuntary servitude"[9] for African Americans. Brown also disagreed with Tourgée's contention that segregation discriminated against blacks or relegated them to a position of second-class citizenship. After all, he pointed out, the law also prohibited whites from riding in cars reserved for blacks. It required railroads to provide cars that were "separate but equal." "We consider the underlying fallacy of the plaintiff's argument to consist in the assumption that the enforced separation of the two races stamps the colored race with a badge of inferiority," Brown stated. "If this be so, it is not by reason of anything found in the act, but solely because the colored race chooses to put that construction upon it."[10]

Finally, Brown asserted that the Separate Car Law qualified as reasonable regulation, and the Louisiana legislature had acted within its authority when it enacted the law. He said that segregation by race reflected public opinion. To prove his point, Brown mentioned a number of legal precedents that supported segregation laws, including some that had been passed in the North prior to the Civil War. He claimed that these rulings proved that individual states were "at liberty to act with reference to the established uses, customs, and traditions of the people, and with a view to the promotion of their comfort, and the preservation of the public peace and good order."[11]

A Lone Dissenter

The only justice who disagreed with the majority opinion in *Plessy v. Ferguson* was John Marshall Harlan (see biography, p. 120). At first blush, Harlan seemed like an unlikely person to support Plessy's fight against segregation. Harlan hailed from Kentucky, where his family had owned slaves before the Civil War. He had opposed secession, however, and joined the Union Army. Harlan was appointed to the Supreme Court by President Rutherford B. Hayes in 1877, at the end of Reconstruction. He surprised many observers by frequently disagreeing with his colleagues in matters of African-American rights. In fact, Harlan opposed the majority so regularly that he became known as the "Great Dissenter."

Harlan detailed his objections to the Court's *Plessy v. Ferguson* ruling in a strongly worded dissenting opinion (see "Justice Harlan Delivers a Scathing Dissent," p. 165). Although he acknowledged that blacks and whites may not be equal in terms of education or wealth, Harlan declared that the U.S. Constitution extended the same civil rights protections to all American citizens, regardless of race. "Our Constitution is color blind and neither knows nor tolerates classes among citizens," he stated. "In respect to civil rights, all citizens are equal before the law."[12] Harlan rejected the legal precedents Brown had cited in upholding the Separate Car Law, asserting that

"If the civil and political rights of both races be equal, one cannot be inferior to the other civilly or politically," Justice Henry Billings Brown stated. "If one race be inferior to the other socially, the Constitution of the United States cannot put them on the same plane."

they did not apply because they came from a time when slavery and racial prejudice were officially sanctioned. He argued that the Civil War and Reconstruction had fundamentally altered the legal standing of African Americans and eliminated race as a legitimate distinction to be made by government.

Harlan agreed with Tourgée's argument that government authorities had no business inquiring about a citizen's race, as the state of Louisiana did under the Separate Car Law. "The constitution of the United States does not, I think, permit any public authority to know the race of those entitled to be protected in the enjoyment of such rights," he wrote. "Indeed, such legislation as that here in question is inconsistent not only with that equality of rights which pertains to citizenship, national and state, but with the personal liberty enjoyed by every one within the United States."[13]

In a scathing dissent, Justice John Marshall Harlan warned that the Court's *Plessy* decision would encourage states to pass new segregation laws.

Instead of promoting the common good, as Morse had contended, Harlan insisted that segregation did the opposite by granting legal sanction to racial prejudice and hatred. "What can more certainly arouse race hate than state enactments which ... proceed on the ground that colored citizens are so inferior and degraded that they cannot be allowed to sit in public coaches occupied by white citizens?"[14] he asked. Harlan also supported Tourgée's claim that segregation amounted to a new form of slavery by abridging the rights of African Americans and branding them with a "badge of servitude." He argued that the ruling gave the states power "to interfere with the full enjoyment of the blessings of freedom; to regulate civil rights, common to all citizens, on the basis of race; and to place in a condition of legal inferiority a large body of American citizens."[15]

Finally, Harlan warned that the majority decision would lead to the enactment of similar segregation laws throughout the South. He even claimed that it gave states the legal authority to segregate citizens by nationality, religion, or any other distinction they cared to make. Harlan also predicted that the separate facilities provided to blacks and whites would never be equal. Instead, he said that segregation laws would further reinforce the social dominance of whites and relegate blacks to a position of second-class citizenship. "The thin disguise of 'equal' accommodations for passengers in railroad coaches will not mislead any one, nor atone for the wrong this day done,"[16] he declared.

Reaction to the Ruling

The *Plessy v. Ferguson* ruling did not attract widespread newspaper coverage. The *New York Times,* for instance, only mentioned it on page 3 in a column about railroads. Several papers in the South published editorials praising the majority for confirming states' rights to regulate activities within their borders. For the most part, though, the verdict was met with shrugs of indifference. "Based on precedent, most contemporary commentators had concluded that racial segregation was permissible," noted historian Michael J. Klarman. "Given the strong legal case for sustaining segregation, the justices were unlikely to resist powerful public opinion endorsing the practice."[17]

A few papers in the North did criticize the Court's ruling and express concern about its implications for the rights of African Americans. "The announcement of this decision will be received by thoughtful and fair-minded people with disapproval and regret. It is not in harmony with the principles of this republic or with the spirit of our time," noted a former abolitionist journal out of Rochester, New York. "It puts the official stamp of the highest court in the country upon the miserable doctrine that several millions of American citizens are of an inferior race and unfit to mingle with citizens of other races."[18]

Many average Americans, though, simply viewed the *Plessy v. Ferguson* ruling as reasonable and appropriate. They believed that blacks and whites were basically different, and they accepted the segregation laws spreading across the South as a manifestation of this belief. The Supreme Court thus ruled in the manner most people expected, and the decision did not significantly change Americans' attitudes about race. "The *Plessy* Court's race decisions reflected, far more than they created, the regressive racial climate of the era," wrote Klarman. "The rulings can be criticized, of course, but not on the

JIM CROW LAW.

UPHELD BY THE UNITED STATES SUPREME COURT.

Statute Within the Competency of the Louisiana Legislature and Railroads—Must Furnish Separate Cars for Whites and Blacks.

Washington, May 18.--The Supreme Court today in an opinion read by Justice Brown, sustained the constitutionality of the law in Louisiana requiring the railroads of that State to provide separate cars for white and colored passengers. There was no interstate commerce feature in the case for the railroad upon which the incident occurred giving rise to case—Plessey vs. Ferguson—East Louisiana railroad, was and is operated wholly within the State, to the laws of Congress of many of the States. The opinion states that by the analogy of the laws of Congress, and of many of states requiring establishment of separate schools for children of two races and other similar laws, the statute in question was within competency of Louisiana Legislature, exercising the police power of the State. The judgment of the Supreme Court of State upholding law was therefore upheld.

Mr. Justice Harlan announced a very vigorous dissent saying that he saw nothing but mischief in all such laws. In his view of the case, no power in the land had right to regulate the enjoyment of civil rights upon the basis of race. It would be just as reasonable and proper, he said, for states to pass laws requiring separate cars to be furnished for Catholic and Protestants, or for descendants of those of Teutonic race and those of Latin race.

Newspaper coverage of the *Plessy v. Ferguson* ruling did not reflect its momentous impact on race relations in America.

grounds that they butchered clearly established law or inflicted racially regressive results on a nation otherwise inclined to favor racial equality. It is also unlikely that contrary rulings would have significantly alleviated the oppression of blacks: Such rulings probably could not have been enforced, and, in any event, the oppression of blacks was largely the work of forces other than law."[19]

The unfavorable Supreme Court verdict struck the final blow to the long campaign by Plessy, Tourgée, and the Citizens' Committee to end segregation. The members of the Citizens' Committee issued a final statement before disbanding their organization. "Notwithstanding this decision," they wrote, "we, as freemen, still believe that we were right and our cause is sacred…. In defending the cause of liberty, we met with defeat, but not with ignominy."[20]

Plessy's eight-year legal drama came to an official end on January 11, 1897, when he appeared before Judge Ferguson again, pleaded guilty to violating the Separate Car Law, and paid a $25 fine. "Separate but equal" became the law of the land, and it would remain so for the next fifty years. Opponents of segregation took some solace in Justice Harlan's eloquent dissent, however. In fact, wrote Medley, Harlan's fierce defense of equal rights for all citizens regardless of race "became a beacon for future civil rights lawyers who would later challenge segregation."[21]

Notes

[1] Martinet, Louis A. Letter to Albion W. Tourgée, May 30, 1893. Quoted in Medley, Keith Weldon. *We as Freemen:* Plessy v. Ferguson. Gretna, LA: Pelican, 2003, p. 177.

[2] Tourgée, Albion W. "*Plessy v. Ferguson.* Brief for Plaintiff in Error." Westfield, NY: Albion W. Tourgée Collection, Chautauqua County Historical Society. Available online at http://nyheritage.nnyln.net/cdm/compoundobject/collection/NYCCH/id/703/rec/5.

[3] Tourgée, Albion W. "*Plessy v. Ferguson.* Brief for Plaintiff in Error."

[4] Tourgée, Albion W. "*Plessy v. Ferguson.* Brief for Plaintiff in Error."

[5] Tourgée, Albion W. "*Plessy v. Ferguson.* Brief for Plaintiff in Error."

[6] Quoted in Aaseng, Nathan. Plessy v. Ferguson: *Separate but Equal.* Farmington Hills, MI: Lucent Books, 2003, p. 50.

[7] *Plessy v. Ferguson,* 163 U.S. 537 (1896). Records of the Supreme Court of the United States. Available online at http://www.ourdocuments.gov/doc.php?flash=true&doc=52&page=transcript.

[8] *Plessy v. Ferguson,* 163 U.S. 537 (1896).

[9] *Plessy v. Ferguson,* 163 U.S. 537 (1896).

[10] *Plessy v. Ferguson,* 163 U.S. 537 (1896).

[11] *Plessy v. Ferguson,* 163 U.S. 537 (1896).

[12] *Plessy v. Ferguson,* 163 U.S. 537 (1896).

[13] *Plessy v. Ferguson,* 163 U.S. 537 (1896).

[14] *Plessy v. Ferguson,* 163 U.S. 537 (1896).

[15] *Plessy v. Ferguson,* 163 U.S. 537 (1896).

[16] *Plessy v. Ferguson,* 163 U.S. 537 (1896).

[17] Klarman, Michael J. *From Jim Crow to Civil Rights: The Supreme Court and the Struggle for Racial Equality.* New York: Oxford University Press, 2004, p. 21.

[18] *Democrat and Chronicle* [Rochester, NY], May 20, 1896. Quoted in Esty, Amos. *The Civil Rights Movement:* Plessy v. Ferguson. Greensboro, NC: Morgan Reynolds, 2012, p. 88.

[19] Klarman, p. 9.

[20] "Statement of the Citizens' Committee." In *Report of the Proceedings of the Citizens' Committee.* New Orleans, LA: 1891, p. 7.

[21] Medley, p. 205.

Chapter Five

LIVING IN TERROR

It is necessary that this principle [segregation] be applied in every relation of Southern life. God Almighty drew the color line and it cannot be obliterated. The negro must stay on his side of the line and the white man must stay on his side, and the sooner both races recognize this fact and accept it, the better it will be for both.

—*Richmond Times* editorial, January 12, 1900

The U.S. Supreme Court's controversial *Plessy v. Ferguson* ruling gave white racists in the South legal sanction to pass a fresh tidal wave of repressive Jim Crow laws in the early twentieth century. These laws segregated people by race in every conceivable location or situation in which blacks and whites might interact socially. Segregation laws also forced blacks to accept facilities and services that were inferior in every way. African Americans had little choice but to accept such inequality—and the position of second-class citizenship it conferred upon them—because white segregationists enforced Jim Crow laws with threats, intimidation, and violence.

Segregation Spreads across the South

When Homer Plessy first launched his challenge to Louisiana's Separate Car Law in 1892, similar laws segregating railway travel already existed in eight other states. Once the U.S. Supreme Court announced its decision upholding the law in 1896, five more states quickly took steps to segregate public transportation within their borders (see "A Kentucky Newspaper Claims That Segregation Benefits Blacks," p. 150). In addition, as Justice John Marshall Harlan

A man approaches the colored entrance at the back of a segregated movie theater in Mississippi.

had warned in his dissenting opinion, many people interpreted the *Plessy v. Ferguson* ruling to mean that *all* forms of racial segregation were now legal. As a result, states, cities, and towns passed a flurry of new segregation laws through the remainder of the 1890s and into the 1900s. These laws governed nearly every aspect of daily life. They forced blacks and whites to use separate drinking fountains, restrooms, parks, libraries, theaters, restaurants, schools, hospitals, and cemeteries.

Most segregation laws were passed in the South—especially within the eleven former Confederate states—because that was where the vast majority of African Americans lived. In 1900, the population of this region consisted of 10 million whites and 6 million blacks, out of a total African-American population of 8.8 million nationwide. The size and potential strength of the South's black population contributed to white supremacists' determination to use every available means to keep African Americans subordinate and politically powerless. "The measure of a man's estimate of your strength is the kind of weapons he feels that he must use in order to hold you fast in a prescribed place,"[1] wrote black theologian Howard Thurman.

The rise of the Populist Party in the 1890s made white Democrats even more concerned about maintaining their grip on political power in the South. The Populists presented themselves as representing the interests of the common man, including farmers, factory workers, and African Americans. White Democrats recognized that such an alliance posed a threat to their dominance of Southern politics. Many state legislatures responded by restricting the voting rights of these groups through a new wave of literacy tests, poll taxes, and property-ownership requirements. In the 1898 case *Williams v. Mississippi,* the U.S. Supreme Court ruled unanimously that such restrictions did not violate the Fifteenth Amendment because they applied equally to all voters, regardless of race. In practice, however, the restrictions were applied in a discriminatory manner that disenfranchised hundreds of thousands of black voters. In Louisiana, for instance, the number of registered black voters dropped from 130,000 in 1896 to 1,500 in 1904. Without voting rights, African Americans could do nothing to prevent the passage of segregation laws throughout the South.

The so-called border states that had once allowed slavery but remained loyal to the Union during the Civil War—including Delaware, Kentucky, Maryland, Missouri, and West Virginia—also passed a number of segregation laws. States in the North, Midwest, and West only accounted for about 20 percent of all segregation laws. The most common types of statutes passed in these regions called for segregated schools. Some of the segregation measures targeted Asians or American Indians rather than—or in addition to—African Americans. Even in the absence of formal segregation laws, though, blacks outside of the South still experienced discrimination in housing, employment, education, health care, and other areas.

Whether formal or informal, segregation created a caste system in American society in which blacks always occupied a lower social status than whites. Blacks automatically had fewer rights and opportunities than whites, regardless of their respective levels of intelligence and talent. This reality

"I knew [as a teenager] that I could never aspire to be President of the United States, nor Governor of my State, nor mayor of my city," said a man who grew up in the Jim Crow South. "I knew that the front doors of white homes in my town were not for me to enter, except as a servant; I knew that I could only sit in the peanut gallery at our theatre, and could only ride on the back seat of the electric car."

weighed heavily on the minds of many African Americans. "At fifteen, I was fully conscious of the racial difference, and while I was sullen and resentful in my soul, I was beaten and knew it," recalled Albon Holsey, an African American who grew up in the South in the early 1900s. "I knew then that I could never aspire to be President of the United States, nor Governor of my State, nor mayor of my city; I knew that the front doors of white homes in my town were not for me to enter, except as a servant; I knew that I could only sit in the peanut gallery at our theatre, and could only ride on the back seat of the electric car."[2]

Separate but Not Equal

Although the Supreme Court's *Plessy v. Ferguson* decision had required segregated public accommodations to be "separate but equal," in reality the facilities provided to blacks were almost always inferior to those provided to whites. African Americans lived in less desirable housing, received inadequate public services, attended inferior public schools, were restricted to working in less lucrative jobs, and received substandard health care. The blacks-only railroad cars in which Plessy was forced to ride, for example, lacked the soft cushions, luxurious appointments, and other amenities found in whites-only cars. "The differences between white and black railroad cars at that time were obvious," noted human rights advocate Harvey Fireside. "The only evident similarity was that they were both headed to the same destination."[3] One resident of Maryland described the cars set aside for blacks as "scarcely fit for a dog to ride in"[4] (see "A Black-Owned Newspaper Criticizes Segregation," p. 153).

Some of the most blatant examples of inequality occurred in segregated public schools. African-American children often attended school in dilapidated, unheated buildings with overcrowded classrooms and underpaid teachers. They also usually used old, worn-out textbooks, desks, and other materials—some of which had been discarded by white schools. In state after state, the amount of funding provided to public schools depended on the race of the students educated there. Beaufort County, South Carolina, for instance, spent $40.68 per white pupil and only $5.95 per black pupil in 1910. The average value of a school building for white students was $30,056 that year, while the average value of a black school was $3,953.

Many whites justified the limited resources provided to black schools by claiming that blacks were intellectually inferior and thus would not benefit from education. Others pointed out that the range of jobs typically available to

Schools for black children, like this one in Kentucky, received less funding and fewer resources than schools for white children in the segregated South.

blacks—which included farming, factory work, and domestic service—did not require much education. In fact, black children were often required to miss school in order to work for their white employers. Ann Pointer, who attended a two-room school in Macon County, Georgia, in the 1930s, remembered that "one teacher taught [grades] one through three, the other taught four through six. And we could not go to school until October.... And you know why? Because Mr. Childer's cotton had to be picked and gathered before the black children went to school."[5] In some cases, black students only attended school a couple of days per week or a few months per year.

Many African Americans responded to the inferior public education offered to black children by supplementing it outside of school. Some communities and churches held informal classes that were taught by respected elders. These individuals shared their experiences under slavery, recalled the achievements of African Americans during Reconstruction, and related stories about friends and family members who had maintained their dignity and strength in the face of severe trials. Since public schools in the South ignored or misrepresented black history, this oral tradition helped preserve a sense of racial pride and community spirit. This type of community assistance helped many black children overcome the problems associated with segregated schools and attend college, either at integrated universities in the North or at historically black colleges like Tuskegee University in Alabama. These institutions of higher learning helped create a small but influential group of middle-class black professionals.

Despite such gains, however, African Americans faced widespread discrimination in employment during the first half of the twentieth century. In the South, only certain types of jobs were open to blacks. Many of these jobs revolved around serving whites as domestic servants, cooks, maids, nannies, and porters. Many other jobs—in mines, fields, and factories—involved hard, physical labor that few middle-class whites were interested in performing. Even in the North, many industries only hired black workers for unskilled positions. These workers often encountered animosity from white co-workers, who worried that an influx of African Americans willing to accept low wages and long hours would cause working conditions to deteriorate for everyone.

Many blacks in the South worked as farmers, but few owned their own land. Instead, they worked as tenant farmers or sharecroppers on land owned by whites. The landowners furnished their tenants with land, tools, seeds, clothing, and other supplies on credit, in exchange for a share of the crops at harvest time. Many sharecroppers could not read or do math, however, so it was easy for landowners to cheat them. In addition, sharecroppers could not repay the landowners in seasons when crop yields suffered due to problems like drought or insect damage. As a result, this system served to keep black farmers in perpetual debt and firmly under the control of whites. In fact, it returned many African Americans to a situation that resembled plantation life during slavery. "If they'd catch you trying to leave, they'd take you back there and whip you, fasten you up in the barn and whip you," recalled Willie Harrell, who worked as a sharecropper on a Mississippi plantation in the 1930s. "It's just like old slavery time."[6]

Segregation and discrimination also affected the housing and living conditions available to African Americans. Throughout the South, those who lived in urban areas were relegated to all-black sections of town where houses tended to be old, small, and poorly maintained. James Robinson, who lived in the black section of Knoxville, Tennessee, remembered that houses in his neighborhood "were hardly more than rickety shacks clustered on stilts like Daddy

The sharecropping system kept black farming families in perpetual debt to white landowners.

Long Legs, along the slimy bank of putrid and evil-smelling 'Cripple Creek.'"[7] Black neighborhoods and communities typically received inadequate public services, which meant that residents struggled with poor drainage, shortages of fresh drinking water, and problems with garbage and sewage disposal. These issues left black residents susceptible to infections and diseases that were much less common in white areas. Partly as a result, the death rate for blacks in the city of Atlanta, Georgia, was 69 percent higher than it was for whites in 1900 (see "The NAACP Offers a Harsh Assessment of the Status of Blacks," p. 80).

Everyday Humiliations

In addition to the blatant discrimination and inequality they endured in segregated schools, neighborhoods, and workplaces, African Americans experienced the everyday humiliation of second-class citizenship in the South dur-

Signs prohibiting African Americans from using public restrooms and other facilities served as a constant reminder of their second-class citizenship.

ing the first half of the twentieth century. They had to defer to whites in every conceivable social situation and behave in a humble, subservient manner at all times. "We came to know that whatever we had was always inferior," said civil rights activist Pauli Murray. "We came to understand that no matter how neat and clean, how law abiding, churchgoing, and moral [we were,] it made no essential difference in our place."[8]

Knowing that the penalties for disobeying the unwritten social etiquette of segregation could be severe, many black parents in the South cautioned their children to avoid interacting with white people as much as possible (see "An Alabama Man Experiences Daily Humiliations under Segregation," p. 178). "When my mother would send me to this grocery store that was approximately a mile away," recalled Charles Gratton of his childhood in Birmingham, Alabama, "she would give me instructions before I'd leave home and tell me, 'Son, now you go on up to [the] store and get this or that for me. If you pass any white people on your way, you get off the sidewalk. Give them the sidewalk. You move over. Don't challenge white people.'"[9]

African Americans understood that they could not enter through the front doors of stores, theaters, restaurants, and other business establishments that served the public. Instead, they were forced to go around back and accept any inferior form of service that white business owners were willing to provide. "I remember this little place near the bus station that sold the best hot dogs I ever ate," recalled Charles Epps of his hometown in North Carolina in the 1940s. "If you were a white person, you could just go in, sit down, and enjoy your hot dog. But if you were black, you had to go around back. There was a little hole, about twelve inches by twelve inches, and you put your money through the opening. Then they would pass you a hot dog through the hole."[10]

"It was two separate worlds," acknowledged a white man from the segregated South. "You know, you just didn't become part of their world, you didn't go into their houses, they worked in your house, but it was just the way it was. It had always been that way."

Many white Southerners never gave much thought to the unfairness of the Jim Crow system. Having grown up in a segregated society, they simply accepted the separation of races and never questioned whether it discriminated against blacks. "It was two separate worlds," said Leonard Barrow Jr., a white man who lived in Louisiana in the 1920s. "You know, you just didn't become part of their world, you didn't go into their houses, they worked in your house, but it was just the way it was. It had always been that way."[11]

Jim Crow Enforced with Violence

Staunch segregationists and white supremacists, on the other hand, believed that blacks were inferior to whites and did not deserve equality. They were determined to maintain strict social and physical boundaries between the races—by force, if necessary. They frequently used threats, intimidation, and violence to enforce segregation laws and keep blacks "in their place." Anyone who dared to disobey or resist Jim Crow laws and customs could be arrested, beaten, shot, or lynched—and the whites responsible for these acts of violence were rarely held accountable (see "A Georgia Native Remembers Jim Crow Tragedies," p. 182).

Even the slightest infraction could result in violence. One contributor to the oral history collection *Remembering Jim Crow* recalled a black teenager being shot and killed for crossing through a white neighbor's watermelon patch. Another described what happened when whites discovered the true racial identity of a light-skinned African-American boy who had often passed for white. After beating him to death, his killers chained his body to the rear of a

This 1935 photo shows a group of spectators at a lynching in Fort Lauderdale, Florida.

car and dragged it until it was unrecognizable. The constant threat of violence made it extremely dangerous for African Americans to come to the aid of people who became the targets of white rage. "We went on about our way, because, you know, okay, you better not stop. Or you are going to get the same thing or worse," said Joanne of Georgia, who witnessed a lynching in 1942. "When you see something happening and you in the deep South, you afraid to say anything about it, so you are going to hush-hush."[12]

Lynching was the most terrifying form of violence used to enforce Jim Crow laws and customs. African Americans could be lynched for any violation of the racial code of the South, from conversing with a white woman to attempting to register to vote. They even placed their lives in danger by wearing fashionable clothing, driving a new car, or living in a nice home. White supremacists viewed any signs of prosperity among African Americans as an indication that they did not "know their place" and thought they were equal to whites (see "A Black Reporter Recalls a Lynching," p. 187).

Lynching took a total of 4,715 black lives from 1882 to 1946. Many lynchings were public events that were attended by cheering mobs of white spectators. Occasionally these mobs would riot in middle-class black neighborhoods, burning down homes and buildings and beating or killing any black residents they encountered. The members of lynch mobs who actually committed the murders were rarely brought to justice. Some law enforcement officials shared the perpetrators' racist attitudes, while others worried that cracking down on racial violence might ruin their hopes for reelection (see "*The Birth of a Nation* Fans the Flames of Race Hate," p. 74).

Still, a few courageous activists spoke out against the practice. One of the best-known opponents of lynching was the black journalist Ida B. Wells. She launched her anti-lynching campaign in 1892, after three of her friends were murdered in Memphis, Tennessee, for opening a grocery store that competed with a white-owned business. Wells investigated the crimes and published details in her newspaper, *Free Speech and Headlight*. White supremacists retaliated by destroying the newspaper offices. When it became too dangerous for her to remain in the South, Wells moved to Chicago and continued raising public awareness of lynching through articles, speeches, and pamphlets such as *Southern Horrors: Lynch Law in All Its Phases*.

Resistance and Exodus

Wells was not the only African American to resist segregation and the suggestion of inferiority that it entailed. On February 12, 1909, the black writer W. E. B. Du Bois and other activists formed a civil rights organization called the National Association for the Advancement of Colored People (NAACP). The organization's goals included: securing the rights guaranteed under the Thir-

The Birth of a Nation Fans the Flames of Race Hate

As repressive Jim Crow laws took root across the South in the first decades of the twentieth century, a theatrical film contributed to the racial atmosphere of fear, hatred, and conflict. The 1915 epic *Birth of a Nation,* directed by D. W. Griffith, was considered a technical and artistic masterpiece at the time of its release. But it also aroused heated controversy, and it is still regarded as racially offensive and politically reprehensible.

Griffith based his film on *The Clansman,* a book by Thomas Dixon that glamorized the Ku Klux Klan (KKK). The story also reflected the struggles of the filmmaker's father, a former Confederate cavalry officer, to deal with the social upheaval of the Reconstruction era in the South. *The Birth of a Nation* follows the experiences of two families—the Stonemans from the North and the Camerons from the South—through the devastation of the Civil War and the challenges of Reconstruction. It portrays African Americans as drunken, brutish sexual predators who threaten the safety of white women, and it blames Northern Republican "carpetbaggers" for the social, economic, and political problems affecting the postwar South. It presents the hooded KKK raiders as heroes and saviors of the Southern culture and way of life.

The National Association for the Advancement of Colored People (NAACP) protested the release of the film. The group requested that the "vicious" film be banned by the National Board of Censorship of Motion Pictures. After viewing the film at the White House, however, President Woodrow Wilson declared it compelling and historically accurate. *The Birth of a Nation* was so popular among white audiences that it contributed to a revival of the KKK during the 1920s. It also fanned the flames of race hate across the United States in the years after its release.

teenth, Fourteenth, and Fifteenth Amendments to the Constitution; gaining political, educational, social, and economic equality for minorities; and eliminating racial prejudice. The NAACP published an influential newspaper called *The Crisis,* and within ten years its membership had grown to 90,000 (see "The NAACP Demands Equal Rights for African Americans," p. 176).

Millions of blacks in the South endured the everyday humiliations of the Jim Crow era through the support of their families and communities. "What blacks did essentially was to draw inward, to construct in their own communities a separate world," said historian Leon Litwack. "Within very rigidly prescribed boundaries, they improvised strategies for dealing with whites. Most tried to enjoy the personal and family experiences that life had to offer."[13] Black churches, social clubs, and fraternal organizations served as gathering places for people who were not allowed to participate in the amusements available to whites. African Americans also expressed their sadness and frustration at living under segregation—as well as their determination to overcome the barriers to equality—in cultural works such as folktales and blues and gospel music.

Black parents in the South worked hard to counteract the negative messages that their children were exposed to on a daily basis. Although they counseled the younger generation to do what was necessary to stay safe and get along, they also emphasized that they were just as good as whites. They encouraged their children to take pride in their heritage and improve themselves through education. "[Black people] maintained a private inner dignity despite a life that was saturated with indignity," said African-American journalist Vernon Jarrett, who grew up in Tennessee. "My father spent his whole life being considered a second-class citizen. Yet he and my mother taught for a combined one hundred years. People like them radiated pride. I've never had so much admiration for spiritual strength."[14]

Some African Americans maintained their dignity through small acts of defiance against white supremacy. Olivia Cherry, who worked as a maid for a white family in Virginia, insisted that her employer address her by name. "I would be upstairs cleaning the bathroom and she said, 'Susie.' They loved to call me Susie. So I didn't answer," she recalled. "I was a spunky kid then, I was like 13 or 14, and I didn't answer. Finally, she [came] to the steps and said, 'Olivia, you hear me calling you?' I said, 'Now I hear you. Now you said, 'Olivia.' That's my name."[15]

Some African Americans responded to the violence and repression in the Jim Crow South by leaving the region altogether. Between 1900 and 1940 an estimated 1.8 million blacks migrated to the North or West in search of greater equality and better education and employment opportunities. "After twenty years of seeing my people lynched for any offense, from spitting on the sidewalk to stealing a mule, I made up my mind that I would turn the prow of my ship toward the part of the country where the people at least made a pretense

Journalist and civil rights activist Ida B. Wells was an outspoken opponent of lynching in the 1890s and early 1900s.

at being civilized,"[16] explained a man who settled in Chicago. This mass exodus from the South became known as the Great Migration.

For some migrants, the change in racial atmosphere from South to North made the upheaval worthwhile. "When I got to New York, got a cab, and went to Harlem, I looked around," recalled Price Davis, who left North Carolina as soon as he finished high school. "I saw a black policeman directing traffic. I said, 'Oh, my God, this is the Promised Land!'"[17] Many others, however, were disappointed to find that discrimination and prejudice existed in the North as well. As more and more blacks arrived in Chicago, Detroit, and other cities, white residents expressed concern that the new arrivals would increase competition for good jobs and housing. They responded to such fears by taking steps to keep African Americans out of their neighborhoods and workplaces. As African-American historian Carter G. Woodson predicted in 1918: "The maltreatment of the Negro will be nationalized by this exodus [of blacks from the South to the North]. The poor whites of both sectors will strike at this race long stigmatized by servitude but now demanding economic equality. Race prejudice, the fatal weakness of America, will not abate."[18]

Notes

[1] Thurman, Howard. *The Luminous Darkness: A Personal Interpretation of the Anatomy of Segregation and the Ground of Hope.* Richmond, IN: Friends United Press, 1965.

[2] Quoted in Litwack, Leon F. *Trouble in Mind: Black Southerners in the Age of Jim Crow.* New York: Knopf, 1998, p. 16.

[3] Fireside, Harvey. *Landmark Supreme Court Cases: Plessy v. Ferguson, Separate but Equal?* Springfield, NJ: Enslow, 1997, p. 76.

[4] Callcott, Margaret Law. *The Negro in Maryland Politics, 1870-1912.* Baltimore, MD: Johns Hopkins University Press, 1969, p. 135.

[5] Quoted in Chafe, William H., Raymond Gavins, and Robert Korstad. *Remembering Jim Crow: African Americans Tell about Life in the Segregated South.* New York: New Press, 2001, p. 55.

[6] Quoted in Chafe, et al., p. 41.

[7] Quoted in Litwack, p. 336.

[8] Murray, Pauli. *Proud Shoes: The Story of an American Family.* Quoted in Litwack, p. 217.

[9] Quoted in Chafe, et al., p. 7.

[10] Quoted in King, Casey, and Linda Barrett Osbourne. *Oh, Freedom! Kids Talk about the Civil Rights Movement with the People Who Made It Happen.* New York: Knopf, 1997, p. 12.

[11] Quoted in Chafe, et al., p. 320.

[12] Quoted in Ezekiel, Raphael S. *Voices from the Corner: Poverty and Racism in the Inner City.* Philadelphia: Temple University Press, 1984, p. 148.

[13] Quoted in Chafe, et al., p. 314.

[14] Interview quoted in Fremon, David K. *The Jim Crow Laws and Racism in American History.* Berkeley Heights, NJ: 2000, p. 41.

[15] Quoted in Chafe, et al., p. 314.

[16] Quoted in Henri, Florette. *Black Migration: Movement North, 1900-1920.* Norwell, MA: Anchor Press, 1975, p. 320.

[17] Quoted in Chafe, et al., p. 315.

[18] Woodson, Carter G. *A Century of Negro Migration.* New York: AMS Press, 1918, p. 180.

Chapter Six

THE CIVIL RIGHTS MOVEMENT

We conclude that, in the field of public education, the doctrine of "separate but equal" has no place. Separate educational facilities are inherently unequal.

—Chief Justice Earl Warren, U.S. Supreme Court opinion in *Brown v. Board of Education*

Racial prejudice and discrimination did eventually abate in the United States, but achieving equal rights for African Americans required a relentless, decades-long fight by courageous individuals and groups. One of the key early victories in the civil rights movement came in 1954, when the U.S. Supreme Court finally overturned its notorious *Plessy v. Ferguson* decision and declared racial segregation unconstitutional. This ruling encouraged civil rights activists to push for the integration of public schools, transportation, and accommodations, as well as an end to discrimination on the basis of race in employment, housing, and voting rights. Although it faced stubborn and often violent resistance, the civil rights movement made steady progress toward eliminating racial inequalities in American society and forcing the United States to honor its founding principles at last.

The Supreme Court Overturns *Plessy*

The federal government's position on race relations began to shift during the administration of Democratic president Franklin D. Roosevelt. African Americans suffered tremendous hardships during the Great Depression of the 1930s. They had a passionate ally and defender, though, in First Lady Eleanor Roosevelt. She spoke out against prejudice and lynching, for instance, and

The NAACP Offers a Harsh Assessment of the Status of Blacks

On February 12, 1909, on what would have been the one hundredth birthday of President Abraham Lincoln, a coalition of prominent African American leaders and white supporters founded the National Association for the Advancement of Colored People (NAACP). The goals of this new civil rights organization included eliminating racial prejudice and securing political, educational, social, and economic equality for minority citizens in the United States. Upon its founding, the NAACP issued a statement that offered a harsh assessment of the status of African Americans and called for a national commitment to racial justice.

> If Mr. Lincoln could revisit this country he would be disheartened by the nation's failure [to ensure equal rights and opportunities for all citizens].... He would see the black men and women, for whose freedom a hundred thousand of soldiers gave their lives, sit apart in trains, in which they pay first-class fares for third-class service, in railway stations and in places of entertainment, while State after State declines to do its elementary duty in preparing the negro through education for the best exercise of citizenship. Added to this, the spread of lawless attacks upon the negro ... often accompanied by revolting brutalities, sparing neither sex, nor age, nor youth, could not but shock the author of the sentiment that "government of the people, by the people, for the people shall not perish from the earth."

> Silence under these conditions means tacit approval. The indifference of the North is already responsible for more than one assault upon democracy, and every such attack reacts as unfavorably upon whites as upon blacks.... Hence we call upon all the believers in democracy to join in a national conference for the discussion of present evils, the voicing of protests, and the renewal of the struggle for civil and political liberty.

Source

Villard, Oswald Garrison. "Call for the Lincoln Emancipation Conference," National Association for the Advancement of Colored People, February 12, 1909. Retrieved from http://www.glencoe.com/sec/socialstudies/btt/celebratingfreedom/pdfs/181.PDF.

worked with influential black leaders to promote civil rights. Thanks in part to her efforts, federal relief agencies began offering jobs, education, training, and farm subsidies to African Americans. It marked the first time since Reconstruction that the federal government had taken action to support the nation's black citizens and incorporate them into the mainstream of American society.

On June 25, 1941, shortly before the United States entered World War II, President Roosevelt issued Executive Order 8802, which prohibited "discrimination in the employment of workers in defense industries or Government because of race, creed, color, or national origin." During the war, 125,000 African Americans fought bravely overseas in segregated military units. Millions more contributed to the war effort by working in factories that churned out weapons and supplies for the Allied forces. On the home front, black-owned newspapers like the *Chicago Defender* encouraged African Americans to strive for a "Double V": victory in the war, and victory at home in the fight against segregation and racism. President Harry S. Truman gave civil rights activists an important victory in 1948 by integrating the U.S. military. In issuing Executive Order 9981, Truman promised to extend "equality of treatment and opportunity for all persons in the armed services without regard to race, color, religion, or national origin."

As the executive branch shifted toward supporting equal rights for African Americans, the U.S. Supreme Court handed down a series of decisions that chipped away at legalized segregation. Civil rights lawyers realized that the Court might be reluctant to overturn *Plessy* outright, so they worked to establish legal precedents that would gradually lead in that direction. Some of the Court's early decisions merely forced states to enforce the *Plessy* ruling by providing segregated facilities that were truly "separate but equal." In the 1938 case of *Gaines v. Canada,* for instance, NAACP lawyer Charles Hamilton Houston convinced the justices that the University of Missouri could not satisfy this requirement by sending black student Lloyd Gaines to an integrated, out-of-state law school. The Court ruled that Missouri either had to admit Gaines or build a separate law school for black students that was equal to the one it provided to white students. Of course, the university could not afford the cost of building a separate black law school, so the ruling had the desired effect of forcing the integration of Missouri's law school.

A dozen years later, on June 5, 1950, the Court issued a pair of rulings that disallowed segregation in higher education. In *Sweatt v. Painter,* the Court found that a separate law school for black students established in Texas was not equal to the law school available to white students. The justices ruled that this arrangement violated plaintiff Heman Sweatt's constitutional rights under the Fourteenth Amendment. Similarly, in *McLaurin v. Oklahoma Board of Regents*, the Court found that the University of Oklahoma's graduate school violated the Equal Protection clause by treating black student George McLaurin differently (forcing him to sit alone in a separate alcove of the classroom from his white classmates, for instance) solely because of his race.

> *"The only way that this Court can decide this case in opposition to our position … is to find that for some reason Negroes are inferior to all other human beings,"* civil rights lawyer Thurgood Marshall declared. *"Now is the time, we submit, that the Court should make it clear that that is not what our Constitution stands for."*

These rulings established precedents that paved the way for the Supreme Court to overturn *Plessy v. Ferguson* once and for all. In December 1952 the Court agreed to hear a collection of five similar cases involving the segregation of public schools. The lead case, *Brown v. Board of Education of Topeka, Kansas*, concerned eight-year-old Topeka student Linda Brown. Each day, she had to walk a mile and cross through a busy railroad yard to reach the bus stop for her all-black elementary school, while a school for white students was located only a few blocks from her home. Her parents filed a lawsuit against the school district for refusing to admit her to the neighborhood school. The NAACP legal team representing Brown did not argue that the physical school facility she attended was inferior to the local white school. Instead, they presented sociological studies showing that segregation itself caused psychological harm to black students by making them feel inferior to white students.

After the first hearing of the case, the justices had trouble reaching a decision. They eventually asked to rehear the case in December 1953. In the meantime, Chief Justice Fred M. Vinson—who believed that the legality of segregation should be addressed by Congress rather than through the judicial system—died and was replaced by former California governor Earl Warren. During the rehearing of the case, NAACP lawyer Thurgood Marshall (see biography, p. 123) made an impassioned plea for the justices to take the opportunity to ban all forms of racial segregation. "The only way that this Court can decide this case in opposition to our position … is to find that for some reason Negroes are inferior to all other human beings," he declared. "Now is the time, we submit, that the Court should make it clear that that is not what our Constitution stands for."[1]

The Supreme Court announced its decision on May 17, 1954. In a 9-0 unanimous opinion, the justices ruled that the segregation of public schools violated the Equal Protection clause of the Fourteenth Amendment. After more than fifty years of legalized segregation, the Court formally overturned *Plessy v. Ferguson*'s contention that "separate but equal" was allowable under the Constitution. "We conclude that, in the field of public education, the doctrine of 'separate but equal' has no place," Warren declared. "Separate educational facilities are inherently unequal."[2]

The Battle over School Integration

Although Marshall and other opponents of segregation rejoiced upon hearing the Court's opinion, white segregationists responded with outrage. A group of ninety-nine members of Congress from Southern states signed a formal

Civil rights attorneys (from left) George E. C. Hayes, Thurgood Marshall, and James M. Nabrit celebrate the U.S. Supreme Court's 1954 ruling in *Brown v. Board of Education.*

document condemning the Court's ruling. This document, known as the Southern Manifesto, described the *Brown v. Board* decision as a "clear abuse of judicial power." The signers of the manifesto vowed to overturn the ruling, and they encouraged state governments to resist it.

The historic *Brown v. Board* ruling did not say how school desegregation should be achieved, so important questions remained as to how it should be implemented. On May 31, 1955, the Supreme Court attempted to answer these questions in a second ruling, commonly known as *Brown II*. Rather than provide specific timetables for desegregation, however, the Court only advised school districts in the South to integrate "with all deliberate speed."

Many Southern states and school districts used the vague wording of *Brown II* as legal justification for resisting, delaying, or avoiding integration. They used a variety of tactics to prevent black and white students from attending school together, including closing down entire school systems, using state funds to cre-

Six-year-old Ruby Bridges had to be escorted by U.S. marshals in order to attend an all-white elementary school in New Orleans in 1960.

ate segregated "private" schools for white students, and admitting a handful of "token" black students to formerly all-white schools while forcing the rest to remain in inferior all-black schools. As a result, three years after the *Brown v. Board* decision fewer than 700 of the 3,000 segregated school districts in the South had made meaningful progress toward integration.

The outright defiance of the Supreme Court's ruling finally forced the federal government to step in to enforce school desegregation. One tension-filled incident occurred in 1957, when Arkansas governor Orval Faubus mobilized his state's National Guard to prevent nine black students from integrating Central High School in Little Rock. Television audiences across the country watched in horror as angry white mobs and heavily armed troops denied the teenagers access to the school. President Dwight Eisenhower responded to the crisis by deploying U.S. Army soldiers to ensure the safe passage of the black students, who became known as the Little Rock Nine.

A similar confrontation took place in Homer Plessy's hometown of New Orleans, where the local school board staunchly resisted integration for five years after the Court overturned *Plessy v. Ferguson.* In 1960 a six-year-old black student named Ruby Bridges passed a test, as the school board required, in order to qualify for admission to an all-white elementary school. When she showed up on the first day of school, however, she encountered a mob of angry white segregationists who shouted insults and threw objects at her. After federal marshals arrived and escorted Bridges into the school, she discovered that only one teacher, Barbara Henry, was willing to instruct a black student. Bridges ended up being the only student in Henry's classroom that year, because the parents of the white students who would have been her classmates pulled their children out of school in protest. Bridges' courage and persistence eventually paid off, though, and the learning environment grew more accepting the following year. Bridges went on to graduate from the integrated Francis T. Nicholls High School, which was named after the former governor who signed the Separate Car Act into law in 1890.

Alabama governor George Wallace, who famously vowed to uphold a policy of "segregation now, segregation tomorrow, segregation forever" in his inaugural address, was responsible for another notorious stand against school integration. On June 11, 1963, he stood in the doorway of a building on the University of Alabama campus to block the entrance of two African-American students. President John F. Kennedy responded by ordering the Alabama National Guard to intervene on behalf of the students and force the governor to step aside. That evening, Kennedy called upon the American people to support the cause of African-American civil rights in a nationally televised speech. "One hundred years of delay have passed since President Lincoln freed the slaves, yet their heirs, their grandsons, are not fully free. They are not yet freed from the bonds of injustice. They are not yet freed from social and economic oppression. And this Nation, for all its hopes and all its boasts, will not be fully free until all its citizens are free," he declared. "Now the time has come for this Nation to fulfill its promise."[3]

Desegregating Public Transportation

Inspired by their progress in ending segregation in public education, civil rights activists demanded justice in other areas of society. From the time Louisiana passed the Separate Car Law in 1890, the segregation of public transportation had stood as one of the most aggravating examples of racial

Rosa Parks (center) rides on an integrated bus following the successful conclusion of the Montgomery Bus Boycott.

inequality. Shortly after the Supreme Court overturned *Plessy v. Ferguson,* the civil rights movement turned its attention toward challenging this longstanding source of frustration for black commuters and travelers.

On December 1, 1955, an African-American seamstress and volunteer NAACP secretary named Rosa Parks was arrested in Montgomery, Alabama, for violating the city bus system's segregated seating policy. This policy required black passengers to relinquish their seats if the white section of the bus was full. When the bus driver asked Parks to move so that a white man could sit down, she refused. "People always say that I didn't give up my seat because I was tired, but that isn't true. I was not tired physically, or no more tired than I usually was at the end of a working day," she recalled. "No, the only tired I was, was tired of giving in."[4]

The Montgomery Improvement Association (MIA), a civil rights group led by a young black minister named Martin Luther King Jr., rallied the city's

African-American residents behind Parks. The MIA organized a boycott of the city bus system that lasted over a year. Blacks, who accounted for 80 percent of bus ridership, organized carpools, shared cabs, and walked rather than travel on segregated buses. The boycott caused such severe economic hardship for the bus company that its management soon joined protesters in demanding integration. Meanwhile, NAACP lawyers brought the issue before an Alabama court, which ruled that segregation of public transportation was unconstitutional. Montgomery mayor W. A. Gayle appealed to the U.S. Supreme Court, which unanimously upheld the lower court's ruling in *Browder v. Gale* and ordered the city to integrate its bus system. One day later, on December 20, 1956, the Montgomery Bus Boycott ended in triumph, having demonstrated the capacity of nonviolent protest to overcome discrimination.

"One hundred years of delay have passed since President Lincoln freed the slaves, yet their heirs, their grandsons, are not fully free," President Kennedy stated. "And this Nation, for all its hopes and all its boasts, will not be fully free until all its citizens are free."

In 1961 a civil rights group called the Congress of Racial Equality (CORE) mounted a challenge to the segregation of interstate bus travel. Although the Supreme Court had found such segregation unconstitutional in the 1946 *Morgan v. Virginia* case, most states in the South openly defied the ruling. All across the region, African American passengers who traveled from state to state on bus lines were forced to sit in the back of the bus and use separate waiting areas, ticket counters, and restrooms in bus terminals. A group of black and white CORE activists decided to travel through the South together by bus and document the inferior treatment of black passengers. They called these integrated bus trips Freedom Rides.

The Freedom Riders understood that they would likely encounter fierce resistance from white segregationists. They accepted the dangers, though, in order to raise awareness of the ongoing racial discrimination. "We knew we had to get the support of the country behind us to end segregation," said CORE director James Farmer. "We had to have some kind of dramatic project to attract the attention of the press, and especially television."[5]

On May 4, Freedom Riders set out from Washington, D.C., on two buses. They planned to stop in various cities along the way to their final destination of New Orleans. Upon reaching the town of Anniston, Alabama, one of the buses was greeted by a mob of 200 white segregationists who pounded on the sides of the bus and smashed several windows. The bus managed to escape the

The Freedom Riders narrowly escaped the flames when white segregationists in Alabama firebombed their bus.

town, but a flat tire forced it to stop a few miles down the road. When the mob caught up to the Freedom Riders' bus, someone threw a firebomb into the vehicle, setting it on fire. The mob waited to attack the Freedom Riders as they fled from the flames. Fortunately, though, one person on board was an undercover officer for the Alabama State Police. He drew his weapon and managed to prevent any further violence. Although the Freedom Riders were lucky to escape with their lives, they achieved their goal of drawing attention to segregation. Photographs and news footage of the burning bus shocked people across the country and increased support for the civil rights movement.

Demanding Equality

In 1963 King and other civil rights activists launched a series of nonviolent protest actions to draw attention to segregation and discrimination in Birmingham, Alabama. They chose Birmingham as the center of their campaign because it was one of the most racially divided cities in America. Stores, restaurants, and public facilities were strictly segregated. Job opportunities for black residents were limited to manual labor, and the average income for black families was half that of white families. Police Chief Eugene "Bull" Connor authorized his department to use force as needed to intimidate the black community and keep this unfair system in place.

The Southern Christian Leadership Conference (SCLC) used a combination of boycotts, sit-ins, marches, and other forms of nonviolent protest "to create a situation so crisis-packed that it will inevitably open the door to negotiation,"[6] according to King. As expected, Birmingham law enforcement responded angrily to these tactics. They arrested so many protesters that the city jail was filled to capacity. When the SCLC recruited children and teenagers to take the place of adult activists who had been jailed, Connor's police force confronted the peaceful protesters with high-pressure water hoses and snarling police dogs. When people across the country saw footage of these events, it brought national attention to the mistreatment of blacks in the South and generated a great deal of support for the civil rights movement.

One of the high points of the movement came on August 28, 1963, when an estimated 250,000 people participated in the March on Washington for Jobs and Freedom. The stated demands of the peaceful demonstration included the passage of new civil rights legislation, including a law prohibiting racial discrimination in employment; the elimination of segregation in public schools; and protection for civil rights protesters against police brutality. The event culminated at the National Mall, where King delivered his famous "I Have a Dream" speech to a huge crowd of inspired activists and supporters.

John Lewis of the Student Nonviolent Coordinating Committee (SNCC) gave the most forceful speech of the day. "The revolution is at hand, and we must free ourselves of the chains of political and economic slavery," he declared. "By the force of our demands, our determination, and our numbers, we shall splinter the segregated South into a thousand pieces and put them together in the image of God and democracy. We must say: 'Wake up America! Wake up!' For we cannot stop, and we will not and cannot be patient."[7]

The Birmingham campaign and the March on Washington gave new momentum to the push for major new civil rights legislation. President Kennedy had first proposed such legislation in June 1963, but segregationists in Congress

Marches, boycotts, sit-ins, and other forms of nonviolent protest became hallmarks of the civil rights movement.

managed to prevent its passage. After Kennedy was assassinated in November, however, President Lyndon B. Johnson made the civil rights bill his top legislative priority, encouraging Congress to pass it as a way of honoring his predecessor. Although members of Congress from Southern states delayed its passage with an eighty-three-day filibuster, the Civil Rights Act of 1964 was finally enacted on July 2. This landmark legislation prohibited discrimination on the basis of race, color, religion, sex, or national origin in the areas of education, employment, public accommodations, and voting rights. It was the most sweeping civil rights legislation since Reconstruction, and it formally ended the legalized segregation of the Jim Crow era in the South.

Securing Voting Rights

Although the Civil Rights Act of 1964 included a section barring the unequal application of voting requirements, it did not prohibit states from using forms of qualification other than citizenship to restrict voting rights. It also did not address the threats, intimidation, and violence that were often directed at blacks who attempted to exercise their right to vote in the South. In order to preserve the gains made by the civil rights movement, African Americans needed strong new voting rights legislation to ensure that they had an equal voice in the nation's political system.

In 1964 the SNCC and other civil rights groups organized a voter-registration drive in Mississippi, which had long used a variety of racist restrictions to exclude blacks from voting. This effort by white and black activists from the North to register African-American voters in the South became known as Freedom Summer. Like other civil rights campaigns, however, it met with violent resistance from white racists and their allies in local law enforcement. On June 21, three civil rights workers—one black, the others white—disappeared near Philadelphia, Mississippi. They had been arrested by local law enforcement and held in custody until nightfall, when they were turned over to the Ku Klux Klan. A massive FBI investigation uncovered their bodies six weeks later—as well as the remains of eight local black men who had been the victims of racist violence. The incident called national attention to the persecution of black voters in the South and the dangers faced by civil rights workers.

In 1965 the campaign to secure black voting rights shifted to Alabama, where civil rights activists planned a protest march from the city of Selma to the state capital in Montgomery. On March 7—known as Bloody Sunday—a

President Lyndon B. Johnson, shown chatting with Martin Luther King Jr., emerged as a prominent supporter of the civil rights movement.

group of 600 peaceful marchers began their journey eastward out of Selma. When they tried to cross the Edmund Pettus Bridge over the Alabama River, however, they were attacked by 150 state and local law enforcement officers wielding billy clubs, bullwhips, and tear gas. More than fifty marchers received wounds serious enough to require hospital treatment—including Lewis, who sustained a fractured skull. Images of the brutal attack appeared on television newscasts, horrifying viewers across the country.

On March 15 Johnson made an eloquent speech before Congress in which he challenged lawmakers to respond to the violence in Selma by passing strong new legislation to protect African-American voting rights. "Rarely are we met with a challenge, not to our growth or abundance, or our welfare or our security, but rather to the values and the purposes and the meaning of our beloved nation," he stated. "The issue of equal rights for American Negroes is such an issue. And should we defeat every enemy, and should we double our wealth and conquer the stars, and still be unequal to this issue, then we will have failed as a people and as a nation."[8]

A week later, the Selma-Montgomery Voting Rights March proceeded with the Alabama National Guard ensuring the safety of the participants. On March 25 the procession culminated in a rally attended by 30,000 people on the steps of the state capitol. On August 6 civil rights leaders celebrated as Johnson signed the Voting Rights Act of 1965 into law. This landmark legislation, which promised to "enforce the Fifteenth Amendment to the Constitution," prohibited the use of literacy tests, poll taxes, and other racially motivated voting requirements. It also provided for federal supervision of elections in jurisdictions that had used such measures to suppress minority voting rights. Finally, a century after the Civil War ended slavery, African Americans gained access to the full rights of citizenship.

Notes

[1] Quoted in Gottheimer, Josh, ed. *Ripples of Hope: Great American Civil Rights Speeches.* New York: Basic Civitas Books, 2003. Retrieved from http://www.blackpast.org/?q=1953-thurgood-marshall-argument-u-s-supreme-court-brown-v-board-education.

[2] Warren, Earl. "Opinion of the Court: *Brown v. Board of Education of Topeka, Kansas,*" 347 U.S. 483, 1954. Retrieved from http://www.law.cornell.edu/supct/html/historics/USSC_CR_0347_0483_ZO.html.

[3] Kennedy, John F. "Civil Rights Address," June 11, 1963. Retrieved from http://www.americanrhetoric.com/ speeches/jfkcivilrights.htm.

[4] Parks, Rosa. "The Front of the Bus." In Colbert, David, ed. *Eyewitness to America: 500 Years of America in the Words of Those Who Saw It Happen.* New York: Pantheon Books, 1997, p. 456.

[5] Quoted in King, Casey, and Linda Burnett Osborne. *Oh, Freedom! Kids Talk about the Civil Rights Movement with the People Who Made It Happen.* New York: Knopf, 1997, p. 62.

[6] Quoted in Garrow, David. *Bearing the Cross: Martin Luther King, Jr., and the Southern Christian Leadership Conference.* New York: William Morrow, 1986, p. 246.

[7] Lewis, John. "Speech at the March on Washington," August 28, 1963. Retrieved from http://voicesofdemocracy.umd.edu/lewis-speech-at-the-march-on-washington-speech-text/.

[8] Johnson, Lyndon B. "Special Message to Congress: The American Promise," March 15, 1965. Retrieved from http://www.lbjlib.utexas.edu/johnson/archives.hom/speeches.hom/650315.asp.

Chapter Seven

THE LEGACY OF
PLESSY V. FERGUSON

⏤⏣⏤

> If there is anyone out there who still doubts that America is a place where all things are possible; who still wonders if the dream of our founders is alive in our times; who still questions the power of our democracy, tonight is your answer.

> —Barack Obama, upon becoming the first African American to be elected president of the United States, November 4, 2008

*P*lessy *v. Ferguson* had a titanic impact on the lives of millions of Americans, both black and white. The Supreme Court decision relegated generations of African Americans to lives of limited economic opportunity, stunted educational options, and daily humiliations. But the law also shaped the contours of life for white Americans in complicated ways. Whites unquestionably benefited from Jim Crow laws that gave them enormous advantages in employment, education, and housing. Yet the nation in which they lived always operated at less than full strength as long as it consigned its African-American citizens to second-class status, where their talents could not be fully explored and developed. And whether whites acknowledged it or not, Jim Crow's laws of segregation and disenfranchisement were an insult to America's founding ideals of equality, liberty, and fairness.

The legacy of *Plessy v. Ferguson*, though, also encompasses the laws and court decisions that ultimately struck down segregation and affirmed the nation's most sacred civil rights principles. Legal and political milestones such as *Brown v. Board of Education* (1954), the Civil Rights Acts of 1964 and 1968, and the Voting Rights Act of 1965 repudiated Jim Crow and gave the people of America an opening to build a truly color-blind society. "*Brown v. Board* became

Integrated public school classrooms, like this one in Charlotte, North Carolina, were rare until the Supreme Court overturned *Plessy v. Ferguson*.

important for every citizen, not just African Americans," stated Cheryl Brown Henderson, daughter of the plaintiff in the *Brown* case. "It showed that we all had sovereign rights that could not be restricted by state and local governments. That decision impacted the lives of women, people with disabilities, blacks, whites, Hispanics, Asians, everyone living in this country.... Everyone had to start talking about race after the decision. It opened up a dialogue and forced the country to take on greater responsibility [in confronting racism]."[1]

In the half-century since the United States turned away from *Plessy's* noxious "separate but equal" doctrine, though, Americans have voiced sharp disagreements about the nation's progress in removing racism from its blood-stream and reducing racial tensions. Many Americans believe that political, economic, and cultural gains by blacks and other minorities—most notably the election of the nation's first black president in 2008—show that racism in the United States is mostly a thing of the past. Many others, however, contend that the deck is still stacked against black Americans in numerous respects. Tellingly, these different perspectives break down largely along racial lines. The great majority of whites believe that America has attained racial equality in the legal system, the housing and job markets, and other sectors of U.S. society. Most blacks, by contrast, believe that racial inequality still casts a long shadow over numerous aspects of American life.

A Sharp Decline in Blatant Racism

Americans almost universally agree that overt racism against African Americans and other minority groups like Hispanics, Asians, and Jews has plunged dramatically in the last half-century. Vicious stereotypes and ugly names for minorities used to be freely tossed around in public; now such insults are roundly condemned in all but the most bigoted households and communities. Doors that were once padlocked against minorities have been opened in numerous sectors of American society, from corporate boardrooms and concert theatres to the U.S. Senate and the head coaching fraternity of the National Football League. Advertisements and programs on television and in other media broke the color barrier as well, introducing campaigns and shows that featured African-American, Hispanic, and Asian faces.

By the 1990s and into the first decade of the twenty-first century, many African Americans openly entertained professional dreams that would have seemed impossible in the *Plessy*-sanctioned world of Jim Crow. "There are [black] people who say, 'I want to be an engineer. I want to be a firefighter. I want to be a police officer,'" said civil rights icon and longtime U.S. congressman John Lewis. "But you hear more and more, 'I want to be governor. I want to be mayor. I want to be president.' That's a good thing."[2]

These trends extend to the American South, the one-time home of Jim Crow. During the 1980s and 1990s huge numbers of African-American families left economically struggling towns and cities in the Midwest and West to pursue an expanding slate of educational and job opportunities in the South. This so-called return migration, which reversed the northward trend of earlier generations, was also sparked

> *"There are [black] people who say, 'I want to be an engineer. I want to be a firefighter. I want to be a police officer,'" said civil rights icon and longtime U.S. congressman John Lewis. "But you hear more and more, 'I want to be governor. I want to be mayor. I want to be president.' That's a good thing."*

The civil rights movement opened doors for black professionals and led to greater diversity in schools and workplaces throughout the United States.

by the desire to explore ancestral roots and rekindle relationships with relatives who never left the South.

These demographic changes sparked fear and anger from pockets of white bigotry in the region, but they also encouraged many Southern whites to prove that their homeland was no longer a world of Jim Crow laws and anti-civil rights violence. The "common quest" of whites and blacks for a "redefined identity," wrote historian James C. Cobb,

> seems to hold out the prospect for bringing black and white southerners closer together, although contemporary conflicts over songs, symbols, and monuments—either to the Confederacy or to the crusade against Jim Crow—suggest that this may take a while. Still … the South's stateways no longer separate its residents by color, and they are free as never before to determine for

themselves whether, despite their conflict-ridden past, the customs and traditions they share, the folkways of region rather than race, will sustain a new and truly meaningful 'southern way of life.'[3]

Troubling Socioeconomic Currents in Black America

Today, African Americans can point with pride to black entrepreneurs, corporate executives, physicians, writers, lawyers, engineers, educators, and artists who have risen to the highest ranks of their professions. "For an expanded black middle class, which enjoys unprecedented success at work and in school, the times are much better than before *Brown*,"[4] summarized black scholar Michael Eric Dyson. Broadly speaking, however, African-American communities in all parts of the United States—whether rural or urban, North or South—have yet to climb to the level of white communities in key economic and educational measurements. In many ways, their circumstances mirror those of Hispanic Americans, another large minority group that has not yet achieved socioeconomic parity with whites.

These shortfalls extend to virtually every corner of American life. Nationwide, the poverty rate for black families is almost three times that of their white counterparts. A 2012 study by the Pew Charitable Trusts found that 65 percent of black families occupy the bottom 20 percent of America's income ladder, compared to only 11 percent of whites. Unemployment rates for African Americans by gender, education, and age are much higher than those of their white counterparts, while rates of home ownership are much lower. Meanwhile, a 2012 study of government statistics released by Child Trends found that 73 percent of black children are born outside of marriage, compared with 29 percent of white children. In black households, the teen pregnancy rate is twice that of whites.

Huge gaps in educational attainment are also present between whites and blacks. The high school dropout rate for blacks in 2010 was 8 percent, according to U.S. Department of Education statistics; whites, by contrast, posted a dropout rate of 5.1 percent that year. The same stark racial divide can be seen among students who complete high school. Education statistics indicate that the percentage of white seniors who achieve "basic proficiency" in the subjects of math, science, and American history is more than twice that of black seniors. The performance gap between the races is not as significant in the subjects of reading and writing, but even there, white twelfth-graders outperform their black counterparts by sizable margins. About 80 percent of white seniors,

Serious social and economic problems affecting African-American communities have contributed to the stunningly high percentage of black men in the U.S. prison system.

for example, achieve basic proficiency in reading, whereas only one out of two black seniors reach this level.

Even when blacks match whites in educational attainment, they are not rewarded equally in the marketplace. "Both whites and blacks experience increased earnings with each additional level of schooling," noted sociologist Angel Harris. "However, whites earn somewhat more than blacks at each level of schooling. Furthermore, the black-white pay differential widens slightly at higher levels of education."[5] Whites enjoy significantly higher levels of upward economic mobility as well. According to Pew, more than half of blacks raised at the bottom of America's economic ladder remain stuck there as adults, compared to only a third of whites.[6]

Black families and communities also grapple with higher levels of environmental pollution, drug addiction, and gang violence than do white households and neighborhoods. The interrelated problems of the illegal drug trade and gang activity, in fact, have been cited as driving factors in the stunningly high percentage of black men in the American prison system. U.S. Census data from 2010 indicate that whereas African Americans made up 13.6 percent of the U.S. population, adult black males accounted for 40.2 percent of all prison inmates in the United States.

Men and women who complete prison sentences also find that their options are much more limited when they return to the outside world. A criminal record shuts doors to many employment and educational opportunities, and in many states it also bars ex-convicts from entering the voting booth. This form of disenfranchisement has had a major and disproportionate impact on black communities. According to a criminal justice reform organization called the Sentencing Project, 7.7 percent of all African Americans have lost the right to vote because of state bans against ex-convict voting, whereas only 2 percent of non-blacks have been stripped of their voting rights due to these laws.[7]

Prescriptions for Lifting Black Communities

African Americans (and Americans of other races) have been engaged for many years in intense debate about the root causes of these terrible problems that afflict so many black families and communities. Some people believe that most serious problems in black America stem from continued racial inequities in American schools, workplaces, courtrooms, and other institutions. They believe that fundamental reforms to those institutions will remove many of the barriers that trap blacks in positions of socioeconomic inferiority.

In the area of education, for example, black scholars like Stanford education professor Linda Darling-Hammond insist that "outcomes for students of color are much more a function of their unequal access to key educational resources, including skilled teachers and quality curriculum, than they are a function of race."[8] This assertion has been supported by analyses of funding for white and minority schools. In 2012, for example, the liberal policy organization Center for American Progress (CAP) reported that nationally, schools spend an average of $334 more per white student than nonwhite student. CAP's report, *Unequal Education: Federal Loophole Enables Lower Spending on Students of Color,* also found that mostly white schools (defined as 90 percent or more white) spent $733 more per student than mostly nonwhite schools (90 percent or more nonwhite).[9]

Some black scholars and civil rights activists return to alleged discrimination in the American justice system to explain some of these social problems as well. "The mass incarceration of people of color through the War on Drugs is a big part of the reason that a black child born today is less likely to be raised by both parents than a black child born during slavery," wrote Michelle Alexander, an African-American lawyer and college professor. "The absence of black fathers from families across America is not simply a function of laziness, immaturity, or too much time watching Sports Center. Hundreds of thousands of black men have disappeared into prisons and jails, locked away for drug crimes that are largely ignored when committed by whites."[10]

Others, however, assert that blacks need to take greater personal responsibility for their own lives, rededicate them-

> *"It is no surprise that race still divides America," stated a* Newsweek *analysis. "The surprise is that one of the most encouraging signs of racial progress in our nation's history, the election of an African-American president, now seems to be deepening our divisions rather than diminishing them."*

Bill Cosby's Challenge

Bill Cosby has long been one of America's most respected and beloved comedians and television personalities. Born in 1937 in Philadelphia, he grew up to become a popular stand-up comedian and a pioneering figure in the history of television. In 1965 he became the first black person to star in a network TV series when he played one-half of a daring secret agent team in the NBC series *I Spy.*

He starred in or produced several other television series during the next three decades as well. The best-known of these shows was *The Cosby Show,* in which he starred as the head of a wholesome, college-educated, and affluent black family. *The Cosby Show* ran from 1984 to 1992 and was the top-ranked program in the country for much of that time.

In 2004 Cosby attracted a great deal of attention when he delivered a speech attacking the declining morality, irresponsible behavior, and misplaced priorities of many poor blacks. He charged that poor blacks had developed a poisonous culture (exemplified by gangster rap and a rejection of standard English) that "kept them down" far more than white racism. "[Young blacks] think they're hip," he said. "They can't read; they can't write. They're laughing and giggling, and they're going nowhere."[1] Cosby also asserted that these self-destructive attitudes made a mockery of the sacrifices that earlier generations of blacks had made to fight segregation and other forms of discrimination.

Cosby's complaints—which he repeated in subsequent speeches and a 2007 book called *Come On, People: On the Path from Victims to Victors* (co-authored by Alvin F. Poussaint)—ignited a fierce debate among black Americans. African-American journalist Cynthia Tucker said that "across the country, middle-class black Americans are applauding comedian Bill Cosby's insistent campaign to draw attention to the bad habits and poor choices that limit black achievement. There has been little disagreement about his main points—that drug use, poor classroom performance and the embrace of outlaw culture have done nothing but cement the black underclass at the bottom of American society."[2]

Some prominent black commentators on the African-American experience, however, objected to Cosby's characterizations of poor blacks. Professor Michael Eric Dyson asserted that "too often we fail to give [the poor] credit for how they are already being personally and morally responsible, given the conditions they confront in the home, in the neighborhood, in the school, and in society."[3] Journalist Ta-Nehisi Coates expressed appreciation for some of Cosby's blunt talk, but he also criticized the comedian for downplaying the continued impact of institutional racism and condemning what Coates sees as genuine forms of black self-expression (such as rap music). "Cosby's gospel of discipline, moral reform, and self-reliance offers a way out—a promise that one need not cure America of its original sin [of racism] in order to succeed," wrote Coates. "But Cosby often pits the rhetoric of personal responsibility against the legitimate claims of American citizens for their rights. He chides activists for pushing to reform the criminal-justice system, despite solid evidence that the criminal-justice system needs reform. His historical amnesia—his assertion that many of the problems that pervade black America are of a recent vintage—is simply wrong."[4]

Sources

Cosby, Bill, and Alvin F. Poussaint. *Come on, People: On the Path from Victims to Victors.* Nashville: Thomas Nelson, 2007.

Dyson, Michael Eric. *Is Bill Cosby Right? (Or Has the Black Middle Class Lost Its Mind?).* New York: Basic Civitas, 2006.

Notes

[1] Quoted in "Rainbow/PUSH Coalition Holds 33rd Annual Conference in Chicago." *Jet,* July 26, 2004, p. 4.
[2] Tucker, Cynthia. "Call It the Cosby Consensus." *Atlanta Journal-Constitution,* September 27, 2004.
[3] Dyson, Michael Eric. *Is Bill Cosby Right? (Or Has the Black Middle Class Lost Its Mind?).* New York: Basic Civitas, 2006, p. 214.
[4] Coates, Ta-Nehisi. "'This Is How We Lost to the White Man': The Audacity of Bill Cosby's Black Conservatism." *Atlantic,* May 2008. Retrieved from http://www.theatlantic.com/magazine/archive/2008/05/-this-is-how-we-lost-to-the-white-man/306774/.

selves to being good parents and productive members of society, and stop using America's imperfections as an excuse for their own failures. Variations of this message have been delivered by a wide cross-section of prominent black voices. "Wake up everybody," urged a 2003 editorial in the *Chicago Defender,* one of America's most historically prominent black-owned newspapers. "There is a widespread malignancy that is enthralling entirely too much of some areas in the Black community—guns, drugs, and gangs.… It is time for adults of all persuasions, political, community and church leaders … to use influence, common sense, and profundity to bear down and take back our streets from the thuggish minions who would choke the creativity and progress of our people."[11] Elsewhere, the famous black comedian Bill Cosby has drawn considerable attention with his repeated criticisms of the values, priorities, and behavior of low-income blacks (see "Bill Cosby's Challenge," p. 102).

Many African Americans believe that both camps raise legitimate points. In a 2008 Father's Day speech to a black church congregation in Chicago, Barack Obama acknowledged the social and economic disadvantages that still burden many black households and communities: "Yes, we need more cops on the street.… Yes, we need more money for our schools, and more outstanding teachers in the classroom, and more afterschool programs for our children. Yes, we need more jobs and more job training and more opportunity in our communities." But he also said that African-American communities need to make better and more responsible personal choices. Obama asserted, for example, that too many black fathers do not own up to their responsibilities as parents. "If we are honest with ourselves, we'll admit that too many [African-American] fathers are missing—missing from too many lives and too many homes.… They have abandoned their responsibilities. They're acting like boys instead of men. And the foundations of our families are weaker because of it"[12] (see "President Barack Obama Discusses Racial Progress," p. 190).

America's First Black President

The 2008 election of Democratic candidate Barack Obama as America's 44th president—and its first African-American commander-in-chief—is frequently cited as the most obvious indication that the United States has made enormous progress in improving race relations since *Brown v. Board of Education.* Even people who believe that white-black relations remain extremely troubled acknowledge that Obama's election (and his subsequent re-election in 2012) was a landmark event in U.S. history. A mere fifty years before Obama's historic elec-

President Barack Obama (right) with First Lady Michelle Obama and Vice President Joe Biden at the White House, 2012.

tion, more than half of Americans participating in a Gallup public opinion poll had declared that they would never vote for a black presidential candidate. To move from that stance to one in which Obama could cruise to a comfortable election victory over a white opponent showed not only that American race relations had evolved, but also that the nation had removed many discriminatory barriers to minority voters (who supported Obama by large margins).

After congratulating themselves for being enlightened enough to elect a black president, though, the American people found to their surprise that the milestone failed to dissolve racial tensions that still afflicted the country (see "A Journalist Considers Obama's Impact on Race in America," p. 195). After Obama's 2008 election, 52 percent of Americans in a Pew Research poll said that they expected race relations to get better. By April 2012, however, a *Newsweek* poll found that only 32 percent of Americans believed that race relations improved during Obama's first term in office—and 30 percent believed that race relations actually worsened. "It is no surprise that race still divides America,"

Keith Plessy and Phoebe Ferguson, descendants of the key men involved in *Plessy v. Ferguson*, are co-founders of an organization dedicated to civil rights education and outreach.

stated *Newsweek* analysts Andrew Romano and Allison Samuels. "It has divided us since the first settlers landed on our shores.... The surprise is that one of the most encouraging signs of racial progress in our nation's history, the election of an African-American president, now seems to be deepening our divisions rather than diminishing them."[13]

Romano and Samuels attributed the nation's continued racial divide to disagreements about whether discrimination against blacks remains a serious problem in the United States. They pointed out that according to the poll, 70 percent of whites but only 35 percent of blacks believe that blacks have equal access to affordable housing. Seventy percent of whites also assert that the two races receive equal treatment in the job market, while only 25 percent of blacks agree. Meanwhile, four out of five whites—but fewer than one in two blacks—believe that the American legal system is now color-blind. Blacks are also much more likely to report having been personally victimized by racism in their daily lives. "This is the dilemma Obama inherited: a white America eager to be convinced that racism is a thing of the past and a black America still painfully aware that it is not," wrote Romano and Samuels. "So how is Obama's presence in the Oval Office driving us farther apart? By pushing all of this racial misunderstanding out onto the political playing field, where it is amplified and distorted"[14] by political warfare between Democrats and Republicans.

Still, Romano and Samuels offer an upbeat perspective on the long-term impact of Obama's presidency on American race relations. "These frustrating feuds won't last forever," they wrote. "In the long run, the mere fact of a President Obama—a brown face alongside all those chalky portraits in our history books—will begin to have its own effect. White children will look at black children differently. Black children will look at themselves differently. And that, one hopes, will be more than enough to make up for whatever growing pains we're experiencing right now."[15]

This sort of optimism is supported by symbols of racial reconciliation and friendship that can be found all across the country every day. One such symbol is the establishment in New Orleans of the Plessy and Ferguson Foundation, an organization dedicated to civil rights education and outreach. This organization was founded by descendents of both Homer Plessy, the man who challenged Louisiana's segregationist Separate Car Law back in the 1890s, and John Howard Ferguson, the state judge who upheld the law back in 1892. Phoebe Ferguson is the great-great-granddaughter of Judge Ferguson, while Keith Plessy's great-grandfather was Homer Plessy's first cousin. "I was not a great leader or a great scholar or any of those things," Keith Plessy said when asked about his role in establishing the foundation. "But I have an obligation and a privilege to keep my ancestor's history alive. What my ancestors dreamt about, I'm able to live."[16]

Notes

[1] Henderson, Cheryl Brown. "Reaffirming the Legacy." *The Unfinished Agenda* of Brown v. Board of Education. Editors of *Black Issues in Education.* Hoboken, NJ: John Wiley & Sons, 2004, pp. 167-69.

[2] Quoted in Ifill, Gwen. *The Breakthrough: Politics and Race in the Age of Obama.* New York: Doubleday, 2009, p. 238.

[3] Cobb, James C. "Segregating the New South: The Origins and Legacy of *Plessy v. Ferguson*." *Georgia State University Law Review,* June 1996. Retrieved from http://digitalarchive.gsu.edu/cgi/viewcon tent.cgi?article=2630&context=gsulr.

[4] Dyson, Michael Eric. *Is Bill Cosby Right? (Or Has the Black Middle Class Lost Its Mind?).* New York: Basic Civitas, 2006, p. 61.

5 Harris, Angel L. "The Economic and Educational State of Black Americans in the 21st Century: Should We Be Optimistic or Concerned?" *Review of Black Political Economy,* October 5, 2010, p. 6. Retrieved from http://www.princeton.edu/~angelh/Website/Studies/Article%208%20%28Rev%20of%20Blk%20Pol%20Econ%20%2710%29.pdf.

6 Pew Charitable Trusts. *Pursuing the American Dream: Economic Mobility Across Generations.* July 2012, p. 18. Retrieved from http://www.pewstates.org/uploadedFiles/PCS_Assets/2012/Pursuing_American_Dream.pdf.

7 Gray, Katti. "Banned from Voting Booths: Ex-Convicts." Salon.com, October 22, 2012. Retrieved from http://www.salon.com/2012/10/22/banned_from_voting_booths_ex_convicts/.

8 Darling-Hammond, Linda. "The Color Line in American Education: Race, Resources, and Student Achievement." *Du Bois Review* 1(2), 2004, p. 214.

9 Spatig-Amerikaner, Ary. *Unequal Education: Federal Loophole Enables Lower Spending on Students of Color.* Center for American Progress, August 2012, p. 4. Retrieved from http://www.americanprogress.org/wp-content/uploads/2012/08/UnequalEduation.pdf

10 Alexander, Michelle. "Where Have All the Black Men Gone?" *Huffington Post,* February 22, 2010. Retrieved from http://www.huffingtonpost.com/michelle-alexander/where-have-all-the-black_b_469808.html.

11 "Black-on-Black Crime Must Be Made a Thing of the Past" [editorial]. *The Chicago Defender,* October 1, 2003.

12 Obama, Barack. "Text of Obama's Fatherhood Speech." *Politico.com,* June 15, 2008. Retrieved from http://www.politico.com/news/stories/0608/11094.html.

13 Romano, Andrew, and Allison Samuels. "A *Newsweek* Poll Shows Americans Still Divided over Race." *Newsweek,* April 9, 2012. Retrieved from http://www.thedailybeast.com/newsweek/2012/04/08/a-newsweek-poll-show-americans-still-divided-over-race.html.

14 Romano and Samuels, "A *Newsweek* Poll Shows Americans Still Divided over Race."

15 Romano and Samuels, "A *Newsweek* Poll Shows Americans Still Divided over Race."

16 Barnes, Robert. "Plessy and Ferguson: Descendants of a Divisive Supreme Court Decision Unite." *Washington Post,* June 5, 2011. Retrieved from http://www.washingtonpost.com/politics/plessy-and-ferguson-descendants-of-a-divisive-supreme-court-decision-unite/2011/06/02/AGji3hJH_story.html.

BIOGRAPHIES

Henry Billings Brown (1836-1913)
Supreme Court Justice Who Wrote the Majority Opinion in Plessy v. Ferguson

Henry Billings Brown was born in the small town of South Lee, Massachusetts, on March 2, 1836. His parents were Mary Tyler Brown and Billings Brown, who owned flour and lumber mills in South Lee. In 1845 Brown's father sold his businesses and took his family to Stockbridge, Massachusetts. Four years later, the Brown family relocated again, to Ellington, Connecticut.

Brown posted good grades at the private schools that his parents enrolled him in, and at age sixteen he enrolled at Yale College (now Yale University) in New Haven, Connecticut. After Brown earned a bachelor of arts degree from Yale in 1856, his father rewarded him with a trip to Europe, where he stayed for the next year.

Pursuing a Law Career

Upon returning to the United States in 1857, Brown found work as a law clerk in Ellington. He also resumed his studies, taking courses at the law schools of both Yale and Harvard University, located in Cambridge, Massachusetts. In 1859 Brown moved to Detroit, Michigan. He quickly was admitted to the state bar, meaning that he received legal authorization to work as a lawyer in Michigan. He then established a successful law practice in Detroit, and in fairly short order he developed a reputation as an expert in shipping laws pertaining to the Great Lakes.

Brown's status as one of Detroit's most prominent citizens was further enhanced by a series of professional and personal milestones. In 1860 Brown was named a deputy U.S. marshal for Detroit, and three years later he was appointed an assistant U.S. attorney for the Eastern District of Michigan (he held the latter position for five years). In 1864 he married Caroline Pitts, a young woman who hailed from one of Detroit's wealthier families. Her father died a few years after the marriage and left his daughter a substantial inheritance. This money enabled Brown and his wife to build a very comfortable life for themselves. Between this money and his own income, Brown was able to put together the necessary funds to hire a substitute to serve in his place in the Union Army during the Civil War. This practice was widely employed by wealthy American Northerners during the war, so Brown did not suffer any damage to his public reputation for avoiding military service.

In 1868 Michigan's Republican governor appointed Brown to fill a vacant circuit judge seat for Wayne County. Brown held the seat for only a few months, however, before losing it to a Democratic nominee in an election. He returned to the life of a lawyer, working as an attorney for the firm of Newberry, Pond & Brown for the next seven years. Brown's only attempt to return to government work during this time was an unsuccessful 1872 bid for the Republican nomination for a seat in the U.S. House of Representatives.

Taking a Seat on the Supreme Court

In 1875 President Ulysses S. Grant appointed Brown to the U.S. District Court for Eastern Michigan, and he served as a federal district judge for the next fourteen years. Brown also lectured on maritime law at the University of Michigan Law School for several years. During the 1880s he openly acknowledged to friends and colleagues that his career ambition was to gain an appointment to the U.S. Supreme Court. This was not an unattainable dream, for Brown was recognized as a fine legal mind, and he had cultivated friendships over the years with many prominent business leaders and politicians around the country.

When Supreme Court justice Samuel F. Miller died in 1890, Brown was widely recognized as a strong candidate to replace him. It came as no surprise, then, when Republican president Benjamin Harrison nominated Brown to fill the vacant Court seat on December 23, 1890. The U.S. Senate confirmed Brown's appointment seven days later.

Author of *Plessy* Majority Opinion

Brown served as an associate justice on the U.S. Supreme Court for the next fifteen years, during which time he authored more than 450 majority opinions. He is regarded by historians as a fairly moderate justice on a politically conservative Court. He usually sided with conservative justices who placed a higher value on private property rights than on government's authority to regulate business, but he also held that the federal government did have a legitimate role to play in overseeing some business practices. In *Holden v. Hardy* (1898), for instance, Brown wrote a majority opinion that upheld a state law limiting the number of hours per day that mining companies could force employees to work.

Brown spent most of his Supreme Court career operating in the shadows of more famous and influential justices like Stephen Field, John Marshall Harlan, and Oliver Wendell Holmes Jr. Brown's status as the author of the majority opinion in the 1896 *Plessy v. Ferguson* case, though, ensured that he would not be entirely forgotten by future generations of legal experts and historians.

The Supreme Court decided in *Plessy v. Ferguson* that segregation of the races into "separate but equal" facilities, establishments, and institutions was legally and morally sound. Brown's majority opinion reflected the judgment of the Court—and most whites of that period—that whites were biologically superior to blacks, which meant that whites should not have to associate with "colored people." Nonetheless, Brown denied that "the enforced separation of the two races stamps the colored race with a badge of inferiority." He said that anyone who interpreted the Court's decision in that way was just looking to stir up trouble.

The Supreme Court's decision in *Plessy v. Ferguson* is now regarded as one of the worst moments in the entire history of the Court. At the time, though, the decision—and Brown's explanation for it—were not seen as particularly outrageous by white Americans. As one biography noted, "So representative were his views on the subject of race that the nation scarcely blinked when Brown established the blueprint for the edifice of Jim Crow segregation that would tower over the South for half a century."[1]

Brown retired from the Court on May 28, 1906, five years after the death of his wife. By the time of his retirement he was almost blind. In 1904 he was remarried, to Josephine E. Tyler. He died in New York City on September 4, 1913.

Sources

Broad, Trevor. "Forgotten Man in a Tumultuous Time: The Gilded Age as Seen by United States Supreme Court Associate Justice Henry Billings Brown." *Michigan Journal of History,* Winter 2005.

Brown, Henry Billings. *Memoir of Henry Billings Brown: Late Justice of the Supreme Court of the United States.* New York: Duffield and Company, 1915.

Hall, Timothy L., ed. *Supreme Court Justices: A Biographical Dictionary.* New York: Facts on File, 2001.

Urofsky, Melvin I., ed. *Biographical Encyclopedia of the Supreme Court: The Lives and Legal Philosophies of the Justices.* Washington, DC: CQ Press, 2006.

Note

[1] Hall, Timothy L., ed. "Henry Billings Brown (1836-1913)." *Supreme Court Justices: A Biographical Dictionary.* New York: Facts on File, 2001, p. 206.

Rodolphe Desdunes (1849-1928)
*Creole Civil Rights Activist Who Challenged
Louisiana's Separate Car Law*

Rodolphe Lucien Desdunes was born on
November 15, 1849, in New Orleans,
Louisiana. He was raised in the Vieux
Carré, a vibrant Creole neighborhood in New
Orleans, by his father, a cigar manufacturer of
Haitian descent, and his Cuban mother.
French, Creole, and English were all spoken in
the streets and shops Desdunes frequented as
a youth, and as a young adult he attended
Reconstruction-era schools and other public
facilities that were fully integrated. This ethni-
cally diverse environment exposed him to a
wide array of cultural influences and ideas,
and it undoubtedly contributed to his later
activism for the cause of racial equality.

Desdunes briefly explored a career in law as a young man, studying the
subject at Straight University (now Dillard University) in New Orleans in the
1870s. In 1879, though, he took a job as a messenger at the U.S. Customs House
in New Orleans. Desdunes worked in that capacity for the next six years, when
he left the customs house to work as a journalist. Desdunes also started a family during this period with Mathilde Chaval, a fellow Louisiana native. Their
marriage ultimately produced six children (two boys and four girls).

Desdunes became best known during the late 1880s for his regular contributions to *The Crusader,* New Orleans's weekly black newspaper. Desdunes
and Louis A. Martinet, the newspaper's founder and managing editor, worked
together closely to speak out against the wave of new segregation laws that was
cresting all across the Deep South at that time.

Fighting the Separate Car Act

In 1891 Desdunes returned to the employ of the U.S. Customs House in
New Orleans as a clerk, but he remained at the forefront of the city's civil rights
activist community. He gained particular prominence for his vocal criticisms of
the Separate Car Act, an 1890 Louisiana law that segregated all rail passenger

cars used for travel within the state by race. "Every honorable person knows that the law was passed to discriminate against the colored people so as to degrade them,"[1] declared Desdunes.

In September 1891 Desdunes joined with Martinet and other black community leaders to establish the Citizens' Committee to Test the Constitutionality of the Separate Car Law, an organization dedicated to challenging the legality of the new statute. This group, headquartered at the downtown offices of *The Crusader*, quickly emerged as the biggest threat to the white legislators who wanted to impose Jim Crow laws across Louisiana. The committee was able to enlist the support of men like Alexandre Aristide Mary, a wealthy New Orleans businessman of mixed white and black descent, and Albion Tourgée, a white lawyer and journalist from the North.

Martinet and Desdunes recognized that the only way to strike down the law was through a court challenge. In February 1892 one of Desdunes's sons, Daniel, defied the Separate Car Law by sitting in a "whites only" rail car. He was promptly arrested, but he was acquitted at his trial because his travel took him over state lines (the Separate Car Law applied only to trains that stayed within Louisiana).

Undaunted, the Citizens' Committee convinced another supporter, a man of mixed white and black descent named Homer Plessy, to challenge the law. In June 1892 Plessy was arrested for sitting in a whites-only rail car on a train that was not engaged in interstate travel. Desdunes and his allies finally had the court case they wanted. "Rodolphe Desdunes was fighting this one to win it," said historian Rebecca Scott. "But he was also fighting this one for the record. So that if anyone claimed that what forced racial segregation was simply a customary means of southern life, there would be an indisputable record that this group of people had fought it tooth and nail."[2]

In November 1892 district judge John Howard Ferguson found Plessy guilty. He rejected the arguments of Plessy's attorneys, who said that the Separate Car Law amounted to a clear violation of the Thirteenth and Fourteenth Amendments to the Constitution. The Citizens' Committee refused to admit defeat, however. It advanced the case—now known as *Plessy v. Ferguson*—all the way to the U.S. Supreme Court. In 1896, though, that Court issued a 7-1 decision that upheld the legality of the Separate Car Law. This ruling paved the way for states all across the South to impose all sorts of discriminatory Jim Crow laws against their black citizens.

Documenting the World of Louisianans of Color

Desdunes and his allies expressed great pride in their efforts to fight Jim Crow, but the *Plessy* decision was a terrible blow. Segregationist laws and violence against blacks proliferated all across the South in the wake of the judgment, and it became impossible for African Americans to agitate for civil rights without risking their lives and those of their families. *The Crusader* and other newspapers associated with blacks or Republicanism ceased publication, and the Citizens' Committee disbanded in defeat.

Desdunes stepped away from political activism, but he never lost the pride he felt about his heritage. In 1911 he published a book called *Nos Hommes et Nostre Histoire (Our People and Our History)* in Montreal, Quebec, Canada, the largest French-speaking city in North America. Desdunes's book contained biographical profiles of fifty prominent Creole artists, musicians, writers, physicians, lawyers, teachers, and philanthropists from New Orleans.

Desdunes continued to support his family through work at the U.S. Customs House, but in 1911 he suffered a terrible workplace accident. While supervising the unloading of granite from a cargo ship, a spray of granite dust blew into his eyes. The incident left him mostly blind, and he was forced to retire from his customs job in 1912. Efforts to restore his eyesight failed, and he was virtually blind for the last seventeen years of his life. He died from cancer of the larynx on August 14, 1928, at the home of his son, Daniel, in Omaha, Nebraska.

Sources

Desdunes, Rodolphe Lucien. *Our People and Our History: Fifty Creole Portraits.* Reprint. Translated and edited by Sister Dorothea McCants. Baton Rouge: Louisiana State University, 1973.

Medley, Keith Weldon. *We as Freemen:* Plessy v. Ferguson. Gretna, LA: Pelican Publishing, 2003.

Scott, Rebecca J. "The Atlantic World and the Road to *Plessy v. Ferguson." Journal of American History,* December 2007.

Notes

[1] Quoted in Medley, Keith Weldon. *We as Freemen:* Plessy v. Ferguson. Gretna, LA: Pelican Publishing, 2003, p. 116.

[2] Quoted in *American Experience: New Orleans.* Program transcript, chapter 6. PBS, 2007. Retrieved from http://www.pbs.org/wgbh/amex/neworleans/program/neworleans_06_trans.html.

John Howard Ferguson (1838-1915)
Louisiana Judge Who Became the Defendant in
Plessy v. Ferguson

John Howard Ferguson was born on June 10, 1838, in Chilmark, a small town on the island of Martha's Vineyard in Massachusetts. He was the third child of Sarah Davis Luce and John H. Ferguson, who supported his family by working as a shipmaster (captain of cargo ships). As a young man, Ferguson did not show much interest in following in his father's career footsteps. Instead, he became a teacher and began studying law in Boston under the instruction of distinguished attorney Benjamin F. Hallett.

Making a Life in New Orleans

After the Civil War ended, Ferguson joined many other ambitious young Northerners who decided to make their fortune in the vanquished South, which needed to rebuild its war-damaged cities, bridges, railroads, and plantations. "Ferguson learned from returning soldiers of the vast opportunities in the defeated South," wrote historian Keith Weldon Medley. "To the victors went the spoils. Eager for new adventure, Ferguson left Boston for a new life in an old city."[1]

Ferguson established law offices in New Orleans, Louisiana, which was policed by federal troops and managed by federal administrators in the years following the Civil War. In July 1866 he married Virginia Butler Earhart, the daughter of an outspoken abolitionist and pro-Union businessman named Thomas Jefferson Earhart. Ferguson wanted to build a quiet home for his bride outside the rough and tumble environment of New Orleans. He settled on a little town called Burtheville located north of the city, and it was here that Ferguson and his wife raised three sons. In 1870, however, the village of Burtheville was annexed into New Orleans and became the city's Fourteenth Ward.

Ferguson thrived in New Orleans in the 1870s and 1880s. He allied himself with the state Democratic party and its Democratic governor, Francis Nicholls, and he even served briefly in the state legislature. Most of his time,

117

though, was devoted to his law practice. On June 30, 1892, he set aside his practice for the robes of a judge. He was appointed to fill a vacancy on the bench in New Orleans's Section A criminal district court. Ferguson took the place of Robert H. Marr, who had mysteriously disappeared the month before. Ferguson was sworn in on July 5, 1892, to fill the remaining four years of Marr's term.

Plessy's Case Comes Before Ferguson

Three months after taking the bench, Ferguson heard the case that would eventually ensnare him in one of the most notorious Supreme Court decisions in U.S. history. On October 13, 1892, Ferguson opened the trial known as *Homer Adolph Plessy v. The State of Louisiana.* The trial centered around Homer Plessy, a thirty-year-old resident of New Orleans who had been arrested for violating a state law that segregated passenger cars on railroads by race. Plessy's ancestors were mostly white, but since he was officially classified as one-eighth black, the state's Separate Car Law asserted that he could not sit with whites on state railroads. Plessy challenged this law at the urging of a civil rights organization called the Citizens' Committee. He took his stand on June 7, 1892, when he spurned the "Colored" car of the East Louisiana Railroad and sat in its "White" car instead.

When Plessy and his lawyers appeared before Ferguson, they argued that Louisiana's Separate Car Law violated the Thirteenth and Fourteenth Amendments to the Constitution. Ferguson, however, decided that the state had the right to impose such regulations on railroad operations that operated only within Louisiana. On November 18 he rendered a guilty verdict on Plessy for refusing to leave the white rail car. His legal decision also provided a firm defense of state laws that segregated people by race. "[Plessy] was not in a proper sense deprived of his liberty," said Ferguson. "He was simply deprived of the liberty of doing what he pleased and of violating a penal statute with impunity."[2]

Plessy and his allies appealed Ferguson's verdict to the Louisiana State Supreme Court. It was at this point that the case became known as *Plessy v. Ferguson.* The state Supreme Court sided with Ferguson, affirming that the Separate Car Law was in fact constitutional. Unwilling to accept defeat, Plessy petitioned the U.S. Supreme Court to strike down the judgment against him and invalidate Louisiana's segregationist rail car law. Instead, the U.S. Supreme Court in 1896 issued its infamous *Plessy v. Ferguson* decision, which provided legal cover for imposing "separate but equal" segregationist laws all across the South and in other parts of the United States.

Ferguson lived and worked in New Orleans for the rest of his life. He died in the city on November 12, 1915, two months after his wife of forty-nine years passed away.

Sources

Allured, Janet, and Michael S. Martin. *Louisiana Legacies: Readings in the History of the Pelican State.* Malden, MA: Wiley Maxwell, 2013.

Medley, Keith Weldon. *We As Freemen:* Plessy v. Ferguson. Gretna, LA: Pelican, 2003.

Notes

[1] Medley, Keith Weldon. *We As Freemen:* Plessy v. Ferguson. Gretna, LA: Pelican, 2003, p. 45.

[2] Quoted in Lofgren, Charles A. *The* Plessy *Case: A Legal-Historical Interpretation.* New York: Oxford University Press, 1987, p. 48.

John Marshall Harlan (1833-1911)
Supreme Court Justice Who Wrote the Famous
Plessy v. Ferguson *Dissent*

John Marshall Harlan was born in rural Boyle County, Kentucky, on June 1, 1833. His parents were Elizabeth Davenport Harlan and James Harlan, who was a prominent attorney, politician, and slaveholder in the region. An excellent student, Harlan graduated from Centre College in Danville, Kentucky, in 1850 at the age of seventeen. He then moved on to Transylvania University in Lexington, where he studied law for two years. In 1853 Harlan was admitted to the state bar and began his professional career as a lawyer in his father's firm.

Harlan quickly advanced to a position of legal and political prominence in Kentucky. He served from 1854 to 1856 as city attorney for Danville, and he made many friends and allies in the state's Whig political party. In 1856 he married Malvina French Shanklin, with whom he eventually had six children. Two years later he was appointed county judge for Franklin County, Kentucky. One of his few disappointments came in 1859, when he narrowly lost his bid for a seat in the U.S. Congress.

From Union Officer to Supreme Court Justice

In 1861 Harlan remained allegiant to the Union despite his family's long history of slaveholding. He signed up with the Union Army and commanded the Tenth Kentucky Infantry, a volunteer regiment. He served as colonel of the Tenth Kentucky until early 1863, when his father's death led him to resign his commission and return home to take the reins of the family law practice. Later that year he was elected attorney general of Kentucky, and he served the people of his state in that capacity for the next four years.

In 1871 and 1875 Harlan conducted unsuccessful campaigns for Kentucky's governorship. These political setbacks did nothing to tarnish his reputation as a brilliant legal mind, however. On October 17, 1877, Republican president Rutherford B. Hayes nominated Harlan—who had campaigned for Hayes in the 1876 presidential election—to the U.S. Supreme Court. The Senate confirmed the appointment a little more than one month later, on November 29, 1877. Harlan thus began a nearly thirty-four-year stint on the Supreme Court, the sixth-longest tenure in the entire history of the Court.

During his first several years on the Court, Harlan occasionally entertained the idea of resigning. He was concerned about his personal finances, which were drained considerably by the expense of putting his three sons through college. But he eventually managed to relieve some of this financial pressure by earning additional income as a professor of constitutional law in Washington, D.C., at the Columbian Law School (later the law school of George Washington University).

Harlan was a popular member of the Court. He crafted deep friendships with several fellow justices over the years, and he possessed a colorful personality that set him apart from other members. He became well known, for example, for his constant tobacco chewing and spitting. Harlan's enduring reputation as one of the nation's great Supreme Court justices, however, stemmed not from his manner, but from his willingness to take unpopular stands on racial equality cases. In fact, Harlan earned the nickname "The Great Dissenter" for his frequent lonely stands against the Court majority on important court cases.

The Great Dissenter

Harlan frequently dissented from his colleagues' opinions on court cases, and at times he expressed his views fiercely. "In private he was quiet, courteous, and good-humored, devoted to his family and the Presbyterian church, revered by his students," wrote one biographer. "But he was a passionate jurist. As he himself once admitted, his deep feelings about a case could show up in his voice and manner as he delivered an opinion from the bench.... A number of his dissents are classics. They range over many issues, but it is the dissents in civil rights cases that have won him a place on some modern lists of the court's greatest justices."[1]

Harlan's record on the subject of racial equality was not spotless. In 1883, for example, he voted with the majority in *Pace v. Alabama*, which upheld the constitutionality of laws outlawing interracial marriage. Harlan also reportedly harbored deeply prejudiced feelings toward people of Chinese descent. Nonetheless, on several occasions he spoke passionately about the importance of protecting equal rights at a time when the American legal system was endorsing all sorts of laws that attacked African-American civil rights.

In 1883, for example, the Supreme Court ruled in a set of five cases known collectively as *The Civil Rights Cases* that the Civil Rights Act of 1875 was unconstitutional. This judgment was a severe blow to African Americans, because the Civil Rights Act of 1875 had, for the first time, granted them the same rights to use public institutions and facilities as white Americans. Harlan was the lone dissenter on this ruling. He also issued one of only two dissents in *Giles v. Harris* (1903), a Supreme Court ruling that gave Southern states legal justification to establish voter registration requirements that suppressed the black vote.

Harlan is best known, however, as the only dissenter in *Plessy v. Ferguson* (1896), a Supreme Court ruling that upheld a Louisiana law that segregated blacks and whites into separate railroad cars. The author of the Court's majority opinion, Justice Henry Billings Brown, insisted that states could adopt "separate but equal" facilities for different races. Harlan ridiculed the "separate but equal" doctrine, declaring that "in the eye of the law, there is in this country no superior, dominant, ruling class of citizens. There is no caste here.... The thin disguise of 'equal' accommodations for passengers in railroad coaches will not mislead anyone, nor atone for the wrong this day done."

Harlan remained on the Court until October 14, 1911, when he died in Washington, D.C. One of his grandsons, John Marshall Harlan II, later followed in his legal footsteps. Harlan II served as an associate justice of the Supreme Court from 1955 to 1971, during which time he became known as one of the Court's leading conservative thinkers.

Sources

Beth, Loren P. *John Marshall Harlan: The Last Whig Justice.* Lexington: University Press of Kentucky, 1992.

Przybyszewski, Linda. *The Republic According to John Marshall Harlan.* Chapel Hill: University of North Carolina Press, 1999.

Thompson, Charles. "*Plessy v. Ferguson:* Harlan's Great Dissent." *Kentucky Humanities,* no. 1, 1996. Retrieved from http://www.law.louisville.edu/library/collections/harlan/dissent.

Note

[1] Thompson, Charles. "*Plessy v. Ferguson:* Harlan's Great Dissent." *Kentucky Humanities,* no. 1, 1996. Retrieved from http://www.law.louisville.edu/library/collections/harlan/dissent.

Thurgood Marshall (1908-1993)
Attorney Who Helped Overturn Plessy v. Ferguson *and First African-American Supreme Court Justice*

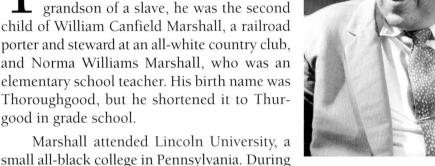

Thurgood Marshall was born on July 2, 1908, in Baltimore, Maryland. The grandson of a slave, he was the second child of William Canfield Marshall, a railroad porter and steward at an all-white country club, and Norma Williams Marshall, who was an elementary school teacher. His birth name was Thoroughgood, but he shortened it to Thurgood in grade school.

Marshall attended Lincoln University, a small all-black college in Pennsylvania. During his enrollment at Lincoln he met his first wife, Vivian "Buster" Burey, at a church service. They married on September 4, 1929. A year later, Marshall graduated with honors with degrees in American literature and philosophy. Marshall then applied to the University of Maryland School of Law, but his application was rejected because he was black. Marshall subsequently enrolled at Howard University School of Law in Washington, D.C.

Finding a Mentor and a Cause

As it turned out, the University of Maryland's racist admission policies led Marshall down a path to a man who would become his mentor, friend, and colleague. The dean at Howard University Law School was Charles Hamilton Houston, an energetic administrator and talented lawyer who was in the process of turning Howard into a national center for the study of civil rights law. Marshall dove into his studies with great enthusiasm, spurred on by Houston's inspiring calls for racial justice in America.

In 1933 Marshall graduated as valedictorian of his law school class. He then passed the Maryland bar and opened a law practice in Baltimore. Over the next several years Marshall represented a number of African-American clients who had been victimized by segregation laws and other discriminatory practices. Marshall did not win all of these cases, but the skill and passion he displayed elevated him to the top ranks of American activists for civil rights. In

1936 the National Association for the Advancement of Colored People (NAACP)—the leading African-American civil rights organization in the country—asked him to join its legal staff. Two years later, Marshall established the NAACP Legal Defense and Educational Fund (LDF) to represent the organization in its efforts to reform discriminatory laws across the United States.

As chief counsel of the LDF, Marshall won several important U.S. Supreme Court cases that struck down state laws that discriminated against blacks. These triumphs included *Smith v. Allwright* (1944), in which the Court struck down a Texas law that excluded blacks from primary elections; *Morgan v. Virginia* (1946), which erased a Virginia state law that segregated passengers on interstate buses and trains; *Shelley v. Kraemer* (1948), which outlawed housing contracts in white neighborhoods that discriminated against black buyers; and *Sweatt v. Painter* (1950) and *McLaurin v. Oklahoma* (1950), which found that states were constitutionally obligated to admit black students to their graduate and professional universities. All of these Supreme Court decisions helped Marshall and the LDF undercut the legal justifications for *Plessy v. Ferguson*, the notorious 1896 Supreme Court decision that was the basis for segregation laws that remained in place all across the South in the mid-twentieth century.

Bringing *Plessy v. Ferguson* Crashing Down

On May 17, 1954, Marshall and a team of LDF attorneys won one of the most important cases in U.S. Supreme Court history. In *Brown v. Board of Education of Topeka, Kansas*, they successfully lobbied the Court to strike down *Plessy v. Ferguson* as unconstitutional. For more than a half-century, Southern states had relied on *Plessy's* "separate but equal" doctrine to justify their segregation of public school systems by race. According to the unanimous *Brown v. Board* decision, however, public school segregation violated the Fourteenth Amendment's guarantee of equal protection and civil rights for all citizens. The landmark *Brown* case, which actually consisted of six separate cases in five jurisdictions (Kansas, South Carolina, Virginia, the District of Columbia, and Delaware), tore down segregation barriers in schools all across the country and relegated *Plessy v. Ferguson* to the dustbin of history.

Marshall continued his legal crusade for minority rights for the remainder of the 1950s. During that time, he and his fellow LDF lawyers won several important court cases that placed additional legal pressure on Southern states to end their segregationist practices. In February 1955 Marshall lost his wife

Vivian to cancer. He remarried in December of that year, taking Cecilia Suyat as his second wife. They had two sons together.

In 1961 President John F. Kennedy nominated Marshall for a judgeship on the Second U.S. Court of Appeals for the State of New York. Several Southern Senators delayed his confirmation for a few months, but Marshall was eventually confirmed, and he served his country in that capacity for the next four years. In 1965 President Lyndon B. Johnson appointed Marshall to the office of U.S. solicitor general, the top legal position in the federal government. Marshall was the first African-American solicitor general in the nation's history. His responsibilities in that post included representing the U.S. government in cases being considered by the U.S. Supreme Court.

Supreme Court Justice

Marshall left the position of solicitor general in 1967, when Johnson nominated him to the U.S. Supreme Court. This was a momentous nomination, since the Court had never before had an African-American justice. "I believe he has already earned his place in history," explained Johnson in announcing the nomination on June 13. "But I think it will be greatly enhanced by his service on the Court.… He is best qualified by training and by very valuable service to the country. I believe it is the right thing to do, the right time to do it, and the right man and the right place."[1] Marshall was confirmed two months later, on August 30, by a 69-11 Senate vote.

Marshall served on the Supreme Court for the next twenty-four years. During that time he became known as one of the Court's most liberal members. He steadfastly supported abortion rights, opposed the death penalty, and cast numerous votes to expand civil rights and preserve new environmental protections. Marshall retired from the Court in 1991 due to a variety of health problems. He died of heart failure on January 24, 1993, at the age of eighty-four. Later that year Marshall posthumously received the Presidential Medal of Freedom, the highest civilian honor awarded by the U.S. government, from President Bill Clinton.

Sources

James, Rawn, Jr. *Root and Branch: Charles Hamilton Houston, Thurgood Marshall, and the Struggle to End Segregation.* New York: Bloomsbury, 2010.

Marshall, Thurgood. *Thurgood Marshall: His Speeches, Writings, Arguments, Opinions, and Reminiscences.* Edited by Mark V. Tushnet. Chicago: Lawrence Hill Books, 2001.

Tushnet, Mark. *Making Civil Rights Law: Thurgood Marshall and the Supreme Court, 1936-1961.* New York: Oxford University Press, 1994.

Note

[1] Johnson, Lyndon B. "Remarks to the Press Announcing the Nomination of Thurgood Marshall as Associate Justice of the Supreme Court," June 13, 1967. American Presidency Project. Retrieved from http://www.presidency.ucsb.edu/ws/index.php?pid=28298.

Louis Martinet (1849-1917)
Black Newspaper Publisher and Civil Rights Advocate

Louis André Martinet was born on December 28, 1849, in St. Martinville, a small city in St. Martin Parish, Louisiana. Martinet grew up in a large family that included seven siblings. His parents were Hipolite Martinet, a Belgian carpenter, and Marie Louise Benoit, a native of Louisiana and a free woman of color.

Smart and ambitious, Martinet spent his twenties hopping back and forth between the worlds of politics and law. From 1872 to 1875 he represented St. Martin Parish in the state legislature. Martinet also studied law at Straight University (now Dillard University) in New Orleans, and in 1875 he passed the Louisiana bar. One year later he graduated from Straight with a law degree. In 1877 he served on the Orleans Parish School Board. In 1882 Martinet married Lenora Miller, a schoolteacher and a native of New Orleans. They had two children together before divorcing sometime around 1900. Martinet also later received a medical degree from Flint Medical College in New Orleans.

Martinet was able to secure a variety of public employment positions through his political connections. These postings in the early and mid-1880s included a clerical job with the U.S. Customs Office, a deputy surveyor position with the Port of New Orleans, and a stint as a U.S. Postal Service mail carrier. In 1888 he opened a notary public office. Martinet's notary work, which involved processing deeds, wills, and other public documents, provided him with a steady source of income until his death in 1917.

Martinet started his life in politics during Reconstruction. He initially cast his lot with the Democratic Party, in part because he believed that the presence of black party members might keep it from becoming dominated by white supremacist leaders and racist ideology. But as the Reconstruction era passed and Democratic leaders felt increasingly free to trumpet their racist beliefs, Martinet realized that he did not have a home in the party. He subsequently changed his affiliation to the Republican Party, which was much more supportive of black rights. Martinet also became a prominent member of the American Citizens Equal Rights Association (ACERA), which was dedicated to protecting the liberty and rights of Americans of every color and creed against rising levels of racism in post-Reconstruction America. His involvement in this group deepened as the national Republican Party showed little ability or appetite to oppose discriminatory laws and racist attitudes in the South.

Editor and Publisher of *The Crusader*

In 1889 Martinet began publishing *The Crusader,* a weekly newspaper aimed at Creole and African-American readers in New Orleans. Martinet's paper included the standard features of newspapers across the country, such as local news, sports scores, and information about social events of potential interest to readers. From its first issue, however, *The Crusader* also championed Republican policies and ideals of racial equality and respect. "The paper was militant about the rights of blacks as American citizens," reported historian Keith Weldon Medley. "[*The Crusader*] reported on acts of racial violence and kept them before the public eye."[1]

Martinet voiced particular anger about the Separate Car Law, an 1890 piece of legislation that required state railroads to segregate passengers by race. He added his name to an ACERA statement of formal protest against the law. "Such legislation is unconstitutional, un-American, unjust, dangerous, and against sound public policy.… [It gives] a free license to the evilly-disposed that they might with impunity insult, humiliate, and otherwise maltreat inoffensive persons, and especially women and children who should happen to have a dark skin."[2]

Martinet came to feel, though, that ACERA was not doing enough to fight the Separate Car Act and other Jim Crow laws looming on the horizon. He wanted to do more than just issue statements of protest. He wanted to challenge the law in the courts, expose its unconstitutional provisions, and strip it out of the Louisiana legal code.

To that end, Martinet helped found a new civil rights organization called the Citizens' Committee to Test the Constitutionality of the Separate Car Law in 1891. This group of prominent African-American and Creole residents of New Orleans immediately set out to mount a legal assault on the Separate Car Act. Martinet even convinced officials of the East Louisiana Railroad to participate in this effort, as long as their cooperation was not publicized. At Martinet's urging, the officials agreed to arrest a black person handpicked by the committee to occupy a "whites only" East Louisiana rail car. The person in question was Homer Plessy, who was classified as black even though most of his ancestors were white. Plessy's carefully orchestrated arrest took place on June 7, 1892.

As the Plessy case wound its way through the courts, where it acquired the official name *Plessy v. Ferguson*, Martinet worked tirelessly to keep the case in the public eye. His main tool in this mission was *The Crusader.* By 1894, in fact, the newspaper's popularity reached the point that Martinet was able to turn it into a daily—the only black daily newspaper in the entire United States during the 1890s.

The editorial tone of *The Daily Crusader* during the mid-1890s was encouraging and uplifting. Historians Joseph Logsdon and Caryn Cossé Bell described it as a "vehicle of racial protest … [that] helped encourage a new assertive spirit in the city as its founders had hoped."[3] In his private correspondence, however, Martinet often expressed despair about the deep roots of racism in American society. He was disappointed but not surprised when the U.S. Supreme Court upheld the legality of the Separate Car Law and segregation in general with its 1896 *Plessy v. Ferguson* decision. A short time after that notorious ruling was handed down, Martinet shuttered the offices of *The Daily Crusader* and it ceased publication.

Martinet lived in New Orleans for the rest of his life, supporting himself with his notary public work. He died in the city on June 17, 1917. His civil rights legacy was recognized forty years later when an organization of African-American lawyers in the New Orleans metropolitan area decided to call itself the Greater New Orleans Louis A. Martinet Legal Society.

Sources

Elliott, Mark. *Color-Blind Justice: Albion Tourgée and the Quest for Racial Equality from the Civil War to* Plessy v. Ferguson. New York: Oxford University Press, 2006.

Medley, Keith Weldon. *We as Freemen:* Plessy v. Ferguson. Gretna, LA: Pelican Publishing, 2003.

Notes

[1] Medley, Keith Weldon. *We as Freemen:* Plessy v. Ferguson. Gretna, LA: Pelican Publishing, 2003, p. 106.

[2] Quoted in Woodward, C. Vann. "*Plessy v. Ferguson*: The Birth of Jim Crow." *American Heritage,* April 1964.

[3] Logsdon, Joseph, and Caryn Cossé Bell. "The Americanization of Black New Orleans, 1850-1900." Edited by Arnold Richard Hirsch and Joseph Logsdon. *Creole New Orleans: Race and Americanization.* Baton Rouge: Louisiana State University Press, 1992, p. 256.

Photo Credit: The Historic New Orleans Collection, Acc. No. 1993.76.113.

Francis Nicholls (1834-1912)
Governor and State Supreme Court Justice of Louisiana

Francis Redding Tillou Nicholls was born on August 20, 1834, in Donaldsonville, Louisiana. His parents were Thomas Clark Nicholls, a judge and state legislator, and Louisa Hannah Drake Nicholls. As a young man, Nicholls received schooling at Jefferson Military Academy and the U.S. Military Academy at West Point. After graduating from West Point in 1855, he served in the U.S. Army for one year at postings in Florida and California. He then resigned his commission to pursue a law career, enrolling at the University of Louisiana (now Tulane University) in New Orleans. Nicholls subsequently established a legal practice in Napoleonville, Louisiana, that he maintained until the beginning of the Civil War. In 1860 he married Caroline Guion, with whom he eventually had six children.

From Confederate General to Louisiana Governor

Southerners like Nicholls—a West Point graduate with army experience—were highly prized by the Confederacy. He joined the Confederate Army as an infantry captain, and over the next two years he rose to the position of brigadier general. During that time, Nicholls took part in several of the war's major battles, including the First Battle of Bull Run, the Shenandoah Valley Campaign, and the Battle of Chancellorsville. He suffered a serious injury to his arm at the May 1862 Battle of Winchester, and doctors eventually amputated the mutilated limb. He returned to duty, though, until the Chancellorsville Campaign, when his left foot was virtually ripped off by an enemy shell. Confederate surgeons once again had no choice but to amputate the damaged limb. This second injury disqualified Nicholls from returning to combat service. He was transferred to the Confederacy's Trans-Mississippi Department and directed its Volunteer and Conscript Bureau until the war ended in 1865.

In the postwar era known as Reconstruction, federal troops and administrators oversaw policymaking, law enforcement, and other affairs in the South. Nicholls's legal practice, to which he returned after the war, thrived during this period. Increasingly, though, the decorated former general devoted time to state politics. He became a powerful figure in Louisiana's Democratic Party, and in 1876 state party leaders nominated him to be their candidate for governor in the upcoming election. He was opposed by Republican candidate Stephen Packard, a native of Maine.

When the election was held, Nicholls won the most votes. But corrupt Republican officials who controlled vote certification rejected the votes of Nicholls supporters on one technicality or another until they could declare Packard the victor. This series of events outraged Nicholls and his supporters, who inaugurated him at a raucous public ceremony on January 9, 1877. Packard was sworn in as governor in a separate proceeding, but he was forced to stay in the State House under the protection of federal troops.

The state of Louisiana remained in this state of political limbo for four months, until the famous Compromise of 1877. This far-reaching deal to resolve the disputed 1876 presidential election included a requirement that Democrat-dominated Louisiana give its electoral votes to Republican presidential candidate Rutherford B. Hayes. In return for these electoral votes, Hayes officially recognized Nicholls as the victor in his gubernatorial contest against Packard.

Two Very Different Terms

Nicholls's first term as governor of Louisiana lasted from 1877 to 1880. During that time his promises to respect the political rights of African-American citizens and his efforts to stamp out corruption in the state's lottery system brought him the support of a number of Republican legislators. He also chaired the state's 1870 Constitutional Convention, which lowered taxes, made reforms to the legislature, and relocated the state capital to Baton Rouge from New Orleans, which had served as the state capital during Reconstruction.

In 1880 Nicholls returned to his law practice. As the 1880s unfolded, however, continued political turbulence in the state—and especially ongoing drama over the corrupt state lottery—sparked a movement to return Nicholls to the governor's office. Nicholls consented, and in April 1888 he easily won a second term as Louisiana's governor.

131

This time around, though, Nicholls no longer felt obligated to maintain protections for his state's black citizens. White public opinion had turned increasingly hostile to laws and regulations that had elevated blacks to positions of equality, and racist views and attitudes toward African Americans were on the rise. In 1890 the Democrat-dominated state legislature passed the Separate Car Act, which segregated passengers into "white only" and "colored only" rail cars. Nicholls signed the bill into law on July 10, 1890.

The Separate Car Law was the legislation that ultimately resulted in the U.S. Supreme Court's 1896 *Plessy v. Ferguson* decision. When Nicholls signed the act into law, it was immediately challenged on constitutional grounds by civil rights activists Louis Martinet, Rodolphe Desdunes, and the Citizens' Committee of New Orleans. This legal challenge, which was carried out by white attorneys Albion Tourgée and James C. Walker, made its way to the Louisiana Supreme Court.

State Supreme Court Justice

Remarkably, Nicholls had by this time become chief justice of the court. After concluding his second term as governor in 1892, he had almost immediately been appointed to serve as chief justice by Democratic governor Murphy Foster, a longtime friend and political ally. This appointment gave Nicholls the opportunity to vote on the legitimacy of a statute that he himself had signed into law only two years earlier. Critics of the law urged Nicholls to recuse himself from the case since he had such an obvious conflict of interest, but he refused. Instead, he joined every other justice on the court in upholding the statute.

Nicholls served as chief justice for twelve years, which was the state's legal limit for serving in that capacity. At that point he was sworn in as an associate justice, and he remained on the court until his retirement in 1911. He died on January 4, 1912, on his estate in Thibodaux, Louisiana. Nicholls State University, which is located in Thibodaux, is named after him.

Sources

Cowan, Walter G. "Francis R. T. Nicholls, Governor, 1877-1880, 1888-1892." In *Louisiana Governors: Rulers, Rascals, and Reformers.* Walter G. Cowan and Jack B. McGuire, eds. Jackson: University Press of Mississippi, 2008.

Dawson, Joseph G., III. "Francis R. T. Nicholls, Governor, 1877-1880, 1888-1892." In *The Louisiana Governors.* Joseph G. Dawson III, ed. Baton Rouge: Louisiana State University Press, 1990.

Homer Plessy (1862-1925)
New Orleans Resident Who Volunteered to Challenge Segregation in Louisiana

Homer Adolph Plessy was born in New Orleans, Louisiana, on March 17, 1862. His parents were Rosa Debergue, a seamstress and housekeeper, and Joseph Adolphe Plessy, a carpenter who died when his son was five years old. Plessy's mother remarried two years later, taking a local postal clerk named Victor Dupart as her husband. Young Homer Plessy's legal status was that of a free person of color, despite the fact that his ancestry was primarily white European and he could "pass" for white. He was classified as black because one of his great-grandmothers had been black.

As a young man Plessy established a shoemaking business with his step-brother, Formidor Dupart. Shoemaking at that time was recognized as a skilled craft, and the profession gave Plessy the money necessary to start a family. In 1888 he married Louise Bourdenave, a fellow native of New Orleans. They settled in a middle-class section of the city called Faubourg Tremé, where families of different ethnic heritages freely worked and socialized together. Plessy was actively involved in his community, which was widely recognized as one of the most vibrant and diverse neighborhoods in New Orleans. In the late 1880s, for example, he served as an officer in a neighborhood organization devoted to reforming the city's public school system.

Becoming a Civil Rights Symbol

Plessy had grown up during the 1860s and 1870s, when blacks enjoyed most of the same freedoms as whites in Louisiana. They were fully engaged in the political, cultural, and economic life of the state, and they rejoiced at Reconstruction-era measures that lifted bans on interracial marriage and integrated schools. During the 1880s, though, Plessy saw that all of these gains were slipping away. The close of Reconstruction in 1877 ended federal oversight of political and legal affairs in the South. White supremacists in the region seized this opportunity to re-impose laws that relegated blacks to an inferior position in Louisiana and elsewhere.

One of the most disturbing early examples of state-sanctioned discrimination came on July 10, 1890, when Louisiana governor Francis Nicholls signed the Separate Car Act into law. This bill, which passed by overwhelming margins in Louisiana's white-dominated state legislature, mandated that all railroads operating in the state separate their passengers into "white only" and "colored only" rail cars.

In 1892 Plessy was approached by an African-American civil rights organization called the Citizens' Committee to Test the Constitutionality of the Separate Car Act. The group, which was led by New Orleans newspaper publisher Louis A. Martinet, was looking for a respected citizen who looked white—but was officially classified as black—and was willing to be arrested for sitting in a "white only" rail car. Once such an arrest was made, the Citizens' Committee could use the case to challenge the constitutionality of the law in the courts.

Plessy agreed to the committee's request. On June 7, 1892, Plessy walked to the Press Street Rail Station in New Orleans and bought a first-class ticket on an East Louisiana Railroad train bound for Covington, a small city located about forty miles north. Plessy got on board, sat in the "white only" section, and informed the conductor that he was actually legally classified as "colored." He then refused the conductor's request that he leave the train (it was not even equipped with a "colored" car, meaning that blacks were for all practical purposes not permitted to use the train at all). When Plessy refused to leave, the train was stopped and a private detective hired by the Citizens' Committee boarded the train. He formally arrested Plessy for violating the Separate Car Act, then took him off the train and delivered him to a local police station. Several members of the committee were waiting at the station. They provided a $500 bond, which freed Plessy while he waited for his court trial.

Namesake of a Notorious Supreme Court Judgment

On October 30 the case of *Homer Adolph Plessy v. The State of Louisiana* formally opened before district judge John Howard Ferguson. Plessy's lawyers, who had been secured by the Citizens' Committee, asserted that Louisiana's Separate Car Law violated the Thirteenth and Fourteenth Amendments to the Constitution. On November 18, though, Ferguson ruled that the state had the right to impose such regulations on railroad operations that operated only within Louisiana—and that Plessy was guilty.

The Citizens' Committee appealed this decision all the way to the U.S. Supreme Court, by which time the case had become known as *Plessy v. Ferguson*. In 1896 the Court returned a 7-1 decision that sided with Ferguson. It agreed with Ferguson that the Separate Car Law and other statutes that separated people by race were constitutional, as long as they provided equal accommodations to everyone. This decision endorsing the "separate but equal" doctrine became the foundation for Jim Crow laws all across the South. It is thus regarded as one of the worst decisions ever rendered in the history of the U.S. Supreme Court.

The Court's *Plessy v. Ferguson* ruling left Plessy and the Citizens' Committee with no other legal options. In January 1897 Plessy stood before a Louisiana court and pleaded guilty to violating the Separate Car Law. He paid the required $25 fine and left the courthouse. Plessy lived the rest of his life quietly, working as a warehouse laborer and clerk before becoming an insurance salesman with a black-owned insurance company. He died in New Orleans on March 1, 1925.

Source

Fireside, Harvey. *Separate and Unequal: Homer Plessy and the Supreme Court Decision That Legalized Racism*. New York: Carroll & Graf, 2004.

Albion W. Tourgée (1838-1905)
Republican Writer, Civil Rights Activist, and Lawyer Who Argued Plessy v. Ferguson

Albion Winegar Tourgée was born into a Williamsfield, Ohio, farming family on May 2, 1838. His parents were Valentine Tourgée and Louisa Emma Winegar Tourgée. He grew up in Kingsville, a small town in northeastern Ohio's so-called Western Reserve, a center of abolitionist sentiment in mid-nineteenth century America. By his late teens, Tourgée had adopted strong antislavery views that would become a guiding star in many of his life decisions.

In 1859 Tourgée enrolled at Rochester University in New York, but his education was interrupted by the arrival of the Civil War in the spring of 1861 (in 1862 the school bestowed a degree on him in recognition of his military service). In May he enlisted in the Union Army as a private with the 27th New York Volunteers. Two months later, he suffered a serious spinal injury at the First Battle of Bull Run in Virginia. The injury took him out of active service for many months, but in July 1862 he re-enlisted as an infantry lieutenant in the 105th Ohio. Tourgée fought in several battles over the next three months, but in October 1862 he was captured in Kentucky at the Battle of Perryville. He spent four months in a Confederate prison before gaining his release in a prisoner exchange. Upon gaining his freedom he returned to Ohio and married his long-time sweetheart, Emma Lodoilska Kilbourne. Tourgée then returned to the army, but complications from his back injury finally forced him to leave military service for good (with the rank of lieutenant) in December 1863.

Battling for Black Rights in North Carolina

After the war ended in 1865, Tourgée and his wife moved south to Greensboro, North Carolina. The relocation was partly due to advice from a physician who thought that a milder climate might relieve some of the pain he was experiencing from his wartime injuries. But Tourgée was also drawn to the idea of helping North Carolina recover from its wartime wounds and rejoin the Union. He spent the next two years working in Greensboro as editor on a Republican newspaper called the *Union Register*, which regularly ran editorials endorsing Negro rights and "radical Republican" political reforms.

In 1868 Tourgée was elected as a delegate to North Carolina's Constitution Convention, where he tirelessly promoted progressive political, economic, and judicial reforms. That same year, he was elected to a six-year state superior court judgeship. As a judge, he became well known for his push to include Negroes in jury pools and his loathing for the Ku Klux Klan. In 1873 Tourgée played a leading role in founding a Negro school that eventually became Greensboro's Bennett College, one of the nation's oldest colleges for black women. Tourgée also adopted a mixed-race girl, despite the misgivings of his wife.

All of these actions made Tourgée extremely unpopular with racist whites in the region. According to some accounts, in fact, he ranked "for many years [as] the most thoroughly hated man in North Carolina."[1] Biographer Otto Olsen wrote, though, that "despite ostracism, persecution, and frequent danger, Tourgée proved himself an able and involved citizen of his adopted state, and much in his conduct and achievement demanded respect. There were some remarkable exchanges of mutual admiration between Tourgée and his Southern foes, but Reconstruction politics and the issue of race drove an implacable wedge between them."[2] These tensions also took a heavy toll on Tourgée's marriage, which became increasingly strained.

Tourgée left North Carolina in 1880, one year after he published an autobiographical novel called *A Fool's Errand* that reflected his strong convictions about racial equality. In 1881 he settled in Mayville, New York, where he enjoyed moderate financial success as a novelist, lecturer, and journalist. Again and again in this work—and especially in a nationally syndicated newspaper column called "A Bystander's Notes"—he crusaded for racial equality and social reform. By the late 1880s, Tourgée was one of the most famous white critics of racism and dedicated advocates for Negro equality in the entire country. His outspoken nature and radical reputation, though, also made him somewhat of an outcast in Republican Party circles. In 1891 Tourgée founded the National Citizens' Rights Association, an organization devoted to securing full equality for African-American and mixed-race citizens.

Tourgée Joins the *Plessy* Legal Fight

Tourgée's reputation as an advocate for black equality extended all the way to Louisiana, which in 1890 had passed a Separate Car Law that segregated railroad passenger cars by race. Tourgée had even spoken out against the bill that created the law in a number of his "Bystander's Notes" columns. In 1891 a group of black New Orleans residents led by newspaper publisher Louis A. Martinet formed the Citizens' Committee to Test the Constitutionality of the Separate Car Law. They approached Tourgée to serve as the lead attorney in their legal challenge to the law, and he promptly accepted.

Tourgée and the Citizens' Committee challenged the constitutionality of the law through Homer Plessy, a New Orleans resident who volunteered to violate the act. Plessy was officially classified as one-eighth black, which under the provisions of the Separate Car Law meant that he could not sit in whites-only rail cars in the state. When Plessy was arrested on June 7, 1892, by sitting in a whites-only rail car, Tourgée and the Citizens' Committee had the case they needed to challenge the law in court.

When Plessy appeared before district judge John Howard Ferguson, his lawyers asserted that Louisiana's Separate Car Law violated the Thirteenth and Fourteenth Amendments to the Constitution. Judge Ferguson, however, disagreed. He ruled that the state had the right to insist on "separate" accommodations in state railroad operations as long as they were "equal." His guilty verdict against Plessy amounted to a ringing defense of state laws that segregated people by race.

Tourgée and his allies did not give up. They took their case, now known as *Plessy v. Ferguson*, all the way to the U.S. Supreme Court. In the legal briefs Tourgée prepared for the Court, he emphasized the importance of making America a "color blind" society—a term that he had coined several years earlier. But the Court did not accept his arguments. In 1896 it handed down a 7-1 decision against Plessy that gave racist lawmakers the legal justification they needed to incorporate "separate but equal" segregationist laws into numerous aspects of daily life. These Jim Crow laws became particularly numerous in the American South.

The Supreme Court's *Plessy v. Ferguson* decision was an enormous psychological blow to the idealistic Tourgée. Discouraged and disillusioned by his country's continued embrace of racist beliefs and laws, Tourgée largely abandoned his crusade for racial justice. He even made peace with Republican leaders who had long been wary of Tourgée's firebrand style. Tourgée subsequently received an appointment from Republican president William McKinley to serve as U.S. consul in Bordeaux, France. Tourgée remained in this diplomatic post until his death on May 21, 1905.

Sources

Elliott, Mark. *Color-Blind Justice: Albion Tourgée and the Quest for Racial Equality from the Civil War to* Plessy v. Ferguson. New York: Oxford University Press, 2006.

Gross, Theodore. *Albion W. Tourgée*. Boston: Twayne, 1963.

Olsen, Otto H. "Albert Winegar Tourgée, 1838-1905." *Dictionary of North Carolina Biography.* William S. Powell, ed. Chapel Hill: University of North Carolina Press, 1996.

Notes

[1] Olsen, Otto H. "Albert Winegar Tourgée, 1838-1905." *Dictionary of North Carolina Biography.* William S. Powell, ed. Chapel Hill: University of North Carolina Press, 1996.

[2] Olsen.

PRIMARY SOURCES

Albion Tourgée Describes Reconstruction-Era Violence in the South

After the Civil War ended, abolitionist, attorney, and author Albion W. Tourgée moved to Greensboro, North Carolina, in order to assist in the federal government's Reconstruction efforts. An outspoken supporter of African-American civil rights, Tourgée served as a judge and helped rewrite the state constitution. He grew disillusioned, however, with the racial intimidation and violence employed by white supremacist groups like the Ku Klux Klan (KKK) to prevent blacks from exercising their rights. The KKK even targeted white Republicans who, like Tourgée, came to the South to promote justice and equality for newly freed slaves. In the following letter to Republican senator Joseph C. Abbott, Tourgée describes the Reconstruction-era atmosphere of hatred and brutality in North Carolina, laments the influence of the KKK (which he calls the Ku-Klux), and offers suggestions for how the federal government can address the problem.

Greensboro, N.C. May 24, 1870
Gen. Jos. C. Abbott

My Dear General:

It is my mournful duty to inform you that our friend John W. Stephens, State Senator from Caswell, is dead. He was foully murdered by the Ku-Klux [Klan] in the Grand Jury room of the Court House on Saturday or Saturday night last. The circumstances attending his murder have not yet fully come to light there. So far as I can learn, I judge these to have been the circumstances: He was one of the Justices of the Peace in that township, and was accustomed to hold court in that room on Saturdays. It is evident that he was set upon by someone while holding this court, or immediately after its close, and disabled by a sudden attack, otherwise there would have been a very sharp resistance, as he was a man, and always went armed to the teeth. He was stabbed five or six times, and then hanged on a hook in the Grand Jury room, where he was found on Sunday morning.

Another brave, honest Republican citizen has met his fate at the hands of these fiends. Warned of his danger, and fully cognizant of the terrible risk which surrounded him, he still manfully refused to quit the field. Against the advice of his friends, against the entreaties of his family, he constantly refused to leave those who had stood by him in the day of his disgrace and peril. He was accustomed to say that 3,000 poor, ignorant, colored Republican voters in that county had stood by him and elected him, at the risk of persecution and star-

143

vation, and that he had no idea of abandoning them to the Ku-Klux. He was determined to stay with them, and either put an end to these outrages, or die with the other victims of Rebel hate and national apathy.

Nearly six months ago I declared my belief that before the election in August next the Ku-Klux would have killed more men in the State than there would be members to be elected to the Legislature. A good beginning has been made toward the fulfillment of this prophecy.... There have been twelve murders in five counties of the district during the past eighteen months, by bands of disguised villains. In addition to this, from the best information I can derive, I am of the opinion that in this district alone there have been 1,000 outrages of a less serious nature perpetrated by the same masked fiends. Of course this estimate is not made from any absolute record, nor is it possible to ascertain with accuracy the entire number of beatings and other outrages which have been perpetrated. The uselessness, the utter futility of complaint from the lack of ability in the laws to punish is fully known to all. The danger of making such complaint is also well understood. It is therefore not infrequently by accident that the outrage is found out, and unquestionably it is frequently absolutely concealed. Thus, a respectable, hard working white carpenter was working for a neighbor, when accidentally his shirt was torn, and disclosed his back scarred and beaten. The poor fellow begged for the sake of his wife and children that nothing might be said about it, as the Ku-Klux had threatened to kill him if he disclosed how he had been outraged. Hundreds of cases have come to my notice and that of my solicitor....

These crimes have been of every character imaginable. Perhaps the most usual has been the dragging of men and women from their beds, and beating their naked bodies with hickory switches, or as witnesses in an examination the other day said, "sticks" between a "switch" and a "club." From 50 to 100 blows is the usual allowance, sometimes 200 and 300 blows are administered. Occasionally an instrument of torture is owned. Thus in one case two women, one 74 years old, were taken out, stripped naked, and beaten with a paddle, with several holes bored through it. The paddle was about 30 inches long, 3 or 4 inches wide, and 1/4 of an inch thick, of oak. Their bodies were so bruised and beaten that they were sickening to behold. They were white women and of good character until the younger was seduced, and swore her child to its father. Previous to that and so far as others were concerned her character was good.

Again, there is sometimes a fiendish malignity and cunning displayed in the form and character of the outrages. For instance, a colored man was placed astride of a log, and an iron staple driven through his person into the log. In another case, after a band of them had in turn violated a young negro girl, she was forced into bed with a colored man, their bodies were bound together face to face, and the fire from the hearth piled upon them. The K. K. K. rode off and left them, with shouts of laughter. Of course the bed was soon in flames, and somehow they managed to crawl out, though terribly burned and scarred. The house was burned.

I could give other incidents of cruelty, such as hanging up a boy of nine years old until he was nearly dead, to make him tell where his father was hidden, and beating an old negress of 103 years old with garden palings because she would not own that she was afraid of the Ku-Klux. But it is unnecessary to go into further detail. In this district I estimate their offenses as follows, in the past ten months: Twelve murders, 9 rapes, 11 arsons, 7 mutilations, ascertained and most of them on record. In some no identification could be made. Four thousand or 5,000 houses have been broken open, and property or persons taken out. In all cases all arms are taken and destroyed. Seven hundred or 800 persons have been beaten or otherwise maltreated. These of course are partly persons living in the houses which were broken into.

And yet the Government sleeps. The poor disarmed nurses of the Republican party—those men by whose ballots the Republican party holds power— who took their lives in their hands when they cast their ballots for U.S. Grant and other officials—all of us who happen to be beyond the pale of the Governmental regard—must be sacrificed, murdered, scourged, mangled, because some contemptible party scheme might be foiled by doing us justice. I could stand it very well to fight for Uncle Sam, and was never known to refuse an invitation on such an occasion; but this lying down, tied hand and foot with the shackles of the law, to be killed by the very dregs of the rebellion, the scum of the earth, and not allowed either the consolation of fighting or the satisfaction that our "fall" will be noted by the Government, and protection given to others thereby, is somewhat too hard. I am ashamed of the nation that will let its citizens be slain by scores, and scourged by thousands, and offer no remedy or protection. I am ashamed of a State which has not sufficient strength to protect its own officers in the discharge of their duties, nor guarantee the safety of any man's domicile throughout its length and breadth. I am ashamed of a party which, with the reins of power in its hands, has not nerve or decision enough to arm its own adherents, or to protect them from assassinations at the hands of their opponents.

A General who in time of war would permit 2,000 or 3,000 of his men to be bushwhacked and destroyed by private treachery even in an enemy's country without any one being punished for it would be worthy of universal execration, and would get it, too. How much more worthy of detestation is a Government which in time of peace will permit such wholesale slaughter of its citizens? It is simple cowardice, inertness, and wholesale demoralization. The wholesale slaughter of the war has dulled our Nation's sense of horror at the shedding of blood, and the habit of regarding the South as simply a laboratory, where every demagogue may carry on his reconstructionary experiments at will, and not as an integral party of the Nation itself, has led our Government to shut its eyes to the atrocities of these times. Unless these evils are speedily remedied, I tell you, General, the Republican party has signed its death warrant. It is a party of cowards or idiots—I don't care which alternative is chosen. The remedy is in our hands, and we are afraid or too dull to bestir ourselves and use it.

But you will tell me that Congress is ready and willing to act if it only knew what to do. Like the old Irish woman it wrings its hands and cries, "O Lawk, O Lawk; if I only knew which way." And yet this same Congress has the control of the militia and can organize its own force in every county in the United States, and arm more or less of it. This same Congress has the undoubted right to guarantee and provide a republican government, and protect every citizen in "life, liberty, and the pursuit of happiness," as well as the power conferred by the XVth Amendment. And yet we suffer and die in peace and murderers walk abroad with the blood yet fresh upon their garments, unharmed, unquestioned and unchecked. Fifty thousand dollars given to good detectives would secure, if well used, a complete knowledge of all this gigantic organization of murderers. In connection with an organized and armed militia, it would result in the apprehension of any number of these thugs en masque and with blood on their hands.

What then is the remedy? First: Let Congress give to the U. S. Courts, or to Courts of the States under its own laws, cognizance [legal jurisdiction] of this class of crimes, as crimes against the nation, and let it provide that this legislation be enforced. Why not, for instance, make going armed and masked or disguised, or masked or disguised in the night time, an act of insurrection or sedition? Second: Organize militia, National—State militia is a nuisance—and arm as many as may be necessary in each county to enforce its laws. Third: Put detectives at work to get hold of this whole organization. Its ultimate aim is unquestionably to revolutionize the Government. If we have not pluck enough for this, why then let us just offer our throats to the knife, emasculate ourselves, and be a nation of self-subjugated slaves at once.

And now, Abbott, I have but one thing to say to you. I have very little doubt that I shall be one of the next victims. My steps have been dogged for months, and only a good opportunity has been wanting to secure to me the fate which Stephens has just met, and I speak earnestly upon this matter. I feel that I have a right to do so, and a right to be heard as well, and with this conviction I say to you plainly that any member of Congress who, especially if from the South, does not support, advocate, and urge immediate, active, and thorough measures to put an end to these outrages, and make citizenship a privilege, is a coward, a traitor, or a fool. The time for action has come, and the man who has now only speeches to make over some Constitutional scarecrow, deserves to be damned.

Source

Tourgée, Albion W. Letter to Senator Joseph C. Abbott on Ku Klux Klan Activities, Greensboro, NC, May 24, 1870. Retrieved from http://history.ncsu.edu/projects/cwnc/items/show/34.

Louisiana Passes the Separate Car Law

When Governor Francis Nicholls signed the Railway Accommodations Act into law on July 10, 1890, Louisiana joined a rapidly growing number of states that had enacted formal measures to segregate citizens by race. The text of the Separate Car Law, which is reprinted below, requires railroads to provide "equal but separate accommodations for the white and colored races." In reality, though, the separate schools, restaurants, theaters, parks, restrooms, and other accommodations provided to blacks were always inferior to those provided to whites, both in Louisiana and throughout the South. The discriminatory nature of segregation laws prompted Homer Plessy and the Citizens' Committee to launch the legal challenge against the Separate Car Law that reached the U.S. Supreme Court in 1896.

An Act to promote the comfort of passengers on railway trains; requiring all railway companies carrying passengers on their trains, in this State, to provide equal but separate accommodations for the white and colored races, by providing separate coaches or compartments so as to secure separate accommodations; defining the duties of the officers of such railways; directing them to assign passengers to the coaches or compartment set aside for the use of the race to which such passengers belong; authorizing them to refuse to carry on their train such passengers as may refuse to occupy the coaches or compartments to which he or she is assigned; to exonerate such railway companies from any and all blame or damages that might proceed or result from such a refusal; to prescribe penalties for all violations of this act; to put this act into effect ninety days after its promulgation, and to repeal all laws or parts of laws contrary to or inconsistent with the provisions of this act.

SEC. 1. *Be it enacted by the General Assembly of the State of Louisiana,* That all railway companies carrying passengers in their coaches in this State, shall provide equal but separate accommodations for the white, and colored races, by providing two or more passenger coaches for each passenger train, or by dividing the passenger coaches by a partition so as to secure separate accommodations; provided that this section shall not be construed to apply to street railroads. No person or persons, shall be permitted to occupy seats in coaches, other than the ones assigned to them on account of the race they belong to.

SEC. 2. *Be it further enacted, etc.,* That the officers of such passenger trains shall have power and are hereby required to assign each passenger to the coach or compartment used for the race to which such passenger belongs; any passenger insisting on going into a coach or compartment to which by race he does not belong, shall be liable to a fine of twenty-five dollars or in lieu thereof to imprisonment for a period of not more than twenty days in the parish prison and any officer of any railroad insisting on assigning a passenger to a coach or compartment other than the one set aside for the race to which said passenger belongs shall be liable to a fine of twenty-five dollars or in lieu thereof to imprisonment for a period of not more than twenty days in the parish prison; and should any passenger refuse to occupy the coach or compartment to which he or she is assigned by the officer of such railway, said officer shall have power to refuse to carry such passenger on his train, and for such refusal neither he nor the railway company which he represents shall be liable for damages in any of the courts of this State.

SEC. 3. *Be it further enacted, etc.,* That all officers and directors of railway companies that shall refuse or neglect to comply with the provisions and requirements of this act shall be deemed guilty of a misdemeanor and shall upon conviction before any court of competent jurisdiction be fined not less than one hundred dollars nor more than five hundred dollars; and any conductor or other employees of such passenger train, having charge of the same, who shall refuse or neglect to carry out the provisions of this act shall on conviction be fined not less than twenty-five dollars nor more than fifty dollars for each offense; all railroad corporations carrying passengers in this State other than street railroads shall keep this law posted up in a conspicuous place in each passenger coach and ticket office, provided that nothing in this act shall be construed as applying to nurses attending children of the other race.

SEC. 4. *Be it further enacted, etc.,* That all laws or parts of laws contrary to or inconsistent with the provision of this act be and the same are hereby repealed, and that this act shall take effect and be in full force ninety days after its promulgation.

Source

Louisiana Railway Accommodations Act of 1890. Louisiana Laws, No. 111, pp. 153-54. Retrieved from http://railroads.unl.edu/documents/view_document.php?id=rail.gen.0060.

A Kentucky Newspaper Claims That Segregation Benefits Blacks

Around the time that Louisiana passed the Separate Car Law, the state of Texas enacted a similar measure requiring white and black railroad passengers to sit in segregated coaches. The following article, which appeared in a Kentucky newspaper in 1892, describes how the "Jim Crow Car" worked in Texas. The writer rationalizes segregation by claiming that African-American train passengers often benefit from separate seating arrangements.

The only grievance the Texas negroes have is that the law passed by the retiring Legislature requires them to ride in separate coaches on railroads. The traveler about to enter a car anywhere in Texas finds himself confronted at the door by one of two forms. The notice reads: "For Whites," or it reads "For Negroes." For a "white" to ride where it says "For Negroes" is to violate a law which subjects himself … to heavy penalties.

There is nothing optional about the operation of the law. A white person is shut out as completely from the negroes as the negro is excluded from the white car. There may be one negro riding in solitary comfort in the negro coach and 100 white people crowded in discomfort into the white coach. That makes no difference. There can be no mixing.

The railroads are unable to foresee just what the [racial composition of passengers will be at various] times. It happens very frequently that a condition very similar to that just mentioned is the result. There are not seats enough for one race and there are too many for the other race.

A single illustration from actual observation may be interesting. At Amarillo in the Panhandle, two ladies with children, a couple of drummers, and the usual assortment of passengers boarded the southbound train at 4. [The] white coach was full. The negro compartment was occupied by a Chinaman in solitary state. [He] had turned over the seat in front and had disposed of his bags—the heathen always travels with bags—in such a way as to prop himself into a very comfortable position.

There is nothing in the law which says "whites" shall not ride in the "negro" compartment, when there are no negroes on board. So the passengers from Amarillo filed into the negro compartment and proceeded to do as the Chinaman had done. The train had begun to move when a solitary negro got on. He took a seat. The conductor appeared. White men, women, and children were required to get up and move into the crowded white coach. There a general awakening took place. Seats were turned. Those who had full seats were obliged to double up with those who had none. Children cried. Everybody grumbled. A few swore.

In the compartment for negroes the African and the Chinaman rode with two seats apiece and several others unoccupied for more than 100 miles. Not another negro came in all that distance. Chinamen, Mexicans and Indians are not classed. They ride where they please. Probably a very strict and liberal construction of the law would throw all but the African on the white side of the coach dead line, but the railroads only observe the forms to the degree that will protect them from prosecution.

At first whole coaches were set apart for the different races. Now, however, at the end of the year's trial of the law, that is rarely done. Each coach is separated by a partition. In parts of Texas there is almost no negro travel. On such roads a small compartment is cut off at one end by thin partition and reserved for the occasional negro traveler. Half of the time it will be unoccupied. Further south the negro compartments are larger. And in the black belt the coaches are separated in halves. Some roads have the fastenings and grooves so arranged that a partition can be taken out and moved a few seats forward or backward accordingly as the race proportion of travel changes. Negroes do not ride on cars the year round. After cotton picking is well underway and silver begins to circulate freely there is a great deal of negro travel. Later on, when "the crop" must be cared for, the negro travel falls to a small fraction. To accommodate these changes, the partitions are so arranged so that they can be moved.

The law makes one exception in favor of negro nurses for white children. This provision is somewhat elastic. A lady came on the train in San Antonio with a robust little Lord Fauntleroy son and a negro lad. She planted the boy in one seat and told the negro to sit with him while she took the seat in front. The negro protested. "Missus," he said, "I mustn't ride here. There is a place where my people have to sit." "You stay right where you are," the lady said, and proceeded to drill the negro in his temporary duty as nurse to the ten-year-old youngster in the sailor suit and long hair. The negro promptly fell asleep and the boy amused himself by leaning far out the window. The lady, having succeeded in doing something the law said could not be done, took great satisfaction in watching....

The negroes of Texas do not object to the separate coach act. They are assured more comfort in travel than they ever had before. Theoretically they think the law is an outrage because it raises what they call a "class distinction." The well-dressed and well-educated negro doesn't like anything which reminds him that he isn't a white man.

Source

"The Jim Crow Car: How the Separate Coach Law Works in Texas—Negroes Get the Best of It." *Crittenden Press* (Marion, KY), October 13, 1892, p. 1. Retrieved from Library of Congress, *Chronicling America:* Plessy v. Ferguson, http://chroniclingamerica.loc.gov/lccn/sn86069457/1892-10-13/ed-1/seq-1/.

A Black-Owned Newspaper Criticizes Segregation

The city of Richmond, Virginia, passed an ordinance requiring segregated seating on streetcars in 1904. The Richmond Planet, a black-owned newspaper, published a flurry of articles and editorials criticizing the new rule and advising the city's black residents to boycott the streetcar system in protest. The April 30, 1904, edition of the paper describes the Jim Crow car as "a studied effort and a deliberate plot to foment inter-racial strife." It points out that no African-American passengers had been arrested for violating the separate seating arrangement, partly because the number of black streetcar riders had declined dramatically since the rule took effect. It also includes the poem reprinted below, which details some of the problems associated with the colored seating section in the rear of streetcars.

Of all the towns beneath the stars,
Old Richmond beats for Jim Crow cars,
They thread her streets and all around
Her suburbs Jim Crow cars abound.
 And some are fast and some are slow,
 But in the rear all serve Jim Crow.

The smokers on the rear platform
Can joke and smoke when cold or warm;
In wide spread door conductor stands,
That joke and smoke of vilest brands
 Throughout the rear may freely flow
 And fill the space kept for Jim Crow.

In summer time they'll smoke Jim Crow;
In winter time when bleak winds blow,
Jack Frost will stalk through open door,
And killing draughts will always pour,
 Upon those who shall hold the row
 Of seats in rear kept for Jim Crow.

But the summer cars, when they shall go
To the lakes where pleasant breezes blow;
Refreshing air of day or night
Will strike alike the black and white!
 And Jim Crow then will have his rights,
 And fair as well as any whites!

But will he though! But will he though!
Who hold the two rear seats? By Joe!
Those seats belong to him who smokes
And loves to crack his ribald jokes,
    And swift winds from the rear will blow
    These sweet things to our dear Jim Crow.

It is the principle involved,
As all will see when all is solved,
Which now enigmatic may seem
To those who do not wake, but dream:
    'Tis rights of man! Make here no balk—
    Man's rights we claim! For these we walk.

Source

Steward, O. M. "Richmond's Jim Crow Cars." *Richmond Planet (VA),* April 30, 1904, p. 1. Retrieved from http://chroniclingamerica.loc.gov/lccn/sn84025841/1904-04-30/ed-1/seq-1/.

Plessy's Lawyers Present Their Arguments in a Legal Brief

When Plessy v. Ferguson came before the U.S. Supreme Court in 1896, lead attorney Albion W. Tourgée argued on behalf of Homer Plessy, who was formally known as the Plaintiff in Error. In the legal brief excerpted below, Tourgée and his colleague James C. Walker present their case against Louisiana's Separate Car Law, detailing the ways in which they believe the statute violates the constitutional rights of railroad passengers.

The case turns wholly upon the question of the constitutionality of Act No. 111, of the legislature of the State of Louisiana, session of 1890....

The Plaintiff in Error was a passenger on the East Louisiana railroad as charged in the affidavit on which the warrant of arrest was based, from New Orleans to Covington, both points in the State of Louisiana, and was the holder of a first-class ticket. The affidavit states that he is a colored man and that he insisted on entering a white compartment, in violation of the Act. The presentment does not aver anything as to the race of the plaintiff but merely that he insisted on entering a compartment to which by race he did not belong. In his plea in bar, Plaintiff in Error avers that he held a first-class ticket—was orderly and cleanly, which is admitted by the state's demurrer. In his petition for re-hearing, he describes himself as "of mixed Caucasian and African blood, in the proportion of one-eighth African and seven-eighths Caucasian," the African admixture not being perceptible. By his plea the Plaintiff in Error put in issue the constitutionality of this Act, the court sustained its validity, and he brought the question here by his Writ of Error.

Assignment of Errors

The following assignment of errors in the judgment of the court below was filed with the application for the writ, and sets out particularly each error asserted and intended to be urged.

FIRST. The court erred in its opinion and decree maintaining the constitutional validity of the Act ... and that the same is not in conflict with nor a violation of any right under the XIIIth and XIVth Amendments to the Constitution of the United States; that the same is the lawful exercise of the police power of the state; that the subject-matter thereof is a regulation of domestic commerce, and therefore exclusively a state function; enforces substantial equality of accommodation supplied to passengers of both races on railroad trains operated within the limits of the State of Louisiana; that the same is in the interest of public order, peace, and comfort, and impairs no right of passengers of either race.

This was in error (1) for the reason that the statute imports a badge of servitude imposed by the state law; perpetuates the distinction of race and caste among citizens of the United States of both races, and observances of a servile character coincident with the institution of slavery, heretofore enacted by the white race and compulsorily submitted to by the colored race. The said statute discriminates between citizens of the white race and those of the colored race, and does not apply to all white persons and all colored persons alike, and the same abridges the rights, privileges, and immunities of citizens on account of race and color.

(2) The said statute does not enforce substantial equality of accommodation to be furnished to passengers of both races on railroad trains, but authorizes the officers thereof to assign passengers to separate coaches without reference thereto.

(3) The statute impairs the right of passengers of the class to which relator belongs, to wit, octoroons, to be classed among white persons, although color be not discernable in their complexion, and makes penal their refusal to abide by the decision of a railroad conductor in this respect.

(4) The said statute does not extend to all citizens alike the equal protection of the laws, and provides for the punishment of passengers on railroad trains without due process of law, by authorizing the officers of railroad trains to refuse to carry such persons as refuse to abide by their decision as to the race to which said passengers belong, and by making said refusal a penal offense.

(5) The statute is not in the interest of public order, peace, and comfort, but is manifestly directed against citizens of the colored race.

(6) The statute exempts individuals of a certain class, to wit, nurses attending children of the other race, from the operation of the law, and is therefore amenable to the charge of class legislation.

(7) The said statute is an invasion and deprivation of the natural and absolute rights of citizens of the United States to the society and protection of their wives and children traveling in railroad trains when said citizens are married to persons of the other race under the law and sacrament of the church—marital

unions between persons of both races, which are not forbidden by the laws of Louisiana.

(8) The statute deprives the citizen of remedy for wrong, and is unconstitutional for that reason.

(9) Neither the said statute, nor the laws of the State of Louisiana, nor the decisions of its courts have defined the terms "colored race" and "persons of color," and the law in question has delegated to conductors of railway trains the right to make such classification and made penal a refusal to submit to their decision.

(10) The East Louisiana Railroad and other railroads to which said statute applies are organized by the laws of the State of Louisiana as common carriers, acting by virtue of public charters and carrying passengers for hire, and cannot be authorized to distinguish between citizens according to race.

(11) Race is a question of law and fact which an officer of a railroad corporation cannot be authorized to determine.

(12) The state had no power to authorize the officers of railway trains to determine the question of race without testimony, and to make the rights and privileges of citizens depend on such decision, or to compel the citizen to accept and submit to such decision.

SECOND. The court erred in its opinion and decree that the statute in question explicitly requires that the accommodation shall be equal and does not authorize the officers of the railway trains to assign passengers according to their own judgment and without reference as to whether the accommodations are equal or not....

THIRD. The court erred in its opinion and decree that the statute does not authorize the conductor or other officer to assign a passenger to a coach to which by race he does not belong; that it obviously means that the coach to which the passenger is assigned shall be, according to the requirements of the act, the coach to which the passenger by race belongs.

Source

Tourgée, Albion W., and James C. Walker. "Brief for Plaintiff in Error, *Plessy v. Ferguson.*" Briefs and Records, Library of the Supreme Court of the United States, 1896. Retrieved from http://history.nny ln.net/cdm/ref/collection/NYCCH/id/703.

Justice Brown Announces the Majority Opinion in *Plessy v. Ferguson*

After the U.S. Supreme Court heard arguments from both sides in the case of Plessy v. Ferguson, *Justice Henry Billings Brown announced the majority opinion on May 18, 1896. The 7-1 decision upheld the lower court's ruling that racial segregation did not violate the U.S. Constitution, as long as the accommodations provided to black and white citizens were "separate but equal." This controversial ruling—which is excerpted below—gave legal sanction to segregation, which soon spread to encompass virtually all aspects of life in the South.*

This case turns upon the constitutionality of an act of the general assembly of the state of Louisiana, passed in 1890, providing for separate railway carriages for the white and colored races....

The constitutionality of this act is attacked upon the ground that it conflicts both with the thirteenth amendment of the constitution, abolishing slavery, and the fourteenth amendment, which prohibits certain restrictive legislation on the part of the states.

1. That it does not conflict with the thirteenth amendment, which abolished slavery and involuntary servitude, except a punishment for crime, is too clear for argument. Slavery implies involuntary servitude—a state of bondage; the ownership of mankind as a chattel, or, at least, the control of the labor and services of one man for the benefit of another, and the absence of a legal right to the disposal of his own person, property, and services. This amendment was ... intended primarily to abolish slavery, as it had been previously known in this country, and ... the use of the word 'servitude' was intended to prohibit the use of all forms of involuntary slavery, of whatever class or name. It was intimated, however,... that this amendment was regarded by the statesmen of that day as insufficient to protect the colored race from certain laws which had been enacted in the Southern states, imposing upon the colored race onerous disabilities and burdens, and curtailing their rights in the pursuit of life, liberty, and property to such an extent that their freedom was of little value; and that the fourteenth amendment was devised to meet this exigency.

So, too, in the *Civil Rights Cases*, it was said that the act of a mere individual, the owner of an inn, a public conveyance or place of amusement, refusing accommodations to colored people, cannot be justly regarded as imposing any badge of slavery or servitude upon the applicant, but only as involving an ordinary civil injury, properly cognizable by the laws of the state, and presumably subject to redress by those laws until the contrary appears. 'It would be running the slavery question into the ground,' said Mr. Justice Bradley, 'to make it apply to every act of discrimination which a person may see fit to make as to the guests he will entertain, or as to the people he will take into his coach or cab or car, or admit to his concert or theater, or deal with in other matters of intercourse or business.'

A statute which implies merely a legal distinction between the white and colored races—a distinction which is founded in the color of the two races, and which must always exist so long as white men are distinguished from the other race by color—has no tendency to destroy the legal equality of the two races, or re-establish a state of involuntary servitude. Indeed, we do not understand that the thirteenth amendment is strenuously relied upon by the plaintiff in error in this connection.

2. By the fourteenth amendment, all persons born or naturalized in the United States, and subject to the jurisdiction thereof, are made citizens of the United States and of the state wherein they reside; and the states are forbidden from making or enforcing any law which shall abridge the privileges or immunities of citizens of the United States, or shall deprive any person of life, liberty, or property without due process of law, or deny to any person within their jurisdiction the equal protection of the laws.

The proper construction of this amendment was first called to the attention of this court in the *Slaughter-House Cases,* which involved, however, not a question of race, but one of exclusive privileges. The case did not call for any expression of opinion as to the exact rights it was intended to secure to the colored race, but it was said generally that its main purpose was to establish the citizenship of the negro, to give definitions of citizenship of the United States and of the states, and to protect from the hostile legislation of the states the privileges and immunities of citizens of the United States, as distinguished from those of citizens of the states. The object of the amendment was undoubtedly to enforce the absolute equality of the two races before the law, but, in the nature of things, it could not have been intended to abolish distinctions based upon color, or to enforce social, as distinguished from political, equality, or a commingling of the two races upon terms unsatisfactory to either. Laws permitting, and even requiring, their separation, in places where they are liable to be brought into contact, do not necessarily imply the inferiority of either race to the other, and have been generally, if not universally, recognized as within the competency of the state legislatures in the exercise of their police power. The most common instance of this is connected with the establishment of separate schools for white and colored children, which have been held to be a valid exercise of the legislative power even by courts of states where the political rights of the colored race have been longest and most earnestly enforced....

The distinction between laws interfering with the political equality of the negro and those requiring the separation of the two races in schools, theaters, and railway carriages has been frequently drawn by this court. Thus, in *Strauder v. West Virginia,* it was held that a law of West Virginia limiting to white male persons 21 years of age, and citizens of the state, the right to sit upon juries, was a discrimination which implied a legal inferiority in civil society, which lessened the security of the right of the colored race, and was a step towards reducing them to a condition of servility. Indeed, the right of a colored man that, in the selection of jurors to pass upon his life, liberty, and property, there shall be no exclusion of his race, and no discrimination against them because of color, has been asserted in a number of cases.

So, where the laws of a particular locality or the charter of a particular railway corporation has provided that no person shall be excluded from the cars on account of color, we have held that this meant that persons of color should travel in the same car as white ones, and that the enactment was not satisfied by the company providing cars assigned exclusively to people of color, though they were as good as those which they assigned exclusively to white persons.

Upon the other hand, where a statute of Louisiana required those engaged in the transportation of passengers among the states to give to all persons traveling within that state, upon vessels employed in that business, equal rights and privileges in all parts of the vessel, without distinction on account of race or color, and subjected to an action for damages the owner of such a vessel who excluded colored passengers on account of their color from the cabin set aside by him for the use of whites, it was held to be, so far as it applied to interstate commerce, unconstitutional and void. The court in this case, however, expressly disclaimed that it had anything whatever to do with the statute as a regulation of internal commerce, or affecting anything else than commerce among the states.

In the *Civil Rights Cases,* it was held that an act of congress entitling all persons within the jurisdiction of the United States to the full and equal enjoyment of the accommodations, advantages, facilities, and privileges of inns, public conveyances, on land or water, theaters, and other places of public amusement, and made applicable to citizens of every race and color, regardless of any previous condition of servitude, was unconstitutional and void, upon the ground that the fourteenth amendment was prohibitory upon the states only, and the legislation authorized to be adopted by congress for enforcing it was not direct legislation on matters respecting which the states were prohibited from making or enforcing certain laws, or doing certain acts, but was corrective legislation, such as might be necessary or proper for counter-acting and redressing the effect of such laws or acts....

Much nearer, and, indeed, almost directly in point, is the case of the *Louisville, N. O. & T. Ry. Co. v. State,* wherein the railway company was indicted for a violation of a statute of Mississippi, enacting that all railroads carrying passengers should provide equal, but separate, accommodations for the white and colored races, by providing two or more passenger cars for each passenger train, or by dividing the passenger cars by a partition, so as to secure separate accommodations. The case was presented in a different aspect from the one under consideration, inasmuch as it was an indictment against the railway company for failing to provide the separate accommodations, but the question considered was the constitutionality of the law. In that case, the supreme court of Mississippi had held that the statute applied solely to commerce within the state, and, that being the construction of the state statute by its highest court, was accepted as conclusive. 'If it be a matter,' said the court, 'respecting commerce wholly within a state, and not interfering with commerce between the states, then, obviously, there is no violation of the commerce clause of the federal constitution.... No question arises under this section as to the power of the state to separate in different compartments interstate passengers, or affect, in any manner, the privileges and rights of such passengers. All that we can consider is whether the state has the power to require that railroad trains within her limits shall have separate accommodations for the two races. That affecting only commerce within the state is no invasion of the power given to congress by the commerce clause.'

A like course of reasoning applies to the case under consideration, since the supreme court of Louisiana, in the case of *State v. Judge,* held that the statute in question did not apply to interstate passengers, but was confined in its application to passengers traveling exclusively within the borders of the state. The case was decided largely upon the authority of *Louisville, N. O. & T. Ry. Co. v. State.* In the present case no question of interference with interstate commerce can possibly arise, since the East Louisiana Railway appears to have been purely a local line, with both its termini within the state of Louisiana. Similar statutes for the separation of the two races upon public conveyances were held to be constitutional.

While we think the enforced separation of the races, as applied to the internal commerce of the state, neither abridges the privileges or immunities of the colored man, deprives him of his property without due process of law, nor denies him the equal protection of the laws, within the meaning of the fourteenth amendment, we are not prepared to say that the conductor, in assigning passengers to the coaches according to their race, does not act at his peril, or that the provision of the second section of the act that denies to the passenger compensation in damages for a refusal to receive him into the coach in which he properly belongs is a valid exercise of the legislative power. Indeed, we understand it to be conceded by the state's attorney that such part of the act as exempts from liability the railway company and its officers is unconstitutional. The power to assign to a particular coach obviously implies the power to determine to which race the passenger belongs, as well as the power to determine who, under the laws of the particular state, is to be deemed a white, and who a colored, person. This question, though indicated in the brief of the plaintiff in error, does not properly arise upon the record in this case, since the only issue made is as to the unconstitutionality of the act, so far as it requires the railway to provide separate accommodations, and the conductor to assign passengers according to their race.

It is claimed by the plaintiff in error that, in a mixed community, the reputation of belonging to the dominant race, in this instance the white race, is 'property,' in the same sense that a right of action or of inheritance is property. Conceding this to be so, for the purposes of this case, we are unable to see how this statute deprives him of, or in any way affects his right to, such property. If he be a white man, and assigned to a colored coach, he may have his action for damages against the company for being deprived of his so-called 'property.' Upon the other hand, if he be a colored man, and be so assigned, he has been deprived of no property, since he is not lawfully entitled to the reputation of being a white man.

In this connection, it is also suggested by the learned counsel for the plaintiff in error that the same argument that will justify the state legislature in requiring railways to provide separate accommodations for the two races will also authorize them to require separate cars to be provided for people whose hair is of a certain color, or who are aliens, or who belong to certain nationalities, or to enact laws requiring colored people to walk upon one side of the street, and white people upon the other, or requiring white men's houses to be painted white, and colored men's black, or their vehicles or business signs to be of different colors, upon the theory that one side of the street is as good as the other, or that a house or vehicle of one color is as good as one of another color. The reply to all this is that every exercise of the police power must be reasonable, and extend only to such laws as are enacted in good faith for the promotion of the public good, and not for the annoyance or oppression of a particular class....

So far, then, as a conflict with the fourteenth amendment is concerned, the case reduces itself to the question whether the statute of Louisiana is a reasonable regulation, and with respect to this there must necessarily be a large discretion on the part of the legislature. In determining the question of reasonableness, it is at liberty to act with reference to the established usages, customs, and traditions of the people, and with a view to the promotion of their comfort, and the preservation of the public peace and good order. Gauged by this standard, we cannot say that a law which authorizes or even requires the separation of the two races in public conveyances is unreasonable, or more obnoxious to the fourteenth amendment than the acts of congress requiring separate schools for colored children in the District of Columbia, the constitutionality of which does not seem to have been questioned, or the corresponding acts of state legislatures.

We consider the underlying fallacy of the plaintiff's argument to consist in the assumption that the enforced separation of the two races stamps the colored race with a badge of inferiority. If this be so, it is not by reason of anything found in the act, but solely because the colored race chooses to put that construction upon it. The argument necessarily assumes that if, as has been more than once the case, and is not unlikely to be so again, the colored race should become the dominant power in the state legislature, and should enact a law in precisely similar terms, it would thereby relegate the white race to an inferior position. We imagine that the white race, at least, would not acquiesce in this assumption. The argument also assumes that social prejudices may be overcome by legislation, and that equal rights cannot be secured to the negro except by an enforced commingling of the two races. We cannot accept this proposition. If the two races are to meet upon terms of social equality, it must be the result of natural affinities, a mutual appreciation of each other's merits, and a voluntary consent of individuals. As was said by the court of appeals of New York in *People v. Gallagher,* 'This end can neither be accomplished nor promoted by laws which conflict with the general sentiment of the community upon whom they are designed to operate. When the government, therefore, has secured to each of its citizens equal rights before the law, and equal opportunities for improvement and progress, it has accomplished the end for which it was organized, and performed all of the functions respecting social advantages with which it is endowed.'

Legislation is powerless to eradicate racial instincts, or to abolish distinctions based upon physical differences, and the attempt to do so can only result in accentuating the difficulties of the present situation. If the civil and political rights of both races be equal, one cannot be inferior to the other civilly or politically. If one race be inferior to the other socially, the constitution of the United States cannot put them upon the same plane.

It is true that the question of the proportion of colored blood necessary to constitute a colored person, as distinguished from a white person, is one upon which there is a difference of opinion in the different states; some holding that any visible admixture of black blood stamps the person as belonging to the colored race; others, that it depends upon the preponderance of blood; and still others, that the predominance of white blood must only be in the proportion of three-fourths. But these are questions to be determined under the laws of each state, and are not properly put in issue in this case. Under the allegations of his petition, it may undoubtedly become a question of importance whether, under the laws of Louisiana, the petitioner belongs to the white or colored race.

The judgment of the court below is therefore affirmed.

Mr. Justice BREWER did not hear the argument or participate in the decision of this case.

Source

Plessy v. Ferguson, 163 U.S. 537 (1896). Retrieved from http://www.ourdocuments.gov/doc.php?flash=true&doc=52&page=transcript.

Justice Harlan Delivers a Scathing Dissent

The lone dissenter from the U.S. Supreme Court's Plessy v. Ferguson *decision was Justice John Marshall Harlan. Excerpts from his famous dissenting opinion are reprinted below. Describing Louisiana's Separate Car Law as "inconsistent with the personal liberty of citizens, white and black, in that state, and hostile to both the spirit and letter of the constitution of the United States," Harlan correctly predicts that the Court's decision will arouse race hate and lead to the widespread adoption of racial segregation laws in the United States.*

By the Louisiana statute the validity of which is here involved, all railway companies (other than street-railroad companies) carrying passengers in that state are required to have separate but equal accommodations for white and colored persons, 'by providing two or more passenger coaches for each passenger train, or by dividing the passenger coaches by a partition so as to secure separate accommodations.' Under this statute, no colored person is permitted to occupy a seat in a coach assigned to white persons; nor any white person to occupy a seat in a coach assigned to colored persons. The managers of the railroad are not allowed to exercise any discretion in the premises, but are required to assign each passenger to some coach or compartment set apart for the exclusive use of his race. If a passenger insists upon going into a coach or compartment not set apart for persons of his race, he is subject to be fined, or to be imprisoned in the parish jail. Penalties are prescribed for the refusal or neglect of the officers, directors, conductors, and employees of railroad companies to comply with the provisions of the act.

Only 'nurses attending children of the other race' are excepted from the operation of the statute. No exception is made of colored attendants traveling with adults. A white man is not permitted to have his colored servant with him in the same coach, even if his condition of health requires the constant personal assistance of such servant. If a colored maid insists upon riding in the same coach with a white woman whom she has been employed to serve, and who may need her personal attention while traveling, she is subject to be fined or imprisoned for such an exhibition of zeal in the discharge of duty.

While there may be in Louisiana persons of different races who are not citizens of the United States, the words in the act 'white and colored races' necessarily include all citizens of the United States of both races residing in that state. So that we have before us a state enactment that compels, under penalties, the separation of the two races in railroad passenger coaches, and makes it a crime for a citizen of either race to enter a coach that has been assigned to citizens of the other race.

Thus, the state regulates the use of a public highway by citizens of the United States solely upon the basis of race.

However apparent the injustice of such legislation may be, we have only to consider whether it is consistent with the constitution of the United States....

In respect of civil rights, common to all citizens, the constitution of the United States does not, I think, permit any public authority to know the race of those entitled to be protected in the enjoyment of such rights. Every true man has pride of race, and under appropriate circumstances, when the rights of others, his equals before the law, are not to be affected, it is his privilege to express such pride and to take such action based upon it as to him seems proper. But I deny that any legislative body or judicial tribunal may have regard to the race of citizens when the civil rights of those citizens are involved. Indeed, such legislation as that here in question is inconsistent not only with that equality of rights which pertains to citizenship, national and state, but with the personal liberty enjoyed by every one within the United States.

The thirteenth amendment does not permit the withholding or the deprivation of any right necessarily inhering in freedom. It not only struck down the institution of slavery as previously existing in the United States, but it prevents the imposition of any burdens or disabilities that constitute badges of slavery or servitude. It decreed universal civil freedom in this country. This court has so adjudged. But, that amendment having been found inadequate to the protection of the rights of those who had been in slavery, it was followed by the fourteenth amendment, which added greatly to the dignity and glory of American citizenship, and to the security of personal liberty, by declaring that 'all persons born or naturalized in the United States, and subject to the jurisdiction thereof, are citizens of the United States and of the state wherein they reside,' and that 'no state shall make or enforce any law which shall abridge the privileges or immunities of citizens of the United States; nor shall any state deprive any person of life, liberty or property without due process of law, nor deny to any person within its jurisdiction the equal protection of the laws.' These two amendments, if enforced according to their true intent and meaning, will protect all the civil rights that pertain to freedom and citizenship. Finally, and to the end that no citizen should be denied, on account of his race, the privilege of participating in the political control of his country, it was declared by the fifteenth amendment that 'the right of citizens of the United States to vote shall not be denied or abridged by the United States or by any state on account of race, color or previous condition of servitude.'

These notable additions to the fundamental law were welcomed by the friends of liberty throughout the world. They removed the race line from our governmental systems. They had, as this court has said, a common purpose, namely, to secure 'to a race recently emancipated, a race that through many generations have been held in slavery, all the civil rights that the superior race enjoy.' They declared, in legal effect, this court has further said, 'that the law in the states shall be the same for the black as for the white; that all persons, whether colored or white, shall stand equal before the laws of the states; and in regard to the colored race, for whose protection the amendment was primarily designed, that no discrimination shall be made against them by law because of their color.' We also said: 'The words of the amendment, it is true, are prohibitory, but they contain a necessary implication of a positive immunity or right, most valuable to the colored race—the right to exemption from unfriendly legislation against them distinctively as colored; exemption from legal discriminations, implying inferiority in civil society, lessening the security of their enjoyment of the rights which others enjoy; and discriminations which are steps towards reducing them to the condition of a subject race.' It was, consequently, adjudged that a state law that excluded citizens of the colored race from juries, because of their race, however well qualified in other respects to discharge the duties of jurymen, was repugnant to the fourteenth amendment…. At the present term, referring to the previous adjudications, this court declared that 'underlying all of those decisions is the principle that the constitution of the United States, in its present form, forbids, so far as civil and political rights are concerned, discrimination by the general government or the states against any citizen because of his race. All citizens are equal before the law'….

It was said in argument that the statute of Louisiana does not discriminate against either race, but prescribes a rule applicable alike to white and colored citizens. But this argument does not meet the difficulty. Every one knows that the statute in question had its origin in the purpose, not so much to exclude white persons from railroad cars occupied by blacks, as to exclude colored people from coaches occupied by or assigned to white persons. Railroad corporations of Louisiana did not make discrimination among whites in the matter of accommodation for travelers. The thing to accomplish was, under the guise of giving equal accommodation for whites and blacks, to compel the latter to keep to themselves while traveling in railroad passenger coaches. No one would be so wanting in candor as to assert the contrary. The fundamental objection, therefore, to the statute, is that it interferes with the personal freedom of citizens. 'Personal liberty,' it has been well said, 'consists in the power of locomotion, of changing situation, or removing one's person to whatsoever places one's own inclination may direct, without imprisonment or restraint, unless by due course of law.' If a white man and a black man choose to occupy the same public conveyance on a public highway, it is their right to do so; and no government, proceeding alone on grounds of race, can prevent it without infringing the personal liberty of each.

It is one thing for railroad carriers to furnish, or to be required by law to furnish, equal accommodations for all whom they are under a legal duty to carry. It is quite another thing for government to forbid citizens of the white and black races from traveling in the same public conveyance, and to punish officers of railroad companies for permitting persons of the two races to occupy the same passenger coach. If a state can prescribe, as a rule of civil conduct, that whites and blacks shall not travel as passengers in the same railroad coach, why may it not so regulate the use of the streets of its cities and towns as to compel white citizens to keep on one side of a street, and black citizens to keep on the other? Why may it not, upon like grounds, punish whites and blacks who ride together in street cars or in open vehicles on a public road or street? Why may it not require sheriffs to assign whites to one side of a court room, and blacks to the other? And why may it not also prohibit the commingling of the two races in the galleries of legislative halls or in public assemblages convened for the consideration of the political questions of the day? Further, if this statute of Louisiana is consistent with the personal liberty of citizens, why may not the state require the separation in railroad coaches of native and naturalized citizens of the United States, or of Protestants and Roman Catholics?...

The white race deems itself to be the dominant race in this country. And so it is, in prestige, in achievements, in education, in wealth, and in power. So, I doubt not, it will continue to be for all time, if it remains true to its great heritage, and holds fast to the principles of constitutional liberty. But in view of the constitution, in the eye of the law, there is in this country no superior, dominant, ruling class of citizens. There is no caste here. Our constitution is colorblind, and neither knows nor tolerates classes among citizens. In respect of civil rights, all citizens are equal before the law. The humblest is the peer of the most powerful. The law regards man as man, and takes no account of his surroundings or of his color when his civil rights as guaranteed by the supreme law of the land are involved. It is therefore to be regretted that this high tribunal, the final expositor of the fundamental law of the land, has reached the conclusion that it is competent for a state to regulate the enjoyment by citizens of their civil rights solely upon the basis of race.

In my opinion, the judgment this day rendered will, in time, prove to be quite as pernicious as the decision made by this tribunal in the *Dred Scott Case*.

It was adjudged in that case that the descendants of Africans who were imported into this country, and sold as slaves, were not included nor intended to be included under the word 'citizens' in the constitution, and could not claim any of the rights and privileges which that instrument provided for and secured to citizens of the United States; that, at time of the adoption of the constitution, they were 'considered as a subordinate and inferior class of beings, who had been subjugated by the dominant race, and, whether emancipated or not, yet remained subject to their authority, and had no rights or privileges but such as those who held the power and the government might choose to grant them.' The recent amendments of the constitution, it was supposed, had eradicated these principles from our institutions. But it seems that we have yet, in some of the states, a dominant race—a superior class of citizens—which assumes to regulate the enjoyment of civil rights, common to all citizens, upon the basis of race.

The present decision, it may well be apprehended, will not only stimulate aggressions, more or less brutal and irritating, upon the admitted rights of colored citizens, but will encourage the belief that it is possible, by means of state enactments, to defeat the beneficent purposes which the people of the United States had in view when they adopted the recent amendments of the constitution, by one of which the blacks of this country were made citizens of the United States and of the states in which they respectively reside, and whose privileges and immunities, as citizens, the states are forbidden to abridge. Sixty millions of whites are in no danger from the presence here of eight millions of blacks. The destinies of the two races, in this country, are indissolubly linked together, and the interests of both require that the common government of all shall not permit the seeds of race hate to be planted under the sanction of law. What can more certainly arouse race hate, what more certainly create and perpetuate a feeling of distrust between these races, than state enactments which, in fact, proceed on the ground that colored citizens are so inferior and degraded that they cannot be allowed to sit in public coaches occupied by white citizens? That, as all will admit, is the real meaning of such legislation as was enacted in Louisiana.

The sure guaranty of the peace and security of each race is the clear, distinct, unconditional recognition by our governments, national and state, of every right that inheres in civil freedom, and of the equality before the law of all citizens of the United States, without regard to race. State enactments regulating the enjoyment of civil rights upon the basis of race, and cunningly devised to defeat legitimate results of the war, under the pretense of recognizing equality of rights, can have no other result than to render permanent peace impossible, and to keep alive a conflict of races, the continuance of which must do harm to all concerned. This question is not met by the suggestion that social equality cannot exist between the white and black races in this country. That argument, if it can be properly regarded as one, is scarcely worthy of consideration; for social equality no more exists between two races when traveling in a passenger coach or a public highway than when members of the same races sit by each other in a street car or in the jury box, or stand or sit with each other in a political assembly, or when they use in common the streets of a city or town, or when they are in the same room for the purpose of having their names placed on the registry of voters, or when they approach the ballot box in order to exercise the high privilege of voting.

There is a race so different from our own that we do not permit those belonging to it to become citizens of the United States. Persons belonging to it are, with few exceptions, absolutely excluded from our country. I allude to the Chinese race. But, by the statute in question, a Chinaman can ride in the same passenger coach with white citizens of the United States, while citizens of the black race in Louisiana, many of whom, perhaps, risked their lives for the preservation of the Union, who are entitled, by law, to participate in the political control of the state and nation, who are not excluded, by law or by reason of their race, from public stations of any kind, and who have all the legal rights that belong to white citizens, are yet declared to be criminals, liable to imprisonment, if they ride in a public coach occupied by citizens of the white race. It is scarcely just to say that a colored citizen should not object to occupying a public coach assigned to his own race. He does not object, nor, perhaps, would he object to separate coaches for his race if his rights under the law were recognized. But he does object, and he ought never to cease objecting, that citizens of the white and black races can be adjudged criminals because they sit, or claim the right to sit, in the same public coach on a public highway. The arbitrary separation of citizens, on the basis

170

of race, while they are on a public highway, is a badge of servitude wholly inconsistent with the civil freedom and the equality before the law established by the constitution. It cannot be justified upon any legal grounds.

If evils will result from the commingling of the two races upon public highways established for the benefit of all, they will be infinitely less than those that will surely come from state legislation regulating the enjoyment of civil rights upon the basis of race. We boast of the freedom enjoyed by our people above all other peoples. But it is difficult to reconcile that boast with a state of the law which, practically, puts the brand of servitude and degradation upon a large class of our fellow citizens—our equals before the law. The thin disguise of 'equal' accommodations for passengers in railroad coaches will not mislead any one, nor atone for the wrong this day done.

The result of the whole matter is that while this court has frequently adjudged, and at the present term has recognized the doctrine, that a state cannot, consistently with the constitution of the United States, prevent white and black citizens, having the required qualifications for jury service, from sitting in the same jury box, it is now solemnly held that a state may prohibit white and black citizens from sitting in the same passenger coach on a public highway, or may require that they be separated by a 'partition' when in the same passenger coach. May it not now be reasonably expected that astute men of the dominant race, who affect to be disturbed at the possibility that the integrity of the white race may be corrupted, or that its supremacy will be imperiled, by contact on public highways with black people, will endeavor to procure statutes requiring white and black jurors to be separated in the jury box by a 'partition,' and that, upon retiring from the court room to consult as to their verdict, such partition, if it be a movable one, shall be taken to their consultation room, and set up in such way as to prevent black jurors from coming too close to their brother jurors of the white race. If the 'partition' used in the court room happens to be stationary, provision could be made for screens with openings through which jurors of the two races could confer as to their verdict without coming into personal contact with each other. I cannot see but that, according to the principles this day announced, such state legislation, although conceived in hostility to, and enacted for the purpose of humiliating, citizens of the United States of a particular race, would be held to be consistent with the constitution.

I do not deem it necessary to review the decisions of state courts to which reference was made in argument. Some, and the most important, of them, are wholly inapplicable, because rendered prior to the adoption of the last amendments of the constitution, when colored people had very few rights which the dominant race felt obliged to respect. Others were made at a time when public opinion, in many localities, was dominated by the institution of slavery; when it would not have been safe to do justice to the black man; and when, so far as the rights of blacks were concerned, race prejudice was, practically, the supreme law of the land. Those decisions cannot be guides in the era introduced by the recent amendments of the supreme law, which established universal civil freedom, gave citizenship to all born or naturalized in the United States, and residing here, obliterated the race line from our systems of governments, national and state, and placed our free institutions upon the broad and sure foundation of the equality of all men before the law.

I am of opinion that the state of Louisiana is inconsistent with the personal liberty of citizens, white and black, in that state, and hostile to both the spirit and letter of the constitution of the United States. If laws of like character should be enacted in the several states of the Union, the effect would be in the highest degree mischievous. Slavery, as an institution tolerated by law, would, it is true, have disappeared from our country; but there would remain a power in the states, by sinister legislation, to interfere with the full enjoyment of the blessings of freedom, to regulate civil rights, common to all citizens, upon the basis of race, and to place in a condition of legal inferiority a large body of American citizens, now constituting a part of the political community, called the 'People of the United States,' for whom, and by whom through representatives, our government is administered. Such a system is inconsistent with the guaranty given by the constitution to each state of a republican form of government, and may be stricken down by congressional action, or by the courts in the discharge of their solemn duty to maintain the supreme law of the land, anything in the constitution or laws of any state to the contrary notwithstanding.

For the reason stated, I am constrained to withhold my assent from the opinion and judgment of the majority.

Source

Plessy v. Ferguson, 163 U.S. 537 (1896). Retrieved from http://www.ourdocuments.gov/doc.php?flash=true&doc=52&page=transcript.

George H. White Makes His "Defense of the Negro Race" Speech

Sixteen African Americans served in the U.S. Congress during Reconstruction, while hundreds more held positions in state and local governments across the South. To many people, that decade-long post-war period seemed like the dawn of a new era of equality in race relations. As soon as federal troops withdrew from the South in 1877, however, white supremacists moved quickly to reclaim political control and social dominance. By the turn of the twentieth century, racial discrimination, segregation, and violence had reversed nearly all of the civil rights gains that blacks had made during Reconstruction.

George H. White, a Republican from North Carolina, was the sole remaining African-American member of the U.S. House of Representatives in 1901. Given the suppression of black voting rights in his home state, White decided it was pointless for him to run for reelection, so he left public office that year. In his farewell speech on the House floor, which is excerpted below, White offers a spirited defense of African-American accomplishments since the Civil War and makes a passionate plea for equal rights and opportunities for black citizens.

I want to enter a plea for the colored man, the colored woman, the colored boy, and the colored girl of this country. I would not thus digress from the question at issue and detain the House in a discussion of the interests of this particular people at this time but for the constant and the persistent efforts of certain gentlemen upon this floor to mold and rivet public sentiment against us as a people and to lose no opportunity to hold up the unfortunate few who commit crimes and depredations and lead lives of infamy and shame, as other races do, as fair specimens of representatives of the entire colored race....

I would like to advance the statement that the musty records of 1868, filed away in the archives of Southern capitols, as to what the negro was thirty-two years ago, is not a proper standard by which the negro living on the threshold of the twentieth century should be measured. Since that time we have reduced the illiteracy of the race at least 45 percent. We have written and published near 500 books. We have nearly 300 newspapers, 3 of which are dailies. We have now in practice over 2,000 lawyers and a corresponding number of doctors. We have accumulated over $12,000,000 worth of school property and about $40,000,000 worth of church property. We have about 140,000 farms and homes, valued at in the neighborhood of $750,000,000, and personal property valued at about $170,000,000. We have raised about $11,000,000 for educational purposes, and the property per capita for every colored man, woman, and child in the United States is estimated at $75.

We are operating successfully several banks, commercial enterprises among our people in the Southland, including 1 silk mill and 1 cotton factory. We have 32,000 teachers in the schools of the country; we have built, with the aid of our friends, about 20,000 churches, and support 7 colleges, 17 academies, 50 high schools, 5 law schools, 5 medical schools, and 25 theological seminaries. We have over 600,000 acres of land in the South alone. The cotton produced, mainly by black labor, has increased from 4,669,770 bales in 1860 to 11,235,000 in 1899.

All this we have done under the most adverse circumstances. We have done it in the face of lynching, burning at the stake, with the humiliation of "Jim Crow" cars, the disfranchisement of our male citizens, slander and degradation of our women, with the factories closed against us, no negro permitted to be conductor on the railway cars, whether run through the streets of our cities or across the prairies of our great country, no negro permitted to run as engineer on a locomotive, most of the mines closed against us. Labor unions—carpenters, painters, brick masons, machinists, hackmen, and those supplying nearly every conceivable avocation for livelihood have banded themselves together to better their condition, but, with few exceptions, the black face has been left out. The negroes are seldom employed in our mercantile stores. At this we do not wonder. Some day we hope to have them employed in our own stores. With all these odds against us, we are forging our way ahead, slowly, perhaps, but surely. You may tie us and then taunt us for a lack of bravery, but one day we will break the bonds. You may use our labor for two and a half centuries and then taunt us for our poverty, but let me remind you we will not always remain poor. You may withhold even the knowledge of how to read God's word and learn the way from earth to glory and then taunt us for our ignorance, but we would remind you that there is plenty of room at the top, and we are climbing....

Now, Mr. Chairman, before concluding my remarks I want to submit a brief recipe for the solution of the so-called American negro problem. He asks no special favors, but simply demands that he be given the same chance for existence, for earning a livelihood, for raising himself in the scales of manhood and womanhood that are accorded to kindred nationalities. Treat him as a man; go into his home and learn of his social conditions; learn of his cares, his troubles, and his hopes for the future; gain his confidence; open the doors of industry to him; let the word "negro," "colored," and "black" be stricken from all the organizations enumerated in the federation of labor.

Help him to overcome his weaknesses, punish the crime-committing class by the courts of the land, measure the standard of the race by its best material, cease to mold prejudicial and unjust public sentiment against him, and my word for it, he will learn to support, hold up the hands of, and join in with that political party, that institution, whether secular or religious, in every community where he lives, which is destined to do the greatest good for the greatest number. Obliterate race hatred, party prejudice, and help us to achieve nobler ends, greater results, and become more satisfactory citizens to our brother in white.

This, Mr. Chairman, is perhaps the negroes' temporary farewell to the American Congress; but let me say, Phoenix-like he will rise up some day and come again. These parting words are in behalf of an outraged, heart-broken, bruised, and bleeding, but God-fearing people, faithful, industrious, loyal people—rising people, full of potential force.

Mr. Chairman, in the trial of Lord Bacon, when the court disturbed the counsel for the defendant, Sir Walter Raleigh raised himself up to his full height and, addressing the court, said: "Sir, I am pleading for the life of a human being."

The only apology that I have to make for the earnestness with which I have spoken is that I am pleading for the life, the liberty, the future happiness, and manhood suffrage for one-eighth of the entire population of the United States.

Source

White, George H. "Defense of the Negro Race—Charges Answered." Speech of the Honorable George H. White of North Carolina in the U.S. House of Representatives, January 29, 1901. *Congressional Record*, 56th Cong., 2d session, vol. 34, pt. 2. Washington DC: Government Printing Office, 1901. Retrieved from *Documenting the American South*, University of North Carolina at Chapel Hill, 2002, http://docsouth.unc.edu/nc/whitegh/whitegh.html.

The NAACP Demands Equal Rights for African Americans

In the wake of the Supreme Court's 1896 Plessy v. Ferguson *ruling, the legal and social status of African Americans eroded significantly. Legalized segregation, discrimination in employment, suppression of voting rights, and racial violence became the norm for the nation's black citizens in the early twentieth century. In 1909 a group of prominent African-American leaders and white supporters gathered in New York City to discuss ways of addressing these problems. This meeting of the Negro National Committee led to the founding of the National Association for the Advancement of Colored People (NAACP), one of the most influential civil rights organizations in U.S. history. It also produced the document reprinted below, which outlines the group's demands for fairness and equality for African Americans.*

We denounce the ever-growing oppression of our 10,000,000 colored fellow citizens as the greatest menace that threatens the country. Often plundered of their just share of the public funds, robbed of nearly all part in the government, segregated by common carriers, some murdered with impunity, and all treated with open contempt by officials, they are held in some States in practical slavery to the white community. The systematic persecution of law-abiding citizens and their disfranchisement on account of their race alone is a crime that will ultimately drag down to an infamous end any nation that allows it to be practiced, and it bears most heavily on those poor white farmers and laborers whose economic position is most similar to that of the persecuted race.

The nearest hope lies in the immediate and patiently continued enlightenment of the people who have been inveigled into a campaign of oppression. The spoils of persecution should not go to enrich any class or classes of the population. Indeed persecution of organized workers, peonage, enslavement of prisoners, and even disfranchisement already threaten large bodies of whites in many Southern States.

We agree fully with the prevailing opinion that the transformation of the unskilled colored laborers in industry and agriculture into skilled workers is of vital importance to that race and to the nation, but we demand for the Negroes, as for all others, a free and complete education, whether by city, State or nation, a grammar school and industrial training for all and technical, professional, and academic education for the most gifted.

But the public schools assigned to the Negro of whatever kind or grade will never receive a fair and equal treatment until he is given equal treatment in the

176

Legislature and before the law. Nor will the practically educated Negro, no matter how valuable to the community he may prove, be given a fair return for his labor or encouraged to put forth his best efforts or given the chance to develop that efficiency that comes only outside the school until he is respected in his legal rights as a man and a citizen.

We regard with grave concern the attempt manifest South and North to deny black men the right to work and to enforce this demand by violence and bloodshed. Such a question is too fundamental and clear even to be submitted to arbitration. The [recent labor] strike in Georgia is not simply a demand that Negroes be displaced, but that proven and efficient men be made to surrender their long-followed means of livelihood to white competitors.

As first and immediate steps toward remedying these national wrongs, so full of peril for the whites as well as the blacks of all sections, we demand of Congress and the Executive:

(1) That the Constitution be strictly enforced and the civil rights guaranteed under the Fourteenth Amendment be secured impartially to all.

(2) That there be equal educational opportunities for all and in all the States, and that public school expenditure be the same for the Negro and white child.

(3) That in accordance with the Fifteenth Amendment the right of the Negro to the ballot on the same terms as other citizens be recognized in every part of the country.

Source

NAACP. Platform of the National Negro Committee, 1909. NAACP Records, Manuscript Division, Library of Congress (024.00.00). Retrieved from http://myloc.gov/Exhibitions/naacp/earlyyears/Exhibit Objects/PlatformNationalNegro.aspx.

An Alabama Man Experiences Daily Humiliations under Segregation

Richard Rose was born in 1935 in the farming town of Cecil, Alabama, and grew up on the outskirts of Montgomery. In a 1995 interview for Duke University's Behind the Veil oral history project, which is excerpted below, Rose recalls some of his experiences as an African American in the South during the era of legal segregation. He remembers learning from an early age how to behave in a submissive manner toward whites in order to avoid trouble. He also describes several incidents of racial violence and relates how law enforcement officials stood firmly on the side of whites in interracial conflicts.

B eing in a segregated area like that you learn from experience, but [the older generation] told you certain things and tried to direct you. For example, if we were speaking to—it didn't matter whether it was a black, an elderly person—you had to say yes m'am, no m'am, yes sir, no sir. And like when we were riding the buses back then. All the blacks had to go to the back, and if the bus would fill up from the front with whites all the way back then the driver would ask you to get up and let this white person sit down. They told us, they instilled in us, not to cause what you might say trouble and that way protected yourself. You wouldn't be put in jail or beaten by some of the policemen....

When I was old enough, I'd say about nine or ten, if I went to town or somewhere with my grandfather or if an insurance man would come by, instead of calling him by his name they would rather say uncle or preacher, and I noticed then something was wrong here. And then this man could be younger than my grandfather, and he had to say yes sir to [the man, and the man] would say yes and no to my grandfather who was up in age. And I said something wrong here, you know? And then when you would get on the bus I noticed that at an early age we'd have to take a seat in the back. So I knowed something was wrong here. And then when you went to the public places like the five and ten cents stores back then, you had a water fountain that says white and one said colored. Bathrooms—one for black if they had one, and one for white. And if you were traveling you couldn't go in the restaurant. You had to prepare your own lunch and, you know, travel that way. What else I notice. I noticed this at an early age, and as I got older and started traveling it began to register more, you know....

Reprinted by permission from the David M. Rubenstein Rare Book and Manuscript Library, Duke University.

Let me mention one incident. I've seen this riding the bus. Just from Montgomery to my community we had a local bus that would go, would come through, and for twenty-five cents you could go one way to Montgomery. There have been cases where a black would get on and then, like I was telling you, if the front would fill up with whites then the driver would ask the next person, a black, to get up and let the whites sit down. So, there was some fellows, grown men I'd say, had had a drink or two and they wouldn't get up. So then the driver wanted to come back and make them get up and that's when you'd have some fights. That's one incident.

Another incident, I had a good friend of mine's mother was walking from work. She was working for some whites in Montgomery and they didn't bring her home. She had to walk home and sometimes it would get dusk, dark 'fore she could get off the highway. Some young whites passed by and took a quarter of a watermelon and threw it and hit her and just knocked teeth out, you know. Another incident, if the sheriff would come to your house for some reason, he didn't have to show you a search warrant. He'd just go on in and search. You had a lot of trouble out of that.

Oh, I used to work at a short-order café, and they had an area in the back with one table or maybe two about this size and chairs on each side for blacks, and they sold beer and sandwiches and, you know, fast food. Short-order place. And the bathroom was located in the back. So, on the outside, for the men. So some of the whites, they had to get up out of the living room or whatever they were sitting at the bar and go through where these blacks were to go to the bathrooms. So, this particular day this one white guy went through, and he made some smart remark. It was a black soldier in there, and they had a brawl. That black soldier got up and told him what he would do, and they started fighting. The owner had to go back there and stop them. Then he kind of talked to the white guy, you know, 'cause he knew the black guy didn't say anything to him, you know. That's one incident.

They had other incidents where—whites will not come one on one. Back then they wouldn't, they'd come in a group. They had to be two or three. If you stood up for what you believed and didn't let them run over you, they'd say you were crazy. And then if you got in an argument with one, and he probably wouldn't say nothing then, but later on he'd get two or three and come back. And that's when you had a lot of trouble. Then they would beat the guy up, you know, the black up and go on.

But I can say this, I knew of the Ku Klux Klan, but I never did see a cross where they had set up and set it afire. Never did see that. I never did see any in robes and their uniforms, you know, but we knew they were there. Because of some of the other incidents that happened. I can recall I was real young and I heard my people, my parents talking about it. They made one black fellow jump off into the Alabama River for no reason at all. They just stopped him and made him do it, but these were Klansmen. They recently, oh, about ten or fifteen years ago the attorney general in Alabama there recently sentenced one of them to live in prison, but he was an old man then. But anyway, a lot of injustices like that went on during that time.

I had an incident where my uncle and another young black lady was working for this white fellow that owned a short-order, he owned a club. She was cooking. My uncle was car hopping and waiting tables. A white guy was liking the black young lady. My uncle was liking the black young lady. So something happened and my uncle found out about it and he slapped her and she went back and told the white man. That night he sent, the white man sent two car loads of whites. They were mixed. You had men and women like they were looking. They came looking for my uncle. Now my uncle had told my grandfather, his daddy what happened. Well, when the cars drove up and they asked for him, they didn't know that there were two guns on the back of the house pointed at them, but they didn't know that. So anyway, my grandfather decided then that it was time for my uncle to leave and go up east on the east coast, because he was going to [be killed] had he stayed there.

Things like that, and then brutality by policemen. This happened after I left the area. I was in service. If they caught you speeding and they say you were sassing, they subject to shoot you, beat you to death or shoot you. And that did happen in some incidents for no reason at all. And then I was raised up, well, I knew this one fellow. I used to work for his parents. He was just a little baby. I remember when he was a little baby, and I left and went away and he grew up. He became a state trooper, and you talking about hating blacks, he hated blacks. Things like that.

There was some, oh, one other thing too. Back then they could, well, the whites could pick up a black young lady and do whatever they wanted and then nothing was done about it. If she could identify him, still nothing would be done. That has happened. There's others, but I won't go into them.

Source

Interview with Richard Rose (btvct04036), interviewed by Paul Ortiz, Cecil, Alabama, August 3, 1995. *Behind the Veil: Documenting African-American Life in the Jim Crow South,* Digital Collection, John Hope Franklin Research Center, David M. Rubenstein Rare Book and Manuscript Library, Duke University. Retrieved from http://library.duke.edu/digitalcollections/media/pdf/behindtheveil /btvct04036.pdf.

A Georgia Native Remembers Jim Crow Tragedies

Born in 1931 in Moultrie, Georgia, Stine George grew up during the Jim Crow era in the South. He shared memories of several tragic incidents from his youth with researchers from Duke University for the oral history collection Remembering Jim Crow. *In the excerpt reprinted below, George recalls a time when his black sharecropping family got an opportunity to purchase a prime piece of farmland from white landowner Jesse Morgan, who even helped them obtain a loan from the Federal Housing Administration (FHA). This act of generosity had terrible consequences, however, when resentful white neighbors burned George's new house to the ground. George also describes the atmosphere of fear that permeated the lives of African Americans as they went about their daily activities.*

[Mr. Morgan] said [to my father], "You've been a good nigger, so I'll tell you what I'm going to do. I'm going to sell you this farm." Dad said, "Sell me a farm, Mr. Morgan? I can't buy no farm." He said, "The government will buy it for you. In fact, we already started buying it. You just go over there and talk with Brown"—that was the FHA man—"and he'll let you sign the papers. I've already got them made up. We're the government." [Laughter.] That was it. Talk to my daddy, he'll tell you the same. "We're the government," [Morgan] said. "Just go over there and sign the papers."

That's what happened. [Morgan] didn't tell his sons about what he had done. He didn't want to tell [them] until after my dad signed the papers. [That farm was] on the main road at that time, see, and nothing but white folks [there], and good land on a hill, too. See, black folks would always get in the bottom, but this was on a hill, nice hill land, because that was one of his choice farms. But anyway, them sons had a fit. It was two of them. Boy, they had a fit, and they went over there and they were going to stop it because they said [their] daddy was senile, he didn't know what he was doing. The people at the FHA office said, "Well, he's done signed the papers. We can't withdraw it now."

So then they came out to the house mad. See, [one of Morgan's sons] had a fence put all the way around the farm. In fact, my dad did all the work, but he bought the fence and the posts and everything. It was new wire. It had just been up about a year. So they came out there and told my dad, "That's our wire." Said, "You've got to take all that wire down and roll it up and give it back to us." Around that whole farm, see, take up the posts. That's what they wanted.

My dad said, "Yes sir, I'll do that." So my dad went back over there to this Brown man's place and asked the FHA office. [He] said, "Mr. Morgan's son came out here and told me I had to take all that wire down from out there and give it to him because it belonged to him." The man told him, "You don't have to do that. The wire belongs to you because you done bought the farm." Said, "But now if you want to get along with them, you might want to take it down." So that's what my dad did. He had to take up all that wire up. To get along with him.

See, that's when black folks were going north because they said the white folks would either come back and lynch you or do anything, burn your house down. That's another thing. I don't talk about this too much. They built us this government house to live in. All government houses looked alike. You could always tell a government house because all of them were white, and they all looked alike. All over the South [if] you saw one, you saw more.

Anyway, that was a part of the deal in buying this farm. They put a house out there and that was part of the deal in the farm operation. So we had this house out there, but the white folks resented the fact that we were out there and had this frame house out there. We're not so sure what happened, but one night, probably about two o'clock in the morning, my oldest sister started running through the house [yelling], "Hey, daddy, daddy, the house is on fire!" And so the house started burning on the front porch and went all the way around, and when she hollered, we all were asleep. [It was] two o'clock in the morning, and then, of course, my dad ran out and she ran out and my dad thought he could put the fire out.

So then I came out. My baby sister and baby brother didn't ever wake up and got burnt up in that fire. That has hurt so much [that] I've never been able to talk about that much. I've never told but one or two persons in my whole life. We ran out there, and we took water and throwed it in the fire all the way around the house. It was said the white folks gassed our house and caused it to burn down and burn up two children.

[My brother and sister were] about three and four. My sister never waked up; she was still in bed, but the boy got up and got as far as the door and just didn't make it out. It was very painful. It was very painful that this happened.

And of course, white folks came over. In fact, my daddy didn't sleep with is pants on. [Laughter.] Well, a lot of people don't sleep with clothes on, but that's why I sleep with clothes on now because he didn't have any pants on, and he was out there trying to put the fire out because we were in a hurry. My sister, when she came out her hair got burned almost all off. And so a white man that lived across the hill, he brought them some clothes.

They never did anything about it. Nobody ever did anything about it, never tried to find out who did it or anything, but we surmised that the white folks done it. My sister had been ironing that day before. If it had caught from the iron, it would have caught inside the house, not outside. But they said, "Yeah, when did you iron over at that house?" My sister said, "Well, we ironed yesterday, ironed something yesterday afternoon." "Well, that was what it was, [it] was the clothes! That's where it caught." But it didn't catch inside the house. It caught on the front porch, went around the house, and burned the house up. It went around fast, too, burned the house down.

That's why we couldn't go back in and get the others out. But you see, a seven- or eight-year-old child, you couldn't expect him to go back and get nobody. Well, you know, I'm scared. I'm a nervous wreck. See, we had a bucket trying to draw the water out of the well, and my oldest sister was running, throwing the water on there. Shucks, in a little while that fire was all the way around the house, so that ended that little bit. Like I said, white folks came around and they were talkative, but nobody ever tried to apprehend anybody who committed the crime.

I had to walk 12 miles a day [to and from school], and there's a wood bridge, and I was kind of afraid to go across that bridge. Of course, my daddy always told me, "Now if you come up that bridge and somebody's on it, you just go back in the woods and stay in the woods until they leave, and then you come on home or go on to school. I'll never forget there were at least two nights that I had to stay in those woods all night long because white folks were fishing up and down the bridge. They never would go back anywhere so I laid over in the woods till they left. I thought they would throw me in the water, you know, throw me in the river, so I just stayed back off the road in the woods, and I slept in the woods at least two nights.

[My daddy] knew, probably, what it was. He loved me. He knew something had happened, but there was no way of getting in touch with me, so instead of going on home, I'd get up and walk on back to school the next morning. I had no other way to work it. [Laughter.] I got up and went on back to school, and the next evening I'd be able to get home, and they knew what transpired.

184

It was just some white guys on the bridge messing around at night, but they was there until late. I fell asleep in those woods, and so after twelve o'clock, it wasn't no point in going home. [Laughter.] So I just stayed in the woods.

I shall never forget this, and this is something nobody ever knew because we don't tell it. I wouldn't tell it now because it's painful, it will be painful even to tell it, but with what you are doing, I'll tell it. Some Sunday mornings we would get a mule and five or six of us would get the wagon. All of us [were] under ten years old. We'd get the wagon and go up about six miles away to see some of our first cousins. So one Sunday morning, it wasn't but three of us in the wagon, my sister, my brother and myself, and we were going up to see my uncle in Chilton. Like I said, my sister was but nine or ten. Of course, I was driving, and she was sitting in the wagon. So we went by this house where these white guys were out there playing ball. I guess it was eight guys, young white boys probably about 18, 19, 20, something like that.

One of those white guys ran and jumped on the wagon. He said, "I'm going to ride with you, I'm going to ride." We were going by this house, you see; we knew him, see, and he got on the back of the wagon, and he was riding with us. When we got to the house, he took the mule from me and stopped the mule at the house, took the wagon from me and tied the mule to a tree in the yard. Then he made my sister get out and go in the house with him. He raped my sister. Like I said, she was about nine at that time.

When he took her in the house, my brother and I jumped out the wagon and ran through the woods. We were scared. We didn't know where to go, and we were scared because, really, we hadn't been anywhere before. He was about six or seven then. No, he was about four or five years old, and I'm seven or eight. Anyway, he followed me down through them woods and went on down through the woods and briars. We were scared for somebody to see us, and so we finally went on through the woods and tried to get back where we thought our daddy was. See, that house where this guy was, we wouldn't dare go by there and be seen, so that meant we had to go way around through the woods and then come back around. My dad was within seeing distance from where this guy got on the wagon.

So about the time we got halfway back to Gum Branch, almost back where we could see the house, we heard the wagon going back down that road, running. See, what he had done, after he raped my sister, he told her to get in the wagon and go home. So she was driving the wagon and she went on home.

She went by the house where my dad was, and all them go out, and they couldn't understand where I was and what happened. They were alarmed. They didn't know we were down in the woods. We heard that wagon running but the corn was tall. We knew it was her with that wagon, but the corn was tall, and so I was scared and naturally my brother would be [too]. So finally they had her, but they didn't know where we were. They finally called the sheriff, and of course, he didn't do nothing.... We finally came out of the woods, and then we went back down to the house, and we didn't have any more trouble out of them, but they never ... do nothing to that guy for what he did.

Source

"Stine George." In Chafe, William H., Raymond Gavins, and Robert Korstad, eds. *Remembering Jim Crow: African Americans Tell about Live in the Segregated South.* New York: New Press, 2001, pp. 11-15.

A Black Reporter Recalls a Lynching

Arthur Searles was born in Albany, Georgia, in 1915. He grew up in a black neighborhood known as CME because it centered around a Colored Methodist Episcopal church. Like many African Americans in the South, Searles was well acquainted with lynching—the terrifying form of violence used by white segregationists to enforce Jim Crow laws and customs. In the following excerpt from the oral history collection Remembering Jim Crow, *Searles recalls the lynching of a family friend by the local sheriff. When Searles publishes details about the crime in a local black newspaper, he finds himself facing the threat of lynching as well.*

Because of my mama and papa, we were sort of the upper echelon [and] young men over in CME chose me as their leader. If you wanted to come into CME, especially to see our little CME girls, you had to get a pass from me. We issued passes like the sheriff of Baker County does now. You didn't know that, did you? The sheriff of Baker County still has to issue you a pass if you want to go and travel freely in Baker County. If he doesn't issue you one and any of the white folks beat you up, you're just a beat-up nigger. Even today [in 1994, when Searles was interviewed]. Just one step from hell. That's what Congressman Oscar DePriest said about Baker County. Said he was born in Newton, Georgia, which is just one step from hell. [Laughter.]

They had me come down there on one occasion to take some pictures and to do an article on a ham-and-egg show. Now that's normally agricultural agents' big to-do throughout the South, in Georgia and Florida, Alabama and all that. As a matter of fact, the ag[riculture] agent told me, "Searles, we want you to come down here and take some pictures. We don't have any money we can pay you but we'll give you a ham." I said, "All right, I don't mind." I said, "But now, I've got to have a letter of introduction or promotion so that when these folks stop me, I can present this letter to them." And so the sheriff wrote me a letter that I could pass through and walk around in Baker County. I was under the protection of his office, the sheriff. Of course, I went on down there, but I was scared to death all the while I was there.

One of my personal experiences with them was that a young man named Bobby Hall was lynched by the sheriff of Baker County, Screws, Sheriff Screws. See, there was a whole lot of inbreeding or mixing, and the Hall family looked just like white folks because there was some white people in there. That's the heritage. So [the] daddy, him and his son, had a beautiful pearl-handled pistol. And this has been validated so I don't mind putting it on tape. The son [Bobby Hall] would carry the pistol around in his glove compartment, which is legal as long as you're not exposing it or that sort of thing. You don't have to have a license. Well, Sheriff Screws told [Bobby Hall], "Let me see what you've got in your glove compartment." He let him see, and [Sheriff Screws] said, "Oh, this is a pretty pearl-handled pistol. I know you must have stole it." So he said, "No, sir. My daddy gave it to me." He said, "Well, I'm going to take it on in and look over my list of stolen pistols and see if it has been stolen." So he took it on away from him. He carried it on away from down there up to the sheriff's office.

About two months later, [Bobby Hall] came down there and asked him for his pistol. [The sheriff] told him, "You get on away from around here." He ran on away. So about four months after that, he saw him again and he said, "Sheriff, you know you've had plenty of time to see whether that pistol was stolen or not." Sheriff said to him, "Well, you come on down to the courthouse and we'll see about it. Don't come all that early because I'm going to be in and out. But you come down here about six o'clock in the evening, and if I haven't found out anything about it … I even forgot about looking it up." [Bobby Hall] came around there that evening, and that man shot him in the head two times, beat him, [beat] his face bloody, as I put it in my paper, as a ripe tomato, and tied his boy to the back of his truck and drug him around the square.

And they called the funeral home up here. This is how I got into it. O.T. Funeral Home. They called them to come get the body. I went over and took pictures of the body and marked the various places on it and everything. The sheriff had killed him, and we reported it to the Georgia Bureau of Investigation and the FBI, and the sheriff brought his car and siren and parked it in front of my place out here. My place was across the street then. [He] turned the siren on and let it go on all evening. I was in there and knew I better not come out there. And, of course, I didn't go out there, to be honest with you. I don't want to be a dead brave man. I want to live so I can write again, keep writing.

So I wrote the article about the man, Bobby Hall. I knew his father real well, and Bobby Hall was a nice little fellow. Whole family are. And all the sons and the girls' husbands all work together, and they had one man, the big Hall, Mr. Hall, to get all the cotton together and take it to the cotton gin. Things like that. They were very prosperous, very prosperous. Nobody believed the sheriff would kill them. They were white-looking black folks.

Oh, they freed that man. He was doing his official business, and the uppity Negro came in, and they claim he tried to attack the sheriff, which you know is a lie. No black man is going to attack the sheriff when he's got pistols and everything. Ain't too many white folks that would even do that, let alone black folks. So, incidentally, I told you I ain't no coward, but I ain't no hero either. I was scared to go down there when they had the funeral. So I sat at my desk over there and I felt like I'd been to many black funerals. So I knew exactly how that black funeral was going to go. I talked with some other people who were there and they told me how it went. How people came in cars, wagons, motorcycles, any way you could get there. The name of the church was Thankful Baptist Church in Baker County, Newton, Georgia. And everybody seemed to be in sympathy with this boy. Most of the people had tears in their eyes and all. It was a sorrowful day.

But as a result of this and the other publicity that I gave out about it, the Ku Klux Klan marched around my house on several occasions. They threw a brick up there with a note on it. It said, "Tend to your own race and tend to your own business or else you're going to have yourself killed." Of course, I didn't print that because I didn't want anybody to know that they had gone quite that far with it.

Source

"Arthur Searles." In Chafe, William H., Raymond Gavins, and Robert Korstad, eds. *Remembering Jim Crow: African Americans Tell about Life in the Segregated South.* New York: New Press, 2001, pp. 27-29.

President Barack Obama Discusses Racial Progress

Upon his inauguration on January 20, 2009, Barack Obama became the first African-American president of the United States. Many people viewed his election to the nation's highest office as a clear indication that America had made significant progress toward overcoming the racial inequalities that had plagued the country since its founding. On September 26, 2009, Obama assessed this progress in a speech (excerpted below) to members of the Congressional Black Caucus (CBC). While he mentions many positive developments and reasons for optimism, Obama also points out many barriers to equal opportunity that continue to face citizens and communities of color in the United States. He calls on the American people to build on the foundation laid by civil rights pioneers and keep working to achieve full racial equality.

I look out at all of you tonight—on members of Congress, on state and local officials, on leaders of all kinds—and I am reminded of the extraordinary acts of public service being rendered by African Americans today. I'm reminded of the difference each of you is making at every level of government, in the quiet neighborhoods of our small towns and the bustling streets of our big cities.

But I'm also reminded that it wasn't always this way. I'm reminded of a time long before the CBC was formed; long before the Civil Rights Movement was sparked; when just a lone African American was serving in the United States Congress.

A North Carolinian by birth, the child, some say, of slaves, George Henry White was the last of that first generation of African Americans elected to Congress in the aftermath of Appomattox [the town where Confederate general Robert E. Lee surrendered to end the Civil War]. But at the end of the 1800s, with a segregationist Supreme Court handing down "separate but equal"; with African Americans being purged from the voter rolls; with strange fruit growing on the poplar trees, White decided against seeking reelection—meaning that once again, neither the House nor the Senate would be occupied by a single African American member.

At the end of an inspiring farewell address, the gentleman from North Carolina said, "This, Mr. Chairman, is perhaps the Negroes' temporary farewell to the American Congress; but let me say, Phoenix-like he will rise up some day and come again."

Members of the CBC, all of you gathered here today, tonight is a fulfillment of that prophecy. While George Henry White might not have foreseen the exact details of Montgomery and Selma; while he might not have foreseen the precise outlines of the Civil Rights Act, and the Voting Rights Act, and all the struggles to come—he knew that someday, African Americans would sit in our City Halls and State Houses. He knew that someday, the halls of Congress would be walked by Representatives and Senators of every creed and color. He knew, as Frederick Douglass knew, as Harriet Tubman knew, as Martin Luther King, Jr. knew, that the arc of the moral universe is long, but it bends toward justice.

More than a century has passed since Congressman White left Congress. In that time, we have faced a number of difficult tests and bitter trials—as a people and as a nation. There have been dangers to peace and security; there have been barriers to justice and equality; there have been threats to opportunity. So we are by no means the first generation of Americans to be tested, but tested we have been. Most recently we've been tested by an economic crisis unlike any that we've seen since the Great Depression....

[Obama outlines some of the steps his administration has taken to promote economic recovery.]

Because of the actions we've taken so far, we have stopped the bleeding in our economy. So the next time some of these folks come up asking you what the Recovery Act has done, you tell them it has prevented us going into a much worse place. That much we know. That's been confirmed.

But we also know that we've got a long way to go; the progress we've made has been uneven; and that this recession has hit communities of color with a particular ferocity. Today, more than one in seven African Americans are out of work—the highest in nearly a quarter century. More than two out of 10 African Americans—and three out of 10 black children—are living in poverty.

So this economic crisis has made the problems in the communities of color much worse. But we all know that these problems have been there for a long time. Communities were struggling to catch up long before this economic storm came ashore. One study that looked at trends in this country over the past few decades found that while roughly seven out of every 10 middle class white children end up surpassing their parents' income, roughly seven out of every 10 middle class black children do not. Think about that. For the majority of some Americans upward mobility, for the majority of others—stagnation or even downward mobility. That was taking place over the last decade, before the economic crisis. That kind of inequality is unacceptable in the United States of America.

191

Bringing hope and opportunity to places where they're in short supply—that's not easy. It will take a focused and sustained effort to eradicate the structural inequalities in our communities—structural inequalities that make it difficult for children of color to make a success of their lives, no matter how smart or how driven or how talented they are. That's why we're launching Promise Neighborhoods to build on Geoffrey Canada's success in Harlem with a comprehensive approach to ending poverty by giving people the tools they need to pull themselves up. That's why I've created an Office of Urban Affairs to lift up our cities with a coordinated strategy to unleash their potential. That's why my administration—under the leadership of Attorney General Eric Holder—is serious about enforcing our civil rights laws and tearing down barriers to equal opportunity.

But of all the barriers still standing in 2009, few are more unjust, few are more entrenched, few are more inhumane than the barriers to a healthy life and a good education. Barriers that constrain the dreams not only of African Americans, but of all Americans. Barriers that can, and must, and shall be overcome.

For the sake of every American living today and for the sake of every American yet to be born, we must bring about a better health care system—not in 10 years, not in five years, not in one year—this year. I know there are voices out there telling us we're moving too fast when it comes to health insurance reform. They're telling us to slow down. They're telling us to wait....

Let me tell you: We have been waiting for health reform since the days of Teddy Roosevelt. We've been waiting since the days of Harry Truman. We've been waiting since Johnson, and Nixon, and Clinton. We cannot wait any longer. "There comes a time when the cup of endurance runs over." There comes a time to remember the fierce urgency of right now.

Now is the time to enact health insurance reform in the United States of America. Now is the time to offer stability and security to Americans who have insurance. Now is the time to make it affordable for those who don't have health insurance. Now is the time to slow the growth of health care costs for our families, and business, our government. That's the kind of reform that we need. Now is the time. And that's what so many members of Congress here tonight and all across the country are working so hard to produce....

[Obama provides details of his proposed health-care reform program.]

Now, the key to progress for all Americans is not just healthy bodies, it's also a well-educated mind. And we know that the African American community will fall behind in the United States and the United States will fall behind in the world unless we do a far better job than we've been doing of educating our sons and daughters. Unless we close the achievement gap that sees black students and brown students lag behind their white classmates, year after year, decade after decade. Unless we reach all the students who are dropping out of school and giving up on their future.

Today, almost a third of students drop out of high school—a third—and a disproportionate number of them are African American or Hispanic. That's not just a loss for the African American community or the Hispanic community. That's a loss for all Americans. That's the future workforce. In the 21st century—when a good education is a prerequisite for success, when the jobs of tomorrow require a bachelor's degree or more, when the countries that out-educate us today will out-compete us tomorrow—we need the talents, the energy, the contributions of all our children, not just some. We need to prepare every child in America to compete with any worker in the world.

Now, there are a number of things government can do to offer our kids a 21st century education. It can increase Pell Grants and Perkins Loans and simplify financial aid forms. It can establish better standards and assessments in our schools. It can reward teachers who are doing a great job and move bad ones out of the classroom. It can improve quality in early learning initiatives. It can rebuild our crumbling schools. It can offer all our children a complete and competitive education from cradle to the classroom, from college through a career. That's what government can do. That's what government must do. And that's exactly what we've begun to do, here in Washington, across this country.

And I've said it before and I know I may sound like a broken record, but I'm going to say it again: Government alone cannot get our children to the Promised Land. Government can't put away the PlayStation. Government can't put our kids to bed at a reasonable hour. Government can't attend those parent-teacher conferences. Government can't read a book to your child at night. Government can't help them with their homework. Government can't make sure they leave to school on time. These are things only a mother can do and a father can do. These are things that a parent can do.

We need to accept our responsibilities—as parents and community leaders. We need to be good role models and encourage excellence in all our children, every last one of them. We need to let them know there are no excuses for not doing your best, every day, all the time, in order to achieve your dreams.

We've got to push our kids to aim higher. I don't want all our kids aspiring to be ballers and rappers. I want them aspiring to be teachers and doctors—and scientists and engineers. I want them aspiring to be members of Congress and Supreme Court Justices. I want them aspiring to be the President of the United States of America. I want them to have their sights set high.

No excuses for mediocrity. If they come home with a B, don't tell them "that's great." I know some of you all do that. Tell them to work harder and get an A. Set their sights high.

A world-class education. Affordable, quality health insurance. Jobs and opportunity. All of us accepting responsibility for ourselves, and our children, and our common future. That's how we'll make life better for the African American community, and thereby make life better for the larger American community. That is how we will build a new foundation for our economy that yields lasting, shared prosperity. That's how we'll take up the cause of freedom, and justice, and equality in our time, just as earlier generations of Americans took it up in theirs.

Remember what it was like for George Henry White in the early days of the 20th century, as he was bidding farewell to the House of Representatives, the last African American to serve there for a quarter century. Remember the taunts, the threats, and the attacks braved by White, braved by [civil rights leader and Congressman John] Lewis, braved by [Congresswoman Shirley] Chisholm. Remember all they did—all so many others did—to make it possible for us to be here tonight, to make it possible for you to be here tonight, to make it possible for me to be here tonight.

Because I know that if we can act as they did—with the same sense of unity, the same sense of possibility, the same determination, the same sense of purpose—then we will not only help America's people live healthier lives, we won't just help America's children live out their dreams, but it will be said of us, as it is said of our forbearers, that when the need was great, when the moment was hard, when the odds seemed against us, we did our part to perfect our union.

Thank you. God bless you. And God bless the United States of America.

Source

Obama, Barack. Remarks by the President at the Congressional Black Caucus Foundation's Annual Phoenix Award Dinner, Washington, D.C., September 26, 2009. Retrieved from http://www.white house.gov/video/President-Obama-Speaks-at-the-Congressional-Black-Caucus-Foundation-Awards-Dinner#transcript.

A Journalist Considers Obama's Impact on Race in America

After viewing the 2012 film Lincoln, *journalist William Jelani Cobb wrote an article for the* Washington Monthly *(excerpted below) comparing the life and times of America's sixteenth president to those of President Barack Obama. Cobb views the 2008 election of Obama as the first African-American commander in chief as a watershed moment in the nation's history. But he argues that it also exposed persistent racism that threatens to undermine the hard-won racial progress made by earlier generations of Americans.*

In 2007 Barack Obama announced his presidential candidacy in Springfield, Illinois, deliberately conjuring comparisons to that other lanky lawyer who spent time in the state legislature there. There is no shortage of politicians claiming an affinity with Lincoln—George W. Bush saw himself as a Lincolnesque figure when he was prosecuting the war on terror—but rarely have the parallels been as apparent as they are with Obama. The candidate played up that angle, visiting the Lincoln Memorial just before his inauguration, carrying a well-thumbed copy of *Team of Rivals* on the campaign trail, slipping sly riffs on Lincoln's second inaugural address into his own first one, and taking the oath of office on the Lincoln Bible.

Beyond the obvious, though, lies a deeper theme between Obama and Lincoln: the identities of both men are inextricably bound to questions of both disunity and progress in this country. It's worth recalling that Obama's rise to prominence was a product of his 2004 speech to the Democratic National Convention, in which he offered a compelling, if Photoshopped, vision of a United States where there are no red states or blue states, where neither race nor religion nor ideology can undermine national unity. Obama walked onto that stage an obscure state legislator; he left it a virtual avatar of American reconciliation, the most obvious brand of which was racial. Implicit within his subsequent campaign, particularly after the flashpoint of controversy over Jeremiah Wright's sermons, was the possibility of amnesty for the past. Nowhere was this more apparent than in Obama's "More Perfect Union" speech in Philadelphia in March 2008. Delivered at a time when the campaign was virtually hemorrhaging hope, the speech was a deft manipulation of the very human aspiration to break with the messy past, to be reborn in an untainted present....

When Obama cast himself in the mold of Lincoln in 2007, he could not have known how deeply he would find himself mired in the metaphor. As a recent Pew Study revealed, our country is more divided along partisan lines today than at any point since they've been conducting studies. Basic demographic divisions—gender, race, ethnicity, religion, and class—do not predict differences in values more than they have in the past. Men and women, whites, blacks, and Hispanics, the highly religious and the less religious, and those with more and less education differ in many respects, but those differences have not grown in recent years, and for the most part they pale in comparison to the overwhelming partisan divide we see today. This is only partly because of the growth of cable news programs offering relentless blue-versus-red commentary and a la carte current events. It's also because party identity has become a stand-in for all the other distinctions the study explained.

That chasm is the stepchild of the sectionalism of Lincoln's era. Today, we are another House Divided, though the lines are now drawn more haphazardly. And this is where Obama and Lincoln part ways. In future feature films about the current era, it won't be the details of the president's life that will be redacted, but the details of our own. More specifically, it will be the details of those Americans who greeted Obama's reelection with secession petitions; those who reacted to the 2008 election by organizing themselves and parading racially inflammatory banners in the nation's capital; those who sought solace from demagogues and billionaire conspiracy theorists who demanded that a sitting president prove his own citizenship.

The heralded "Age of Obama" began with a sugar high of postracialism, but four years later the number of whites subscribing to explicitly racist ideas about blacks had *increased*, not diminished. The vision of a black person executing the duties of the nation's highest office was supposed to become mundane; we were supposed to take his identity for granted. Somewhere there was a little-voiced hope among black people that his simple existence as president would be a daily brief for our collective humanity, that we would be taken to be every bit as ordinary as the man occupying the Oval Office. At points in the last four years, it seemed as if we could live in a poetic moment, as if our founding documents could be taken at face value. But the numbers tell us it's not true. Many Americans have reacted to the promise of the Obama era as a threat, as a harbinger of the devaluing currency of whiteness. The problem is not that these people want to take their country back, it's that they were loathe to share it in the first place. The recalcitrant racism of the Obama era will be as vexing to the story of American virtue as Lincoln's racial failings were to those of his era. Lincoln was not as flawless as we've been told, and we are not as virtuous as we've begun to tell ourselves.

To be clear, though, something in the nation has changed. At no point prior to 2008 could a presidential aspiration have been so effectively yoked to this yearning for a clear racial conscience. But beneath the high-blown, premature rhetoric of postracialism lies the less inspirational fact that those changes were as much about math as they were about morality. Depending on your perspective, we have either reached a point of racial maturity that facilitated the election of an African American president or we've reached a point where a supermajority of black voters, a large majority of Latino and Asian ones, and a minority of white people are capable of winning a presidential election. Again, these ideas need not be mutually exclusive, but the need for clean lines and easy redemption makes us behave as if they are....

Indeed, the real problem is not that the nation has so consistently sought balm for its racial wounds, and drafted Lincoln—and Obama—for those purposes; it's the belief that we could be absolved from the past so cheaply. No Lincoln, not even an unfailingly moral one who was killed in service of a righteous cause, could serve as an antidote for ills that persisted, and continue to persist, for a century and a half after his demise. We find ourselves now in circumstances where actual elements of racial progress are jeopardized precisely because we've smugly accepted the idea of ourselves as racially progressive.

The Thirteenth Amendment states that "[n]either slavery nor involuntary servitude, except as a punishment for crime whereof the party shall have been duly convicted, shall exist within the United States, or any place subject to their jurisdiction." We are a nation in which a black president holds office while more than half a million duly convicted black men populate the prisons and county and municipal jails hold hundreds of thousands more. The symbolic ideal of postracialism masks a Supreme Court that may undermine affirmative action in higher education and the preclearance clause of the Voting Rights Act. Our most recent election saw both unprecedented black turnout and efforts at black voter suppression that resound with echoes of bad history. Black unemployment, even among the college educated, remains vastly higher than it is for whites. (Among the more hideous hypocrisies of the recent election was Mitt Romney's cynical appeals to black Americans, pointing out that blacks have suffered disproportionately in the Obama economy. The black president, we were to believe, is now also responsible for racism in the labor market.)

Obama himself was wise to these contrasts as far back as 2008, when he gave the speech in Philadelphia that saved his political career.

> [W]ords on a parchment would not be enough to deliver slaves from bondage, or provide men and women of every color and creed their full rights and obligations as citizens of the United States. What would be needed were Americans in successive generations who were willing to do their part—through protests and struggle, on the streets and in the courts, through a civil war and civil disobedience and always at great risk—to narrow that gap between the promise of our ideals and the reality of their time.

The election of an African American president is a watershed in our history. But the takeaway is that what we do during these moments is somehow smaller than what we do between them, that our heroes are no better than we are, nor do they need to be. Harriet Tubman is often cited as saying she could have freed more blacks if only she'd been able to convince them they were slaves. In our own era, the only impediment to realizing the creed of "We Shall Overcome" is the narcotic belief that we already have.

Source

Cobb, William Jelani. "Lincoln Died for Our Sins." *Washington Monthly,* January/February 2013. Retrieved from http://www.washingtonmonthly.com/magazine/january_february_2013/features/lincoln_died_for_our_sins042041.php.

IMPORTANT PEOPLE, PLACES, AND TERMS

Abolitionist
A person who opposes slavery and supports efforts to end the practice.

Accommodations
Food, lodging, transportation, and other services that are supplied to meet a public need.

Black Codes
A series of repressive laws passed in Southern states following the Civil War that were designed to restrict the rights and freedoms of former slaves and prevent them from gaining any political or economic power.

Border states
States that had once allowed slavery but remained loyal to the Union during the Civil War—including Delaware, Kentucky, Maryland, Missouri, and West Virginia.

Brief
A written document that outlines the main legal arguments in a court case.

Brown, Henry Billings (1836-1913)
U.S. Supreme Court justice (1891-1906) who wrote the majority opinion in *Plessy v. Ferguson*.

Brown v. *Board of Education*
The 1954 U.S. Supreme Court ruling that overturned *Plessy v. Ferguson's* "separate but equal" doctrine and declared segregation of public schools unconstitutional.

Caste system
A social structure in which citizens are placed into distinct classes based on heredity or race.

Citizens' Committee
A group of prominent black and mixed-race New Orleans residents who organized and funded a legal challenge to Louisiana's Separate Car Law.

Civil Rights Act of 1875
A federal Reconstruction law that prohibited racial discrimination in businesses that served the public; it was ruled unconstitutional by the Supreme Court in 1883.

Civil rights movement
A decade-long campaign (encompassing the late 1950s and early 1960s) to end discrimination against African Americans and pass laws guaranteeing equal rights and opportunities for all citizens.

Civil War
A conflict that raged from 1861 to 1865 and pitted the Northern half of the United States against the eleven Southern states that seceded from the Union to form the Confederate States of America.

Comité des Citoyens
See Citizens' Committee

Creoles
Descendants of the French colonists who settled Louisiana, including mixed-race people of black and French ancestry.

Desdunes, Rodolphe (1849-1928)
A Creole civil rights activist and journalist who encouraged New Orleans residents to challenge Louisiana's Separate Car Law.

Dissent
A legal opinion that disagrees with or withholds approval from the majority decision.

Ferguson, John Howard (1838-1915)
The Louisiana judge who rendered the original ruling against Homer Plessy and thus was named in the appellate case *Plessy v. Ferguson*.

Fifteenth Amendment
Ratified in 1870, this change to the U.S. Constitution granted African American men the right to vote.

Fourteenth Amendment

Ratified in 1868, this amendment extended the rights of U.S. citizenship to all persons "born or naturalized in the United States," including freed slaves; guaranteed all citizens equal protection under the law; and forbade states from denying citizens their rights without due process of law.

Grandfather clause

A type of law that offered an exemption from voter-registration requirements to anyone who had been eligible to vote prior to 1867 or whose ancestors had voted before that time; during the Jim Crow era these laws protected poor, uneducated whites from requirements intended to disenfranchise blacks.

Great Migration

A mass movement of African Americans from the South to the North and West in search of greater equality and better education and employment opportunities in the early twentieth century.

Harlan, John Marshall (1833-1911)

The U.S. Supreme Court justice (1877-1911) who wrote the famous dissenting opinion in *Plessy v. Ferguson*.

Jim Crow

A system of discriminatory laws and customs that were put in place throughout the South in the late 1800s and early 1900s and relegated African Americans to a position of second-class citizenship.

Johnson, Andrew (1808-1875)

The seventeenth president of the United States (1865-1869) who led the country during the early years of Reconstruction.

Ku Klux Klan

A shadowy terrorist group made up of white supremacists who employed violence in an effort to maintain the dominant position of whites in Southern society.

Lincoln, Abraham (1809-1865)

The sixteenth president of the United States (1861-1865) who led the Union during the Civil War and signed the Emancipation Proclamation.

Lynching

The public murder—often by hanging—of an African American by a mob of whites; this terrifying form of violence was used to enforce Jim Crow laws and customs in the South.

Marshall, Thurgood (1908-1993)

The civil rights attorney who helped overturn *Plessy v. Ferguson* and later became the first African-American Supreme Court justice.

Martinet, Louis (1849-1917)

A New Orleans newspaper publisher and civil rights advocate who helped organize opposition to the Separate Car Law.

NAACP

See National Association for the Advancement of Colored People (NAACP)

National Association for the Advancement of Colored People (NAACP)

A civil rights organization, formed in 1909, that aims to eliminate racial prejudice and achieve political, educational, social, and economic equality for minorities.

Nicholls, Francis T. (1834-1912)

The governor of Louisiana who signed the Separate Car Act into law and later found it to be constitutional as chief justice of the State Supreme Court.

Plessy, Homer (1862-1925)

A mixed-race New Orleans resident who volunteered to challenge the legality of segregation laws.

Precedent

A previous court ruling that judges take into consideration when weighing legal questions.

Public transportation

Services involved in the conveyance of paying passengers, including trains, buses, and subway systems.

Radical Republicans

Members of Congress who sought to destroy the old social order in the South and create a new system based on racial equality during Reconstruction.

Reconstruction

The period (1865-1877) following the Civil War when the federal government helped to rebuild the South's shattered infrastructure and established conditions for the Confederate states to be readmitted to the Union.

Redeemers

White Democrats who sought to reverse the changes of the postwar Reconstruction era and reclaim the South from the influence of freed slaves and their Northern supporters.

Segregation

A system of laws that formally separates people by race in the use of public facilities—such as schools, parks, and restrooms—in order to limit social contact between blacks and whites.

Separate Car Law

An 1890 Louisiana statute that divided railroad passengers into different cars by race and became the subject of the legal challenge in *Plessy v. Ferguson.*

Sharecropper

A system of tenant farming, popularized during Reconstruction, in which large landowners allowed small farmers to work sections of land in exchange for a share of the crops they grew.

Slavery

The practice of owning human beings as property and forcing them into involuntary servitude.

South

A region comprised of the eleven states that seceded from the Union to form the Confederate States of America during the Civil War, as well as (sometimes) several states bordering that region.

Thirteenth Amendment

Added to the Constitution in 1865, this amendment abolished slavery in the United States and freed all slaves in border states who were not covered under the Emancipation Proclamation

Tourgée, Albion W. (1838-1905)

The Republican writer, civil rights activist, and lawyer who argued *Plessy v. Ferguson* before the U.S. Supreme Court.

White supremacist

A person who believes that blacks are inherently inferior to whites and do not deserve equal treatment or civil rights.

CHRONOLOGY

1600s

The first Africans are forcibly brought to North America to serve as slaves for European colonists. *See p. 5.*

1783

The thirteen American colonies gain their independence from England and form a new nation based on the principles of freedom, equality, and democracy; the new U.S. Constitution does not address the issue of slavery. *See p. 6.*

1793

The invention of the cotton gin—a machine that separates seeds from cotton fibers— leads to a massive increase in cotton production in the South, and an accompanying increase in demand for slave labor on large cotton-growing plantations. *See p. 7.*

1803

The Louisiana Purchase doubles the territorial size of the United States. *See p. 34.*

1808

The U.S. Congress outlaws the transatlantic slave trade, making it illegal to import slaves from Africa to the United States. *See p. 8.*

1812

Louisiana is admitted to the Union as the eighteenth state. *See p. 34.*

1857

The U.S. Supreme Court gives legal protection to the institution of slavery with its infamous *Dred Scott v. Sandford* decision. *See p. 9.*

1860

Abraham Lincoln is elected president of the United States; eleven Southern states subsequently announce their intention to secede from the Union and form a new country called the Confederate States of America. *See p. 8.*

1861

The Civil War begins on April 12, when Confederate troops attack a U.S. Army garrison at Fort Sumter in Charleston, South Carolina. *See p. 8.*

1862

Union forces capture New Orleans in April and occupy the city for the remaining three years of the Civil War. *See p. 35.*

On July 17 Congress passes a law allowing black men who were free before the war to enlist in the Union Army. *See p. 10.*

1863

On January 1 Lincoln issues the Emancipation Proclamation, which frees slaves held in Confederate states. *See p. 10.*

1865

The surrender of Confederate general Robert E. Lee on April 9 marks the end of the Civil War. *See p. 11.*

Lincoln is shot and killed by a Confederate sympathizer on April 14; Vice President Andrew Johnson assumes the presidency. *See p. 11.*

On May 29 Johnson signs a Proclamation of Amnesty that pardons Confederate soldiers who take an oath of allegiance to the United States and returns most Southern farmland to white ownership. *See p. 12.*

The Thirteenth Amendment to the U.S. Constitution, formally adopted on December 6, outlaws slavery. *See p. 16.*

1866

A group of former Confederate soldiers form the Ku Klux Klan white supremacist organization in Tennessee. *See p. 20.*

Southern states introduce a series of repressive laws, known as Black Codes, designed to restrict the rights and freedoms of former slaves and prevent them from gaining any political or economic power. *See p. 13.*

1867

The Reconstruction Act divides the former Confederate states into five military districts and establishes the Freedman's Bureau to help former slaves make a successful transition to new lives. *See p. 16.*

African Americans in New Orleans successfully challenge a law that reserves two-thirds of the city's mule-drawn streetcars for the exclusive use of white passengers and relegates African Americans to cars marked with a black star. *See p. 37.*

1868

The Fourteenth Amendment to the U.S. Constitution extends the rights of citizenship to African Americans, guarantees all citizens equal protection under the law, and forbids states from denying citizens their rights without due process of law. *See p. 16.*

1870

The Fifteenth Amendment to the U.S. Constitution extends voting rights to black men. *See p. 16.*

Hiram Revels, a Republican from Mississippi, becomes the first African-American member of the U.S. Senate; twenty more black candidates win election to the U.S. House of Representatives. *See p. 18.*

Albion Winegar Tourgée writes a letter to Republican senator Joseph C. Abbott describing Reconstruction-era violence in North Carolina. *See p. 143.*

1872

Pinckney Benton Stewart (P. B. S.) Pinchback becomes the first African-American governor in U.S. history when he assumes office in Louisiana. *See p. 35.*

1873

A group of prominent African-American, Creole, and white businessmen, military leaders, and politicians form the Louisiana Unification Movement. *See p. 35.*

1875

The federal Civil Rights Act prohibits racial discrimination by businesses that serve the public. *See p. 26.*

1876

As part of a political compromise to resolve a disputed presidential election, Republican Rutherford B. Hayes is declared the winner in exchange for his promise to withdraw federal troops from the South. *See p. 21.*

Democrat Francis T. Nicholls, a Confederate war hero, wins the governorship of Louisiana as part of the Compromise of 1876. *See p. 36.*

1877

Reconstruction ends with the withdrawal of federal troops from former Confederate states. *See p. 21.*

With his Senate confirmation on November 29, John Marshall Harlan begins thirty-four years of service as a justice of the U.S. Supreme Court. *See p. 51.*

1879

Tourgée publishes *A Fool's Errand,* an autobiographical novel that reflects his strong convictions about racial equality. *See p. 137.*

1883

On October 15 the Supreme Court overturns the Civil Rights Act of 1875, ruling that the protections of the Fourteenth Amendment only apply to discrimination by state governments, rather than by individual citizens. *See p. 26.*

1889

Louis Martinet launches the *Crusader,* a weekly African-American newspaper based in New Orleans. *See p. 37.*

1890

Governor Nicholls signs Louisiana's Separate Car Act into law on July 10. *See p. 39.*

On December 23, Henry Billings Brown is nominated to the U.S. Supreme Court by President Benjamin Harrison. *See p. 51.*

1891

A group of prominent New Orleans residents form the Citizens' Committee to Test the Constitutionality of the Separate Car Law. *See p. 39.*

1892

Daniel Desdunes challenges the Separate Car Law on February 24; the case against him is dismissed because it involves interstate travel. *See p. 41.*

On June 7 Homer Plessy is arrested for boarding a whites-only coach on an East Louisiana Railroad train in violation of the Separate Car Law. *See p. 42.*

Judge John Howard Ferguson rules against Plessy on November 18. *See p. 44.*

A record 230 lynchings of African Americans take place in the United States; more than 95 percent of these incidents occur in former Confederate states or border states. *See p. 28.*

Activist Ida B. Wells launches her anti-lynching campaign. *See p. 73.*

1894

The Louisiana state legislature strengthens its railroad segregation law to require separate black and white waiting areas in train stations. *See p. 48.*

1895

On September 15 black educator Booker T. Washington makes his controversial Atlanta Exposition Address. *See p. 29.*

1896

The U.S. Supreme Court hears arguments in *Plessy v. Ferguson* on April 13. *See p. 52.*

On May 18 the U.S. Supreme Court rules 7-1 against Plessy, declaring racial segregation constitutional as long as the facilities provided to blacks and whites are "separate but equal." *See p. 55.*

1897

Plessy appears before Judge Ferguson on January 11, pleads guilty to violating the Separate Car Law, and pays a $25 fine. *See p. 60.*

1898

The Supreme Court provides legal cover to discriminatory voter-registration laws in *Williams v. Mississippi.* *See p. 23.*

1900

The Great Migration begins; over the next four decades an estimated 1.8 million Southern blacks migrate to the North or West in search of greater equality and better education and employment opportunities. *See p. 75.*

1901

George Henry White, the last black man to serve in the U.S. House of Representatives from the South until 1972, makes his famous "Defense of the Negro Race" speech on January 29. *See p. 24.*

1905

Thomas Dixon publishes *The Clansman: An Historical Romance of the Ku Klux Klan. See p. 74.*

1909

The National Association for the Advancement of Colored People (NAACP) is formed on February 12. *See p. 73.*

1911

Rodolphe Desdunes publishes *Nos Hommes et Nostre Histoire* (*Our People and Our History*), which contains biographical profiles of fifty prominent Creoles from New Orleans. *See p. 116.*

1915

The controversial film *Birth of a Nation,* directed by D. W. Griffith, fans the flames of race hate in the United States. *See p. 74.*

1938

The NAACP wins its first Supreme Court ruling against segregation in *Gaines v. Canada. See p. 81.*

1941

On June 25 President Franklin D. Roosevelt issues Executive Order 8802, which prohibits employment discrimination by government agencies and contractors. *See p. 81.*

1948

President Harry S. Truman issues Executive Order 9981, which integrates the U.S. armed services. *See p. 81.*

1950

On June 5 the Supreme Court issues a pair of rulings that disallow segregation in higher education: *Sweatt v. Painter* and *McLaurin v. Oklahoma Board of Regents. See p. 81.*

1952

The Supreme Court agrees to hear *Brown v. Board of Education,* a collection of five similar cases involving the segregation of public schools. *See p. 82.*

1953

The Supreme Court hears a second round of arguments in *Brown v. Board of Education. See p. 82.*

1954

In a 9-0 opinion issued on May 17, the Supreme Court rules that the segregation of public schools violates the Equal Protection clause of the Fourteenth Amendment. *See p. 83.*

1955

On May 31 the Supreme Court issues its *Brown II* ruling, which advises school districts in the South to integrate "with all deliberate speed." *See p. 83.*

On December 1 Rosa Parks is arrested in Montgomery, Alabama, for violating the city bus system's segregated seating policy; her arrest sparks the year-long Montgomery Bus Boycott. *See p. 86.*

1956

On December 19 the Supreme Court finds segregation of public transportation unconstitutional in *Browder v. Gale. See p. 87.*

The Montgomery Bus Boycott ends in triumph on December 20, when city officials agree to integrate the bus system. *See p. 87.*

1957

Arkansas governor Orval Faubus mobilizes his state's National Guard to prevent nine black students from integrating Central High School in Little Rock. *See p. 84.*

1960

Six-year-old black student Ruby Bridges is confronted by a mob of white segregationists as she attempts to enter an all-white elementary school in New Orleans. *See p. 85.*

1961

Civil rights activists launch the Freedom Rides to challenge the segregation of interstate bus travel. *See p. 87.*

1963

Martin Luther King Jr. and other civil rights activists launch a series of nonviolent protest actions to draw attention to segregation and discrimination in Birmingham, Alabama. *See p. 88.*

On June 11 Alabama governor George Wallace stands in the doorway of a building on the University of Alabama campus to block the entrance of two African-American students. *See p. 85.*

President John F. Kennedy makes a nationally televised address on the subject of African-American civil rights. *See p. 85.*

On August 28 an estimated 250,000 people participate in the March on Washington for Jobs and Freedom. *See p. 89.*

1964

On June 21 three civil rights workers involved in a voter-registration drive disappear near Philadelphia, Mississippi; their bodies are found six weeks later. *See p. 91.*

The Civil Rights Act, enacted on July 2, prohibits discrimination on the basis of race, color, religion, sex, or national origin in the areas of education, employment, public accommodations, and voting rights. *See p. 91.*

1965

On March 7—known as Bloody Sunday—a group of peaceful voting-rights marchers are attacked by white state and local law enforcement officers in Selma, Alabama. *See p. 91.*

On March 15 President Lyndon B. Johnson challenges Congress to respond to the violence in Selma by passing strong new legislation to protect African-American voting rights. *See p. 92.*

The Selma-Montgomery Voting Rights March concludes on March 25 in a rally attended by 30,000 people on the steps of the Alabama state capitol. *See p. 93.*

Johnson signs the Voting Rights Act into law on August 6. *See p. 93.*

1967

Thurgood Marshall is confirmed on August 30 as the first African-American U.S. Supreme Court justice. *See p. 125.*

2004

Actor and comedian Bill Cosby delivers a speech attacking what he sees as the declining morality, irresponsible behavior, and misplaced priorities of many poor blacks. *See p. 102.*

2005

June 7 is established as Homer A. Plessy Day in New Orleans.

2008

When Barack Obama is elected as the forty-fourth president of the United States on November 8, he becomes the first African American to hold the nation's highest office. *See p. 104.*

2009

Descendants of the men involved in the famous Supreme Court case establish the Plessy and Ferguson Foundation for Education, Preservation, and Outreach. *See p. 107.*

2012

Obama wins reelection to a second term as president. *See p. 104.*

SOURCES FOR FURTHER STUDY

Esty, Amos. *The Civil Rights Movement:* Plessy v. Ferguson. Greensboro, NC: Morgan Reynolds, 2012. Aimed at students, this book offers an accessible history of the *Plessy v. Ferguson* case and valuable background information about race relations in the South in the late nineteenth century.

Fremon, David K. *The Jim Crow Laws and Racism in American History.* Berkeley Heights, NJ: Enslow, 2000. This book provides a readable overview of a century in black history— from the Reconstruction era, through segregation and Jim Crow, to the civil rights movement.

McNeese, Tim. *Great Supreme Court Decisions:* Plessy v. Ferguson, *Separate but Equal.* New York: Chelsea House, 2007. This volume offers a comprehensive history of the *Plessy v. Ferguson* case and the people involved in it.

Medley, Keith Weldon. *We as Freemen:* Plessy v. Ferguson. Gretna, LA: Pelican, 2003. Meticulously researched and written by a New Orleans native, this book provides a detailed, behind-the-scenes look at the shifting political landscape of Louisiana during the Reconstruction era. It also features valuable background information about members of the Citizens' Committee, including excerpts from correspondence and editorials by Rodolphe Desdunes, Louis Martinet, and Albion Tourgée.

"The Rise and Fall of Jim Crow." PBS, 2002. Retrieved from http://www.pbs.org/wnet/jimcrow /about.html. This Peabody Award-winning, four-part series chronicles segregation in America from the end of the Civil War to the beginning of the civil rights movement. It includes interactive maps and timelines, personal narratives, and tools and activities for students.

Woodward, C. Vann. "The Case of the Louisiana Traveler." In *American Counterpoint.* Boston: Little, Brown, 1971, p. 163. Retrieved from http://www.soc.umn.edu/~samaha/cases/van %20woodward,%20plessy.htm. Written by a prominent historian, this article describes the personalities and legal issues involved in *Plessy v. Ferguson.*

BIBLIOGRAPHY

Books

Aaseng, Nathan. Plessy v. Ferguson: *Separate but Equal.* Farmington Hills, MI: Lucent Books, 2003.

Ayers, Edward L. *Promise of the New South: Life after Reconstruction.* New York: Oxford University Press, 1992.

Blackmon, Douglas A. *Slavery by Another Name: The Re-Enslavement of Black Americans from the Civil War to World War II.* New York: Doubleday, 2008.

Chafe, William H., Raymond Gavins, and Robert Korstad. *Remembering Jim Crow: African Americans Tell about Life in the Segregated South.* New York: New Press, 2001.

Colbert, David, ed. *Eyewitness to America: 500 Years of America in the Words of Those Who Saw It Happen.* New York: Pantheon Books, 1997.

Du Bois, W. E. B. *Black Reconstruction in America, 1860-1880.* 1935. Reprint. New York: Free Press, 1998.

Dyson, Michael Eric. *Is Bill Cosby Right? (Or Has the Black Middle Class Lost Its Mind?).* New York: Basic Civitas, 2006.

Esty, Amos. *The Civil Rights Movement:* Plessy v. Ferguson. Greensboro, NC: Morgan Reynolds, 2012.

Ezekiel, Raphael S. *Voices from the Corner: Poverty and Racism in the Inner City.* Philadelphia: Temple University Press, 1984.

Fireside, Harvey. *Landmark Supreme Court Cases:* Plessy v. Ferguson, *Separate but Equal?* Springfield, NJ: Enslow, 1997.

Fischer, Roger A. *The Segregation Struggle in Louisiana, 1862-77.* Urbana: University of Illinois Press, 1974.

Foner, Eric. *Reconstruction: America's Unfinished Revolution.* New York: Harper and Row, 1988.

Garrow, David. *Bearing the Cross: Martin Luther King, Jr., and the Southern Christian Leadership Conference.* New York: William Morrow, 1986.

Gottheimer, Josh, ed. *Ripples of Hope: Great American Civil Rights Speeches.* New York: Basic Civitas Books, 2003.

Henri, Florette. *Black Migration: Movement North, 1900-1920.* Norwell, MA: Anchor Press, 1975.

Hine, Darlene Clark. *The African-American Odyssey.* Upper Saddle River, NJ: Prentice Hall, 2005.

Ifill, Gwen. *The Breakthrough: Politics and Race in the Age of Obama.* New York: Doubleday, 2009.

King, Casey, and Linda Barrett Osbourne. *Oh, Freedom! Kids Talk about the Civil Rights Movement with the People Who Made It Happen.* New York: Knopf, 1997.

Klarman, Michael J. *From Jim Crow to Civil Rights: The Supreme Court and the Struggle for Racial Equality.* New York: Oxford University Press, 2004.

Litwack, Leon F. *Trouble in Mind: Black Southerners in the Age of Jim Crow.* New York: Knopf, 1998.

Medley, Keith Weldon. *We as Freemen:* Plessy v. Ferguson. Gretna, LA: Pelican, 2003.

Middleton, Stephen. *Black Congressmen during Reconstruction: A Documentary Sourcebook.* Westport, CT: Greenwood Press, 2002.

Olsen, Otto H. *The Thin Disguise: Turning Point in Negro History*—Plessy v. Ferguson. New York: American Institute for Marxist Studies, 1967.

Schwartz, Bernard. *A History of the Supreme Court.* New York: Oxford, 1993.

Stevens, Leonard. *Equal! The Case of Integration vs. Jim Crow.* New York: Coward, McCann, and Geohagen, 1976.

Thurman, Howard. *The Luminous Darkness: A Personal Interpretation of the Anatomy of Segregation and the Ground of Hope.* Richmond, IN: Friends United Press, 1965.

Woodson, Carter G. *A Century of Negro Migration.* New York: AMS Press, 1918.

Woodward, C. Vann. "The Case of the Louisiana Traveler." In *American Counterpoint.* Boston: Little, Brown, 1971.

Periodicals

Barnes, Robert. "Plessy and Ferguson: Descendants of a Divisive Supreme Court Decision Unite." *Washington Post,* June 5, 2011. Retrieved from http://www.washingtonpost.com/politics/plessy-and-ferguson-descendants-of-a-divisive-supreme-court-decision-unite/2011/06/02/AGji3hJH_story.html.

Cobb, James C. "Segregating the New South: The Origins and Legacy of *Plessy v. Ferguson.*" *Georgia State University Law Review,* June 1996. Retrieved from http://digitalarchive.gsu.edu/cgi/viewcontent.cgi?article=2630&context=gsulr.

Darling-Hammond, Linda. "The Color Line in American Education: Race, Resources, and Student Achievement." *Du Bois Review* 1(2), 2004.

Erler, Edward J. "Is the Constitution Color-Blind?" *USA Today Magazine,* July 2004.

Harris, Angel L. "The Economic and Educational State of Black Americans in the 21st Century: Should We Be Optimistic or Concerned?" *Review of Black Political Economy,* October 5, 2010. Retrieved from http://www.princeton.edu/~angelh/Website/Studies/Article%208%20%28Rev%20of%20Blk%20Pol%20Econ%20%2710%29.pdf.

Medley, Keith Weldon. "The Sad Story of How 'Separate but Equal' Was Born in 1896." *Smithsonian,* February 1994.

Romano, Andrew, and Allison Samuels. "A *Newsweek* Poll Shows Americans Still Divided over Race." *Newsweek,* April 9, 2012. Retrieved from http://www.thedailybeast.com/newsweek/2012/04/08/a-newsweek-poll-show-americans-still-divided-over-race.html.

Williams, T. Henry. "The Louisiana Unification Movement of 1873." In *Journal of Southern History,* Vol. IX, No. 1. Nashville, TN: Vanderbilt University Press, 1945.

Web Sites

"Examples of Jim Crow Laws." Jim Crow Museum of Racist Memorabilia, Ferris State University, 2012. Retrieved from http://www.ferris.edu/htmls/news/jimcrow/links/misclink/examples/homepage.htm.

Gray, Katti. "Banned from Voting Booths: Ex-Convicts." Salon.com, October 22, 2012. Retrieved from http://www.salon.com/2012/10/22/banned_from_voting_booths_ex_convicts/.

"Jim Crow in America." Library of Congress, n.d. Retrieved from http://www.loc.gov/teachers/classroommaterials/primarysourcesets/civil-rights/.

"Jim Crow Laws." Martin Luther King Jr. National Historic Site, 2013. Retrieved from http://www.nps.gov/malu/forteachers/jim_crow_laws.htm.

Nystrom, Justin A. "Reconstruction." In *KnowLA Encyclopedia of Louisiana.* Louisiana Endowment for the Humanities, December 21, 2012. Retrieved from http://www.knowla.org/entry.php?rec=463.

Pew Charitable Trusts. *Pursuing the American Dream: Economic Mobility Across Generations.* July 2012. Retrieved from http://www.pewstates.org/uploadedFiles/PCS_Assets/2012/Pursuing_American_Dream.pdf.

Pilgrim, David. "What Was Jim Crow?" Jim Crow Museum of Racist Memorabilia, Ferris State University, 2012. Retrieved from http://www.ferris.edu/jimcrow/what.htm.

Plessy v. Ferguson, 163 U.S. 537 (1896). Records of the Supreme Court of the United States. Retrieved from http://www.ourdocuments.gov/doc.php?flash=true&doc=52&page=transcript.

Spatig-Amerikaner, Ary. *Unequal Education: Federal Loophole Enables Lower Spending on Students of Color.* Center for American Progress, August 2012. Retrieved from http://www.americanprogress.org/wp-content/uploads/2012/08/UnequalEduation.pdf.

Tourgée, Albion W., Collection. Westfield, NY: Chautauqua County Historical Society. Available online at http://nyheritage.nnyln.net/cdm/search/collection/NYCCH.

PHOTO AND
ILLUSTRATION CREDITS

Cover and Title Page: *Negro drinking at "Colored" water cooler in streetcar terminal, Oklahoma City, Oklahoma* (original caption). Photo by Russell Lee, FSA/OWI Black-and-White Negatives, Prints and Photographs Division, Library of Congress, LC-DIG-fsa-8a26761.

Chapter One: Drawing by Thomas Nast, American Cartoon Prints Collection, Prints & Photographs Division, Library of Congress, LC-DIG-pga-03898 (p. 7); Illus. in *Harper's Weekly* (1863 Feb. 21, p. 116), Prints & Photographs Division, Library of Congress, LC-USZ62-112158 (p. 10); Prints & Photographs Division, Library of Congress, LC-DIG-pga-02640 (p. 12); Picture Collection, The New York Public Library, Astor, Lenox and Tilden Foundations (p. 14); Lithograph by Gaylord Watson, Prints & Photographs Division, Library of Congress, LC-DIG-pga-03004 (p. 17).

Chapter Two: Drawing by A. R. Waud, Illus. in *Harper's Weekly* (1868 July 25, p. 473), Prints & Photographs Division, Library of Congress, LC-USZ62-105555 (p. 20); Artist: Frederick Burr Opper, Illus. from *Puck* (1883 July 4 cover), Prints & Photographs Division, Library of Congress, LC-DIG-ppmsca-28402 (p. 23); Prints & Photographs Division, Library of Congress, LC-DIG-ds-00886 (p. 25); Manuscripts, Archives and Rare Books Division, Schomburg Center for Research in Black Culture, The New York Public Library, Astor, Lenox and Tilden Foundations. (p. 26); Illus. in *Puck* (1913 Feb. 26), Prints & Photographs Division, Library of Congress, LC-USZC2-1058 (p. 30).

Chapter Three: Photograph by William Henry Jackson, Detroit Publishing Co. Collection, Prints & Photographs Division, Library of Congress, LC-D418-8102 (p. 34); Brady-Handy Collection, Prints & Photographs Division, Library of Congress, LC-BH826-3467 (p. 35); Picture Collection, The New York Public Library, Astor, Lenox and Tilden Foundations. (p. 38); Louisiana Division/City Archives, New Orleans Public Library (p. 40); The Historic New Orleans Collection, Acc. No. 1974.25.37.57. (p. 43).

Chapter Four: Prints & Photographs Division, Library of Congress, LC-USZ62-104 (p. 49); Courtesy, Chautauqua County Historical Society, Westfield, NY (p. 53); Bain Collection, Prints & Photographs Division, Library of Congress, LC-USZ62-90766 (p. 56); Bain Collection, Prints & Photographs Division, Library of Congress, LC-USZ62-88501 (p. 58); The Granger Collection, New York (p. 60).

Chapter Five: Photo by Marion Post Wolcott, FSA-OWI Photograph Collection, Library of Congress Prints and Photographs Division, LC-DIG-ppmsc-12888 (p. 64); Photo by

INDEX